Feet of
CLAY

Feet of CLAY

A FICTIONAL NOVEL BASED ON THE LIFE
OF DR. JAMES ADDISON BELL

CHERRY W. WARDWELL

FEET OF CLAY

Published by Late Day Publishing
Monticello, Georgia

International Standard Book Number: 978-0692887189

Printed in the United States of America

Unless otherwise noted, Scripture quotations are taken from the New King James version of the Bible.

Dedicated to my mother, Alfreda Bell Warren,
who instilled in me an admiration and love
for a man I never met.

PROLOGUE

The early twentieth century was a transitional era in Georgia's history. Many southerners believed the war had been about states rights, and not about slavery, which they believed the government had made an issue to justify the conflict. The South suffered terrible devastation. In addition to the loss of life, which affected both sides, the South lost most of their homes and businesses. They survived the carpetbaggers and came through reconstruction with little help from the government. Times were hard and many were still bitter about losing the lifestyle of the "Old South." The coloreds were no longer slaves but they were still part of a society in which southern whites presumed themselves to be superior. They worked as paid servants or tenant farmers in the homes or fields of white men. They were loyal to the white families they served, many of whom worked beside them tilling the soil, planting crops and gathering the harvests. The white families provided them with humble housing and a share of the goods. It was a harsh existence for both peoples but provided some security for the dark-skinned people from a faraway land and a different culture.

Love was found in unlikely places and only those who experienced it understood the genuine affection that often existed between the blacks and the whites for whom they labored. White children in the care of black women loved them and these women often returned a genuine affection for their white charges.

The knowledge of medicine was growing during that period but many mistakes were made in the process of diagnosing and treating illnesses and as in every era not all physicians were motivated by compassion.

This is the story of one who was.

The events of this novel are based on the life of Dr. James Addison Bell, a Georgia physician who served the Lithonia and Decatur areas of Georgia from 1907 to 1939. He lived through the transitional era from mail to the telephone, horse and buggy to the automobile and Procaine to Ether. He was alleged by his family to have been the treating physician in the first case of lockjaw ever cured at Wesley Memorial Hospital in Atlanta, Georgia (now Emory University Hospital). He was a man of honor and idealism who had exceptional diagnostic skill and was revered throughout Dekalb County, Georgia, during his lifetime. His family has kept his story alive through their great love and vivid memories to their third generation. Unfortunately, those who knew him best have died. Therefore, the details of my grandfather's education, courtship, marriage, medical practice and the staunch support of his wife are lost to this generation. The incidents related in this story are largely comprised of my memory of the stories related by my grandmother, embellished by figments of my own imagination.

The purpose of this writing is not to suggest my grandfather was without fault, but to present him as the man he was, fraught with human weakness but filled with compassion for the sick and an ardent desire to serve God.

INTRODUCTION

But now, O LORD, thou art Our Father; we are the clay,
and thou our Potter; and we all are the work of Thy hand.
Isaiah 64:8

Tutney, Addison and Walter Blair were the surviving children of the late Lycurgeus McElsworth Blair of Marbleton, Georgia, who hadn't fought in the civil war because he was the youngest of nine brothers, in ill health and had one blind eye. During the war, he remained on the farm to oversee the family's cotton crop. When his brothers dispersed into other regions of Georgia after the war, they deeded to him their father's 1840 farmhouse, where he lived with his wife Louisa and his mother, Granny Blair.

In 1863, Louisa gave birth to their first child, a daughter, who was given her mother's name, Louisa Cordelia. Two years later in 1865, a son, William Everett, was born. William had a crippling deformity and because of his mother's neglect he became more and more timid and slow of speech. She had very little patience with him and when he reached the age of ten, had him committed to the State Mental Hospital at Milledgeville. He developed extreme melancholy and within less than a year he died. This devastated his sister, the young Louisa, who blamed her mother. When her mother died, she changed her name to "Tutney Key" and made it legal as soon as she was of age.

Lycurgeus, by the time of his first wife's death, was a prosperous farmer with 35 head of cattle, 75 pigs and several acres of cotton. It didn't take him long to bring home a new bride, Sally Olivia, his first cousin.

Both Tutney and Granny took to Sally, but Sally was very young and felt threatened by her new fifteen-year-old stepdaughter. She treated Tutney with distrust and contempt. However, this changed when Sally's first child, Addison, was born in 1881. Sally was immature and lazy, and more than happy to let Tutney be her son's nanny. Tutney adored the child and took him under her wing. She clothed, fed and read to him and because she was in her teens, also delighted in teaching him mischief.

Sally went into labor with her second child in the winter of 1884. Earlier that evening Tutney had put a toad in Granny's chamber pot. The poor old woman was so adversely affected, she took to her bed. She and Addison found this quite amusing but because Granny was incapacitated, Tutney became obliged to act as midwife. She managed surprisingly well, helping Sally to deliver another boy, Walter James. Tutney blissfully assumed full care of this infant, as well, and eagerly transitioned into surrogate motherhood.

Granny unexpectedly died of typhoid in the spring of 1889, and Lycurgeus contracted the disease and died only five months later. The children were devastated by the loss of Granny, but had never been close to their father. Sadly, they seemed minimally affected by his death.

Sally soon began courting Dr. Jacob Blair, a widowed cousin, and after only a few months they married. Sally moved into Jacob's home, leaving the boys behind, in Tutney's words, "to root hog or die without a crust of bread between them."

Two years later Sally died in childbirth, along with an infant daughter. As she had failed to leave the children an inheritance and there was no immediate family left to object, Tutney declared Addison and Walter 'her boys'. She assumed full responsibility and in order to provide for them, enrolled in State Normal School and became a teacher. She taught for several years at the grade school in Broad, Georgia, and later took a position at the school in Marbleton. She was frugal with her money and over the years saved enough to provide for both boys' formal educations. When Addison graduated from high school with stellar grades, she enrolled him in Louisville Medical College. Even if the idea hadn't appealed to him, Addison wouldn't have protested, as he had become absolutely submissive to his sister's authority.

At the age of nineteen Addison was into his second year of medical school. He stood six feet four inches tall and had dark brown hair that curled around his large ears and fell into his blue-gray eyes.

His half-sister Tutney, at thirty-seven, was an attractive but foreboding young woman. She never let up pressuring Addison to achieve the highest marks, and he didn't disappoint her. He was an astute academic and particularly excelled in his study of human anatomy. Unfortunately, his reserved nature made social life as a young man more difficult.

PART I

Tutney

CHAPTER ONE

The constant rhythmic puffing of the steam engine would normally have put Addison to sleep but this trip was different. Tutney's letter concerning his brother's illness had been quite urgent. Addison was anxious to see Walter for himself. He left Louisville to remain in Marbleton as long as it took for his brother to recover, and he hoped Tutney wouldn't interfere. He ate an early dinner and remained in the dining car studying for most of the trip.

Back at the Blair farmhouse in Marbleton, Tutney was preparing to travel to the depot. She pulled on her raincoat and scurried to the barn to hitch up the horse. It had been a week since she'd written Addison. She decided to stop by the general store on her way, and when she got there rain was sliding in sheets from the roof of the establishment. She lifted her coat over her head and ran for the door.

"Hello, Miss Blair," said Billy Welch, who was minding the store that day.

"Good morning, Billy," she said cheerfully. I need a few things. Addison is coming home today to help me with Walter."

"Yes ma'am," said Billy. "I heard Walter was sick. I hope it isn't serious."

"It is, Billy, but with Addison's and Dr. Sullivan's help we'll be able to bring him around I'm sure."

Billy gathered up everything Tutney had requested –a ten-pound sack of flour, dried peaches, five pounds of sugar for pies, a country ham, a week's worth of fruit and the most recent issue of "The Marbleton Gazette" for Addison to read while he was at home. She was worried about Walter but very optimistic regarding his recovery. Although his illness had been her reason for asking Addison to come, she was excited about seeing him again after four long months. When Tutney arrived at the station Addison stepped off the train looking distraught.

"How is he?" he asked.

Tutney presented her cheek for Addison's kiss.

"Not good, Brother, but at least he's not digressing. I made him breakfast this morning and asked Amy to sit with him while I bought staples at Jones' store."

"I wish you hadn't left him," said Addison. Tutney rolled her eyes.

"He's all right, Brother. Anyway, he's been desperate to see Amy."

Walter was an outgoing young man, blonde and fair. He was much more comfortable with girls than his older brother, and he and Amy Sullivan had been sweethearts since grade school. His only ambition was to live out his life in Marbleton as a farmer like his father before him. Of course, Tutney had other ideas for her youngest brother. She was hoping to recruit another student for Louisville Medical. In her opinion, there couldn't be too many physicians in the family.

"Let's hurry!" said Addison retrieving his suitcase from the porter.

On the ride home in Tutney's rig they were deluged with rain but even through the downpour Addison could see that Marbleton's hills were already dotted with the first yellow leaves of fall. As they approached the farm, the old house loomed large and stark under its grove of tall oaks, but it was welcoming to Addison. There was no hint of the illness inside.

Tutney drove the rig to the barn and Addison loosened the horse's harness and got him settled in the stall. He and Tutney ran through the rain to the front gate. The latch was loose.

"You need to have this fixed," Addison said. He opened the front door and was inundated by the odor of Benzoin. He'd encountered it often at Louisville Hospital and found it sickeningly sweet. He threw his wet overcoat and derby onto the hall tree and took his suitcase to the bedroom, then went straight to Walter. Although Tutney's letter had been disturbing, he wasn't prepared for his brother's condition.

"Doctor Blair!" said Walter excitedly as Addison entered the room.

"Aren't you getting ahead of things?" Addison protested.

"No. You're going to be rich!"

"Being rich is not enough to handle you!" Addison turned to Amy who sat in a cane chair by the bed.

"Hello, Amy," he said. She rose and kissed him on the cheek. "Addison. I'm so glad you're here. I've been catching Walter up on what's going on in town."

"Well, just seeing you must do wonders for him," Addison replied. "As for you, Walter, what's the idea of your getting sick and upsetting Tutney? You know how she can be when she's upset!"

Walter smiled but Addison could see his desperation. He put his stethoscope to Walter's chest and quickly decided to summon Dr. Sullivan. He asked Tutney to ride to the doctor's office to get him to come right away. He expected her to protest but she complied. She seemed excited to run the errand, even if it meant hitching up the horse and going out into the rain again. Addison went back to the bedroom and spent the next hour telling Amy and Walter all about school while they waited for the doctor.

When Dr. Sullivan arrived, his eyes fixed on Amy.

"Didn't expect to find you here," he said.

"Well, I don't know why not, Daddy," she answered, then bent to kiss Walter. "I'm going home now, love. Try to be a good patient."

As she tiptoed out her father followed her every step, then turned and examined his patient. He checked Walter's throat and listened to his chest.

"You've gotta stay in this bed, boy," he said sternly. "Let Tutney wait on you. She's a good nurse."

"I'll do whatever it takes, Dr. Sullivan."

The doctor motioned for Addison to follow him into the hall and Addison knew it wouldn't be good news.

"He has pneumonia. He's very congested and only time will tell the outcome. You'll have to keep a close watch. This kind of thing can change in the blink of an eye. Don't let his fever get too high--one-hundred-four degrees maximum-any more and you'll need to use ice to cool him down. Listen to his breathing. If there's a significant change let me know. Mustard plasters are probably a good idea. All we can do at this point is hope his body is ready for this fight. He's a strong young man so I feel sure he's going to recover."

He went back into the room and pushed the window curtain aside to let in more light.

"Don't let Tutney overdo the Benzoin," he smiled.

"I'll call if we need you," said Addison.

"Do that!" said Dr. Sullivan, giving him a pat on the shoulder. "T-u-t-n-e-y!"

Addison was surprised at the authority with which the doctor shouted at his sister. She intimidated most of the townspeople in Marbleton. She brought Dr. Sullivan his coat and took him home in the carriage.

Addison determined to do all he could for Walter and immediately went to the kitchen to make a mustard plaster for his chest. After applying it, he took a seat beside his brother's bed.

"I must really be in bad shape," Walter said.

"Walter, have confidence in your caregiver!"

Walter drifted off to sleep and slept for several hours, although restlessly. When he began to rouse, Addison reached for a small towel and dipped it in a bowl of warm water on the night stand. He bathed Walter's forehead and pushed the matted blonde locks away from his pale face.

"Brother," Walter said weakly, "You need to get back to school. Tutney can take care of me."

"You wouldn't deprive me of a chance to be your hero would you?"

"You're already my hero!"

When Tutney entered the room the conversation ceased.

"Brother, you can't stay in here day and night. Let me take over for awhile."

"I'll handle this, Tutney." He didn't leave her space for rebuttal so she huffed off angrily.

"She's right, you know," said Walter.

"She's always right, isn't she?" They both grinned.

Walter closed his eyes and drifted off again.

'Good,' thought Addison.

As he sat there he was flooded with thoughts of the past. Tutney had always been an enigma to him, and he knew her better than anyone. Her eyes were impenetrable but occasionally he sensed something in them that puzzled him--a kind of 'far away-ness' -- perhaps some painful memory she'd tucked away.

Hours passed with Addison lost in thought. The rain stopped and

Addison opened a window. He was surprised when Amy visited again that afternoon.

"Hello, doctor!" she said cheerily. She was petite and fair with deep blue eyes and long honey-colored hair.

"Hello," he replied.

"Walter," Amy whispered, moving closer to the bed. Walter turned in the direction of her voice.

"How are you?" she asked.

"I'm fine," he said. "Brother hasn't left my side."

"I'll let the two of you have a few minutes to yourselves," said Addison. He walked into the kitchen and poured a cup of strong coffee. Tutney came in from the garden and sat down beside him at the table.

"I'm almost done planting the turnips and broccoli," she said gasping for breath. "I planted a twenty by twenty plot and it'll be enough to get us through the winter."

"You know I don't like broccoli," said Addison.

"Well, it's not for you. It's for me and Walter. It's all I can do to pay for your schooling ... and you will need to get back soon!"

"I'll leave when Walter's better."

Suddenly Amy burst into the kitchen.

"Walter needs you!" she blurted, teary-eyed. She threw back the screen door and ran toward home.

Addison hurried back to Walter and found him delirious and burning with fever. At that moment it occurred to him Dr. Sullivan might be wrong about his brother's prospects for recovery. He pulled back the blankets and began to bathe Walter's body underneath the bed sheet so he wouldn't get chilled. He fought the fever till late that evening and when it finally subsided he sat down by the bed exhausted.

He remembered how, as a young boy, he'd been so excited to watch Tutney help his mother bring Walter into the world. He began to reminisce about the shortcuts he and Walter had taken home from school during the last hot days of summer when they were boys. Tutney always stayed late at the schoolhouse to grade papers and plan for the next day, and as soon as she got home she worked tirelessly in her garden until dusk. She then milked her cow, who would not let Addison or Walter near her. Left to amuse themselves the boys always found something to get into, either breaking some treasured item or perusing some forbidden book.

Occasionally, they'd do schoolwork until Tutney called them to supper. After eating she'd make sure they had all their home assignments done.

Addison continued sitting dutifully by the bedside. Tutney interrupted his thoughts once to bring him supper. When he was done he took the plate to the kitchen, told his sister 'good night' and returned to his chair beside Walter's bed. A light breeze blew through the open window and the eyelet curtains ballooned into the room. The clouds had disappeared and the moon was almost full. Shadows began to move on the walls. Tutney finished tidying the kitchen and retired. The house grew very quiet except for Walter's heavy breathing. Addison fell asleep.

On awakening he threw up his hand to deflect the glare from the morning sun. He rose abruptly and noticed the curtains were now still and infiltrated by the morning light. He could hear Tutney in the kitchen getting breakfast. He suddenly was aware of a deadly silence in the room. He didn't hear Walter's breathing. He instinctively bent over the bed.

"Walter," he said touching his shoulder, but there was no response. "Walter!"

He felt his brother's forehead and quickly drew back his hand in fear. Walter's skin was cold.

"WALTER! WALTER!" he repeated over and over, nudging him senselessly. Finally, he fell back into his chair in despair. His cheeks began to burn with tears as he realized the worst had happened.

'How could I have slept?' He asked himself and started to sob uncontrollably. He made a valiant effort to compose himself. After several minutes he reached over and straightened the ragged blanket, pulling it up to his brother's chin.

"Good-bye, Walter," he whispered. He stared at his brother for a long time thinking he looked peaceful with the blanket against his face, and wondered if he gazed intently enough he would suddenly see the slow rise and fall of Walter's chest. He didn't call for Tutney, who had opened the door once, and seeing him sitting there, had softly closed it again. Not knowing how much time had passed he got up and walked to the kitchen.

Tutney turned toward him as he approached the stove.

"How's your patient?" she asked, spooning eggs onto a plate. She reached for a cup from the white-washed cupboard and poured it full of coffee. On seeing her, his tears started again. As she turned around he dropped his head onto her shoulder.

"He's gone, Tutney. He's gone!" He buried his tear-streaked face in her neck.

For a long time she said nothing. Then, she placed her cup of coffee on the table and gave Addison a pat on the arm.

"Well," she said quietly. "The money I put away for Walter is yours now. Eat your breakfast."

Addison watched her walk down the hall in a quiet toe-first gait into Walter's room. She methodically closed the curtains and carefully pulled the covers up over Walter's face. She smoothed her dress over her stomach and hips and swept the loose curls at her neck up toward her bun. She closed the door behind her and walked back into the kitchen. There was no evidence of grief.

Addison looked down at his plate.

"I'm not hungry," he mumbled. He walked out the kitchen door and didn't stop until he had reached the river. He sat down on the bank where he and Walter had fished together so many times. He watched the water tumble over rocks and fallen branches and flow into shallow pools where water sprites darted back and forth. All sense of urgency was gone.

Tutney, practical soul that she was, immediately began to organize her thoughts. Later that afternoon when Addison returned she sent him to the school to tell them she wouldn't be in for a few days.   She also sent him to summon the undertaker who agreed to come to the house later that morning to prepare Walter's body for the wake and subsequent burial. She wasted no time writing an article to send to the newspaper office to notify the community, and spent the rest of the day cleaning and cooking.

The next evening most of Marbleton came to pay their respects. Many of the parents of Tutney's students were there, as were Walter's classmates, Gus and Millie Andrews, and Doc Neal Barnes from the pharmacy, Dr. Sullivan and Amy, and many of Walter and Addison's friends in Marbleton. Dr. Jacob Blair came and brought his daughters. Addison had so resented his mother for leaving him he had never allowed himself to miss her, but he now fervently wished she were alive and there with him.

Tutney was a perfect hostess, seeing to it everyone was served a plate of food. There were special dishes brought by the women in the community, a pork roast from Earline Andrews, collards, a large pan of dressing and all kinds of cakes and pies.

Once during the evening Addison caught a glimpse of Walter's body in the candlelit parlor and for a moment everything seemed surreal. Everyone was kind but he was so glad when they were gone. He went straight to bed without saying a word.

During the night a cold front moved through. Tutney spent the morning pressing a gray pin-striped suit that had belonged to their father for Addison.

"It smells of mothballs, Brother, but that can't be helped."

She had provided the undertaker with a suit she'd given Walter on his birthday and picked a couple of white rosebuds lingering on the English roses, putting one in Walter's lapel and giving the other to Addison. She chose for herself a high-waisted navy blue dress and a wide-brimmed hat with a veil.

Around twelve-thirty p.m. the undertaker, Seth Jackson, arrived and shifted Walter's body onto the lush quilted lining of the pine coffin Tutney had chosen. Addison wasn't surprised cost had been her first consideration. The pallbearers arrived around one-thirty in the afternoon along with a few visitors expressing last-minute condolences. At two o'clock Tutney and Addison along with those in attendance walked in procession out to the field where their father Lycurgeus, Granny Blair, and both of their mothers were buried.

Misty clouds hovered over the mourners gathered by the graveside. A blustering wind shook the multi-colored leaves of two giant water oaks keeping watch over the family cemetery. There were a few arrangements of flowers sent in Walter's memory. It was cool and Addison overlapped the edges of his coat to fend off the wind. Pastor Hodges from the Methodist church said a few words and recited a prayer as workers slowly lowered the coffin.

Tutney seemed in total control but she was angry at God for taking someone from her again and didn't want to give Him the satisfaction of succumbing to her pain.

Addison was oblivious to the low whispers of well-meaning neighbors and friends. His sadness was mingled with strangely comforting memories of his brother and their last fishing trip. Walter had caught a full string of bream and teased Addison about his only fish. In retaliation Addison had poured the last bit of worms down Walter's back and watched him squirm to get them out of his shirt. The two had wrestled in the briars and underbrush and awakened the next morning covered with 'chiggers'.

Walter's was the only affection Addison had ever known. He couldn't help asking God 'why?' He knew Tutney loved him but after Granny had died she cringed from any show of affection. Since his mother left them, Addison had existed more than lived and only his little brother had been able to connect with the lonely boy hidden in his heart. He suddenly longed for the day he might come to know a woman's love.

As the guests began to say their goodbyes and leave, he looked over at Tutney. Her pert lips were closed in resolve but the veil from her hat obscured the rest of her face. When the service was over Addison took the rosebud from his lapel and placed it with the other flowers strewn over the burial site. He thought himself safely hidden behind his quiet reserve but tears betrayed him. He left Tutney standing over the grave. Neither of them spoke.

Addison walked across the field and down Main Street. The wind was still brisk and lifted a few fallen leaves into swirls and slid them across the dusty road to the doorsteps of the granite shop buildings on the other side. Several carriages passed by but Addison didn't look up to see if he recognized anyone. The gas street lights began to glow in the misty afternoon as he reached the granite bridge over McGhee's Mill Road and passed by the First Baptist Church. Addison was weary of depending on Tutney for everything. He decided to approach Dr. Sullivan about taking him on as an intern. He longed to experience an actual practice even if it meant he could no longer conduct the anatomy class at school. He walked three more blocks down Main Street to Dr. Sullivan's home and medical practice at the corner of Main and First Avenue. The green lawn was speckled with brown and gold leaves from the oaks along the walkway. The house was a traditional red brick with a large arched wooden door at the entrance, framed by granite blocks set with cords of mortar that looked like gray toothpaste. There were tall side windows and through them a lamp glimmered and promised refuge from the wind.

Irene Sullivan answered the door and graciously invited Addison inside. Unlike her petite sister Amy, Irene was tall and statuesque. Addison was unsure if she recognized him. The Sullivans were originally from Connecticut and quite personable but were not given to showy sentiments, and only Amy and her father had attended Walter's funeral. Irene took Addison's hat and overcoat and ushered him down the hall to a seat in Dr. Sullivan's office while she went to find her father.

Addison gazed around the walls of bookshelves full of medical volumes. There was a ruby red crystal shot glass on the desk engraved with the words, 'Doc, here's prosperity,' through which the light from the window cast a pink glow. On the desk was a miniature ceramic skull wearing a pink and blue cap, sitting atop its three ceramic books. A stethoscope hung over the back of the doctor's chair. Everything was frightfully cluttered and dusty except for a few medical journals which, apparently, the doctor read from time-to-time.

Addison was startled by Dr. Sullivan's hand on his shoulder.

"Addison!" he said in a fatherly tone. "Are you doing all right? I'm so sorry about Walter. He was a good boy!"

Addison was ambivalent. In his eyes, no one was worthy of assessing his brother's value. He rose from the chair and extended his hand managing a 'Yes, thank you,' as the doctor pushed by him taking his seat behind the desk. Dr. Sullivan carefully removed the stethoscope, placed it around his neck and sat down. Addison straightened his coat and returned to his seat.

"What can I do for you, Son?"

Irene suddenly interrupted them with iced tea, slices of lemon tastefully perched on the rim of each glass. Addison was painfully reserved around women and was actually embarrassed by his growing attraction to a pretty face or full bosom.

"Thank you", he said rather weakly as he bent forward to take the glass from her hand. Addison's eyes fixed on hers for a moment but he deliberately did not disclose any interest. She smiled.

"You're welcome, Addison." The sound of his name surprised him. Apparently, she did recognize him. He had seen her many times in passing but she had never addressed him before. The whole town knew Dr. Sullivan had taken a liking to Addison when his father died and because of Addison's interest in medicine the doctor felt somewhat responsible for him and kept up with his achievements at Louisville

Medical School. He was aware Addison had been conducting the anatomy class for the residing professor of anatomy and often brought up his name in conversations at their family table. Addison slid back into his chair trying to focus on what had brought him there.

"Walter's afternoon job at the pharmacy was a big help to Tutney, and now ... " Addison stopped briefly so as not to reveal his grief.

"Dr. Sullivan," he started again, "I need to do something to help with expenses until I finish school. Your practice is growing and on the weekends I've seen your patients come and go as late as seven in the evening. I thought maybe I could help you by seeing patients on the Saturdays I'm home."

Dr. Sullivan held his pipe between his teeth and lit the bowl. The smell of sweet pungent tobacco filled the room. He looked up at Addison and grinned.

"You'd be willing to accept produce for compensation, of course?" he asked jokingly.

Addison patronized the doctor's attempt at humor with a half-smile. Everyone knew Dr. Sullivan was a frugal man and that most of his patients were the wealthy of Marbleton – no 'poor white trash' and definitely no blacks!

"Seriously, Addison, I couldn't compensate you in the way you deserve, but you must have read my mind. I've been thinking of bringing someone into my practice. It's getting to be too much for an old man!" Actually, the notion of being old was foreign to the doctor who was very proud of himself and would never have admitted truly needing help.

"Can you start this weekend?" he asked.

"Yes," said Addison.

"Then be here early Saturday morning, say about six, so we can go over some things. The patients start arriving at seven." He rose from his chair and offered Addison his hand. "We'll talk more later, if that's all right. I have a patient waiting. Give my best to Tutney!"

Addison shook the hand of Dr. Sullivan, whom he knew was really going out of his way to help him, and for now he was quite willing to accept his help. He started down the hall with the doctor close behind and rambling on about what a wonderful man Addison's father had been, and what a shame it was about poor Walter.

Irene met Addison at the door.

"Your coat." she said. Addison pulled on his overcoat, took his hat from her hand and hastened down the steps.

"You remember Irene, don't you Addison?" Addison paused on the bottom step and turned to look at Irene.

"Yes, I do."

"And I, you!" She said with a big smile. Addison nodded, then turned and walked toward home.

CHAPTER TWO

Addison was glad to be back in Louisville. Its large old maples were breathtaking, their green leaves mixed with shades of orange painted by the cool mornings. Wide stretches of green lawn led up to the tall brick campus halls with their white columns and massive doors, and the students gathered in groups of two and three under the tall stately trees discussing their class professors, their noble ambitions and the girls they'd left behind. It was noon and the chimes rang out from Hamilton Chapel. The pink roses at the entrance were still scantily blooming and cardinals and sparrows flitted under them, scratching at the dirt for worms or seeds. Louisville was quite a contrast to the stark granite town of Marbleton. Many of the homes near the campus were stately and sprawling and almost all had vine-covered arbors, porches, flower gardens and picket fences. Large black lanterns hung from brick and white clapboard carriage houses.

On his way up the dormitory stairs Addison ran into a fellow student, Henry Patterson. Henry was quite the ladies' man and bragged a little too much. He had slicked-back black hair, sparkling blue eyes, a thin mustache and was fairly tall. He was a dapper dresser and wore expensive shoes and clothes in the loudest stripes he could find. Henry liked everyone and everyone liked Henry.

Addison couldn't have been more his opposite. His size made it difficult for him to buy clothes that fit so he wore what he could find, mostly gray and black, and the sleeves were always a little too short. He was quiet, seldom witty but could be when he knew someone well. He was soft spoken, intellectually quick and a voracious learner who often mastered far beyond what was required of him to the chagrin of some of his professors.

Henry expressed his sympathy concerning Addison's loss then quickly barraged him with all that had been happening on campus. Professor Equin had resigned giving no explanation except 'it has become necessary', and everyone believed Addison would be taking over his anatomy class for the remainder of the year. Addison wondered if his letter to the professor informing him of his position with Dr. Sullivan's office had anything to do with his decision.

"You know there's no one else who can handle it," said Henry, "And even if they find someone to take his place, they won't let him start until fall of next year."

"Well, we'll see." said Addison. "I've taken on a part-time position in Marbleton and had planned to give up Anatomy class. There was a short silence.

"Where are you headed?" asked Addison.

"I'm on my way to Bingham Hall for lunch. Care to join me?"

"Be glad to!" Addison answered. As they walked toward Bingham Hall they chatted about what everyone would be doing for the upcoming holiday season. Still feeling the terrible emptiness of Walter's death, Addison was glad to be speaking of lighter things.

"Henry," Addison asked. "Do you have a big family?"

"Too big!" Henry quipped. "Five sisters older than me, two of them twins! My father is quite a taskmaster and my mother only has time for the girls! By the way, what are you planning for the holidays?"

"I'll probably spend Thanksgiving here," Addison replied. "I haven't given much thought to Christmas yet." He was thinking of Tutney, austere and sober, more so at Christmas, and the house always without a tree. Now that Walter was gone there was really no family to share a special meal. Anyway, his sister was an agnostic. She believed strongly in a Creator but as to Jesus, 'I just don't know' she would say, feeling it was sufficient. It was the only subject on which she had never formed a definite opinion.

"I was thinking," mused Henry, "maybe you could spend Christmas with me. My sisters would love it! They can show you off to Charleston society and you'll enjoy our warm days. Maybe you could even say a few words to impress my father with how well I'm doing in medical school.

Heaven knows, I need all the help I can get."

Addison would have liked to be free to accept Henry's invitation but he couldn't do so in good conscience.

"I'd better plan on taking every spare moment to study, especially if I'm going to be expected to cover anatomy class for the rest of the year."

"I know you, Addison, so I won't insist," Henry conceded. "But, my sisters are true belles and they'd love to meet you."

"One day, maybe," Addison replied. "How about spending the afternoon studying with me? It would help us both."

"I think not!" said Henry. "I'm going courting--pretty young thing, too!" Addison knew Henry never studied and would never complete his schooling. It troubled him greatly but he also knew it couldn't be changed. Henry was Henry and sooner or later even Henry's demanding father would have to accept it.

The two sat quietly for the next few minutes finishing their lunches, then went their separate ways. Henry headed for the city and Addison to the library for a few hours of reading.

Miss Wilson sat at the front desk as usual, peering over her reading glasses as Addison entered the door. She was very stern with the students, which had given her a reputation for meanness. She was highly intelligent but had not an ounce of common sense and, thus, no credibility. The students found her almost comical. She ran the library with a rod of iron, however, having found her place but always seeming a little out of place. She didn't speak but Addison could feel her eyes following him as he walked by her desk to the medical journals at the back of the room. He pulled out a few of the most recent volumes and found a table to himself. He had a habit of running the flat of his palm over the leather binding before he opened a book. He perused the contents and turned to an article called "Tetanus, Contemporary Breakthroughs," by Professor Ronald Searcy of Dayton, Ohio. Searcy was developing a therapy for treatment of lockjaw, a terrible disease brought on by the tetanus bacteria and up until now without a cure. Searcy believed it should be treated with nutrition. Addison poured over Searcy's account of the history of the disease, as well as several documented cases from diverse locales and the varied attempts at therapy.

Students slipped in and out of the library but Addison was oblivious to them as he sat reading. The hours ticked by. Starting to become sleepy his head sank closer and closer to the reading table. His eyes slowly shut. He didn't know how long he had dozed when he was suddenly awakened by the jerk of Miss Wilson's sturdy fingers on his sleeve.

"The library is about to close, Mr. Blair," she said snappily, "And it will take some time to return these books to the appropriate shelves." Authority exuded from her pores like sweat.

"S-s-o-r-r-y", Addison garbled, adjusting his eyes.

"Actually, it would be nothing to me if you studied all night. I'd like to see more dedication on this campus. Maybe less people would die from treatment at Louisville," she said cattily, thinking how clever and witty she was.

"However," she added, true to her character, "rules are rules!"

Addison wasn't in the least amused but forced a polite smile and immediately rose. It took him a few minutes to deposit the volumes on Miss Wilson's desk. When he reached the front door he lifted his coat from the rack in the corner and slid his long arms into the too short sleeves. Miss Wilson opened the door and ushered him out.

The Louisville nights were beginning to get very cold. The stars twinkled like sparkling crystals on a clear black sky. Orion was directly above him. The Big Dipper hung over Bingham Hall. It was almost nine o'clock.

CHAPTER THREE

Thanksgiving season came and went without event. Addison spent the time reviewing as planned. Henry returned from the holiday weekend with a photograph of his twin sisters for Addison's approval. He immediately began trying to coax Addison into spending Christmas in Charleston.

The next few weeks sped by. Addison spent two Saturdays helping Dr. Sullivan but still managed to complete the semester with echoes of praise from the school's president, Dr. Bergham. He received news the school had found someone to replace Dr. Equin soon after the New Year. Addison felt a little disappointed but the last few weeks of school had been so intense it would actually be a relief for him not to be subject to a continued grueling schedule of preparing for anatomy and supervising dissections. The school had hired Dr. Anderson Byrd, a professor from Washington University, who had received his medical degree and Ph.D. from Yale. Addison found him to be quite stuffy. He constantly puffed on a rank cigar and often repeated himself, but Addison decided to defer final judgment until after he spent some time under the professor's tutelage.

The Christmas holidays finally arrived and on Saturday morning the street was full of several teams of horses hitched to stylish carriages and awaiting their passengers. The breath of the horses formed large puffs of vapor in the cold air. Students eagerly greeted their relatives and crammed into coaches with tapestry bags, some filled with soft blankets to keep them warm for their journey home.

Henry, along with his twin sisters stopped by Addison's room in a last ditch effort to talk him into accepting an invitation to Charleston.

"Addison," he said cheerily, "I want you to meet my sisters, Rosalie and Marilee." Addison nodded at each girl, respectively.

"Ladies, this is Addison Blair, the brightest student in our class. So bright he's been teaching me anatomy in Dr. Equin's absence."

Rosalie was small-framed, fair and blonde with sky blue eyes like Henry's, while Marilee had Henry's black hair and was tall and slender in stature.

"Good morning," Addison said rather shyly. "Henry's told me a great deal about you."

"Don't listen to Henry," said the blonde sister smiling. "You'll be scared to death of us!" Addison didn't know how to reply.

"We're all hoping you'll change your mind and visit Charleston for the holidays" said Henry. "We have lots planned, don't we girls?"

"That's good of you, Henry," Addison said politely, "But my sister Tutney is expecting me and it'll be our first Christmas without Walter. I hope you understand."

"Of course we do," said the brunette sister, smiling sweetly. "It's so considerate of you to think of your sister ... isn't it Henry?"

Henry ignored her and turned to Addison.

"We do understand, old boy. Still, I thought I'd give it a try. You do need to think of yourself sometimes, you know." He embraced Addison warmly, then they all said good-bye. Henry walked away with a sister on each arm, equally dividing his attentive glances between them as they politely conversed on their way.

Addison would have traveling companions for part of his trip home. George Payne, a fellow anatomy student and the son of a prominent lawyer --a nice enough chap but rather odd-looking-- would accompany him as far as Chattanooga. George had pale freckles and orange hair, was short and thin and wore spectacles. He had a special preference for a dark brown tweed overcoat, which he wore every day, and refused to carry a satchel but lugged his books from class to class in his arms. He had very few friends and spent most of his time studying, so when he learned Addison would also be traveling by train he came by to make arrangements to meet him at nine o'clock Friday morning so they could ride to the station in his uncle's carriage. Bob Hamilton, a graduate student, would be joining them. He would be getting off the train in Nashville, where he was to begin residency with a couple of other graduate physicians. Addison looked at his watch. It was eight-forty-seven a.m. He picked up his suitcase and started toward Bingham Hall. The suitcase was heavily packed with books he was taking to keep at Dr. Sullivan's office. He was glad to see George Payne waiting at the top of the hill beside a carriage hitched to a team of dappled grays.

When Bob Hamilton finally arrived at nine-fifteen, the three of them climbed into the carriage and headed for Louisville Station. They boarded a few minutes before departure and found an empty berth as the train rumbled off through the outskirts of Louisville. At about eleven-thirty they went to the dining car and found a table, where they each ordered the Louisville "Christmas Special" for lunch. On returning to their berth George fell fast asleep, his head back, his mouth wide open and his spectacles dangling treacherously upon his nose. Addison and Bob Hamilton spent some time reviewing their finals and researching information in the areas in which they had shown weakness. Bob was a conscientious sort, very studious and quick to learn. He was one of the brightest in the anatomy class and was always full of questions for Addison so the three hours to Nashville went by quickly. They ran into heavy snow coming into Nashville and by the time they arrived at the Nashville Station the ground was white. Bob left the train and was greeted by several children in bright-colored sweaters and hats. A porter walked up with a Christmas tree Bob had brought from Louisville. Bob tied the tree up and then, he and the children climbed into a sleigh pulled by a tall black Tennessee walking horse who wore a Christmas wreath around his neck and bells that jingled from his harness.

The snow became more sparse as the train approached Chattanooga. The last few miles seemed long and arduous. There was a lot of sumac growing along the tracks, still autumn red, and a few dry leaves clung to the white oak trees. Conversation with George was difficult for Addison, as the two of them had little in common. George was extremely happy to have a good listener and rattled on enthusiastically about his plans to open a practice in Dalton for the indigents in the North Georgia foothills. When George finally departed Addison tried to settle in for a nap but his thoughts turned unhappily toward home. He wasn't looking forward to three weeks with Tutney. He knew she would avoid any mention of Walter, which would make the holidays more painful. He had postponed grieving to meet the difficult demands of school and he longed to share his memories of Walter with her, but Tutney would probably just remind him to put sentiment behind him and focus. Addison had a fleeting thought of Irene Sullivan.

Finally, he arrived at the Marbleton Depot. Gus Andrews offered him a ride in his delivery wagon. It was a rough ride but it got him home. When he got down from the wagon, Gus handed down his heavy luggage.

"What you got in this bag?" Gus asked inquisitively. "Feels like it could be gold! You rich already, Doc?" Gus, like everyone in Marbleton who knew Addison liked calling him 'Doc', however prematurely.

"If I were rich I'd be riding in a stylish carriage instead of your ice wagon! It's books," said Addison as he took his luggage from Gus' rough hands.

"Thanks, Gus! I have a lot of fine folks to thank for getting me here!"

"Oh, it ain't nothin', Doc. I was on my way home from the ice house when I seen you standin' there. Millie and I just got married, and I'm so cheery nothin' seems to put me out."

Millie worked at the pharmacy in Marbleton where Walter had worked, and she concocted the best sodas in Georgia. Gus was a good man, but illiterate like most of his family and had very little ambition. Addison found it difficult to understand why pretty Millie had settled for him.

"Millie's a sweet girl," replied Addison. "Take care of her."

"Aw, you know I will," Gus assured. "Merry Christmas, Doc!"

Addison waved good-bye then turned to open the gate. The latch was still rusty and about to fall off. Tutney hadn't had it repaired as he requested. To his surprise the old house was decorated for the holiday. There was a holly wreath on the door with a white bow and garlands of pine draped on the rails across the front porch. Addison was glad to finally be home and wondered what had gotten Tutney into a festive mood. Tutney heard the key rattling in the front door and rushed to the parlor with excitement. She had spent the last two days decorating and cooking, and was eagerly anticipating the dinner she'd planned. She just knew her brother would be pleased with her.

Addison opened the door and found Tutney on the other side.

"Brother!" she said fondly. "Let me take that suitcase to your room. You head for the bathroom to freshen up before our guests arrive." There was a hug and quick kiss on his cheek, which coming from Tutney was unusually warm. As he had suspected she made no mention of Walter.

"Who on earth is coming?" asked Addison tiredly as she disappeared down the hall with his heavy luggage.

"It's never too early to pave the way for your future," yelled Tutney from the bedroom. "I've invited Dr. and Mrs. Sullivan to join us for dinner." She had made these arrangements after she learned Irene was away visiting her cousins in Greenville and would be indisposed. Tutney had no real reason to be wary of Irene but she had always discouraged any thoughts of Addison's having a social life, especially one that might include the opposite sex.

"Tutney! I was hoping to be able to relax and get to bed early. I was up all night tying up loose ends, and studying on the train coming down kept me from catching a nap. Besides, I thought I'd go through Walter's things. There's something Amy should have."

"Walter is dead," said Tutney returning to the parlor, "and Amy can wait! You have to put the past in its place."

"Don't you miss him?" Addison surprised himself by asking.

"You never appreciate my efforts!" she said curtly, ignoring his question. "But never mind that. I'm more than glad to do my part to help you become an established physician in Marbleton. The short trip from Louisville couldn't have made you that tired!" Tutney's manipulation had started already.

"Oh, you know I appreciate it, Tutney," Addison said patiently, "but I'm exhausted."

He thought about it for a moment,

'I guess I should be glad Dr. Sullivan's coming. I need to talk with him before Saturday about some things I learned this month.'

"I would like to ask Dr. Sullivan if he has ever heard of a Dr. Anderson Byrd from upstate New York."

"Who is he?" asked Tutney returning from the bedroom with a clean towel and washcloth.

Addison took them from her hand.

"Dr. Equin's successor," he replied.

"You mean they didn't give the Anatomy class to you after all you've done to help the other students? No professor could be as meticulous as you are!"

"I'm your brother, Tutney."

"You're a Blair," said Tutney matter-of-factly. "Don't ever forget that!"

Addison walked toward his room so he wouldn't be subjected to Tutney's 'blood is thicker than water' tirade. Feeling a little refreshed after his bath he put on the gray pinstriped suit he had worn to Walter's funeral and borrowed a sprig of holly from Tutney's table arrangement for his lapel.

There was a knock at the door promptly at seven and Addison walked through the parlor into the hall and peered out the stained glass window to see Dr. and Mrs. Sullivan standing there with Irene. The doctor looked quite distinguished and Mrs. Sullivan stood with her gloved hand through his arm. She was a stately woman of five feet ten inches, slightly taller than the doctor. She wore a black velvet skirt and matching high-feathered hat. Beside her stood Irene in a midnight blue taffeta dress, cream-colored pearls dripping from her ivory neck and a soft pink blush on her cheeks. She resembled her mother but had a much softer demeanor. Addison opened the door to welcome them.

"Good evening," he said as he ushered them into the parlor. Tutney greeted them awkwardly, somewhat disarmed by the appearance of Irene.

"Irene's cousin came down with measles and Dr. Sullivan didn't want her exposed," explained Mrs. Sullivan. "Amy had already left and is taking her chances. I assured Irene you wouldn't mind if she came along, dear. I thought she and Addison could visit."

"Yes," said Tutney. "Please have a seat." She pointed toward a chair.

"How nice to see you, Irene," continued Tutney with a forced smile. "I'll have to get down another place setting." Addison was embarrassed by Tutney's rude tone. After adding the plate and silverware, Tutney ushered her guests into the dining room. She directed Addison to the end of the table and seated herself between him and Dr. Sullivan, seating Mrs. Sullivan on the opposite side of Addison, which seemed rather bold even for Tutney. Of course, Irene was seated beside her mother and as far away from Addison as Tutney could manage. The table was covered with a white linen cloth embroidered with red poinsettias.

There were matching napkins and a finger bowl at each place setting, along with tiny individual silver salt and pepper shakers. There was an elaborate centerpiece consisting of three slender red wax tapers skillfully arranged amongst long-needle pine, holly and red velvet ribbons. The candles filled the room with soft, flickering light. With everyone seated Tutney served pork roast, dressing, cranberry salad and homemade rolls. Addison's appetite languished, both at the pain of Walter's absence and at Irene's unexpected presence. Everyone talked quietly and Irene discussed with her mother the exhaustion of shopping in Atlanta to find gifts for her school chums.

"I decided on sterling charm bracelets and wrapped each one in silver paper with one of the silver charms tied to a lacy white ribbon," she said. She smiled sweetly at Addison when she caught him staring at her.

Tutney asked Dr. Sullivan how his practice was going during the holiday season and made a point to compliment him on his success. Addison was rather quiet, as was Mrs. Sullivan, and he hoped she had not been offended by Tutney's coldness toward Irene. When everyone finished eating Addison and Dr. Sullivan retired to the living room while the women attended to the dishes. Dr. Sullivan lit his pipe as he and Addison walked through the parlor. A photograph of Addison's anatomy class caught Dr. Sullivan's eye. In the photograph Addison was supervising a group of students in the dissection of a cadaver.

"Quite impressive, Addison!" he said in a muffled fashion as he puffed. "Strange décor for the parlor, though, don't you think?"

"Tutney's advertisement," quipped Addison with a chuckle. Dr. Sullivan was surprised to learn his quiet protégé had a sense of humor.

"Addison, I'm very pleased with the way it's working out having you in the office on Saturdays," Dr. Sullivan continued. "The patients seem to have taken to you in the worst way."

"Worst way?" Addison asked.

"Just don't forget I'm the top dog!" Dr. Sullivan said laughing. "I can't have them liking you too much!"

"Actually, Dr. Sulllivan, I'm thinking of joining a group in Athens when I finish school," Addison said quickly, spurred on by the doctor's comments.

"Well, I'm sorry to hear that. I was hoping you'd consider joining my practice permanently," said Dr. Sullivan. "I mentioned it at breakfast and my family was quite enthusiastic about the idea--especially Irene."

He puffed on his pipe and planted a reassuring pat on Addison's shoulder. Addison's face grew warm at his reference to Irene and he reached up to loosen his collar. He bent down to stoke the fire and when it flamed up, he settled down on the divan next to the fireplace. Dr. Sullivan seated himself in an overstuffed chair on the opposite side of the room.

The walls of the living room were covered in blue and gold-striped, somewhat faded silk wallpaper, and gold draperies hung heavily from the high ceiling to the floor over three oversized windows on the front of the old house. Reflections of the fire danced in a huge baroque mirror over the divan and, also, in a framed portrait of Lycurgeus Blair, which hung over a chair. Lycurgeus had been a strikingly handsome young man in spite of his ill health and his blind right eye, the target of a playmate's arrow when he was only five. He had been one of the few Blairs to become farmers. Three of his brothers became physicians and one a prominent Atlanta lawyer. All of his sisters had married well and left Marbleton long ago and Addison and Tutney knew little of their families.

Addison and Dr. Sullivan were discussing patients when Irene appeared in the room and seated herself next to Addison on the divan.

"Where do you get the bodies for those horrible experiments?" Irene asked Addison, referring to the somber photograph. "I'm sorry, but it seems absolutely ungodly!"

"We don't do experiments," assured Addison. "But dissection of a cadaver is the best way to learn about the human body. Is healing ungodly, Miss Sullivan?"

Addison's directness made Irene feel ashamed.

"I'm sorry, Addison," she said sincerely. "How foolish of me to get such an impression. You must tell me some of the things you're learning."

Addison was relieved when Mrs. Sullivan brought in a dessert tray followed by Tutney with the tea service.

"Your sister's not only a beautiful young woman, Addison," said Dr. Sullivan. "She's a marvelous cook!" His eyes were fixed on Tutney.

"Yes, she is a good cook!" replied Addison, "as evidenced by my waistline."

After all had enjoyed bread pudding and a cup of hot tea, the Sullivan's prepared to leave. Addison approached Irene in the hallway.

"Irene."

"Yes, Addison," she said as she turned toward him. He slipped a small box into her hand.

"Please give this to Amy. I think she would like to have it, and I very much hope she will accept it." Irene opened the small box.

"Walter's watch!" she said. "It's beautiful. Amy will be so honored."

"We'd better be on our way, darlings," said Dr. Sullivan and the three of them thanked Tutney for the meal and departed.

"See you in the morning!" Dr. Sullivan called back to Addison as he and Tutney watched them disappear over the hill.

"There's more tea, Brother," said Tutney when they were out of sight. "You haven't told me anything about what's been happening at school or how the Saturdays at Dr. Sullivan's office are going."

"I'm sorry, Tutney," said Addison, "but I talked enough about that with Dr. Sullivan tonight. Can't it wait till morning?"

"You seemed anxious enough to converse with Irene," Tutney said sourly, then turned and walked curtly down the hall to her room.

Addison was sure Tutney noticed he had hardly spoken to Irene except to reply to her remarks. He started to say something but stopped short.

"Dinner was nice," he said. When she didn't answer, he walked out onto the porch. He took a seat in the swing and began to move it lazily back and forth. The train whistle blew softly in the distant twilight. It was nice to be in Marbleton, where it was slightly warmer than Louisville. The evening seemed almost balmy. The gaslights on Davis Street were quite bright and almost every front porch displayed a wreath. A small church had constructed a unique nativity under a gaslight intended to represent the Bethlehem star. Its glow fell softly on the courtyard. It had been a good evening, after all!

CHAPTER FOUR

Addison rubbed his eyes and stretched to the side of the bed to see the clock. It was six a.m. He pushed back the covers and stood to his feet, reaching for his robe at the foot of the bed.

He could hear Tutney in the kitchen, running water for coffee. She was becoming a routine-driven old maid. She had opened the shutters, filled the birdfeeders and watered the houseplants. Her Saturday routine was consistent. She cleaned the house, thoroughly swept the windows and corners of the rooms for cobwebs and mopped the floors. When this was done, she made her weekly trip to the general store for kitchen supplies. She had fresh meat one night a week with greens from the small garden in the backyard and a pitcher of milk from her cow consisting of nine-tenths cream. She would choose from among the vegetables she canned each summer for the other nights of the week and always bought at least one piece of fresh fruit a day for she and Addison when he was at home. Every Saturday night she graded papers for the students in her classes. She loved teaching and inspired their best efforts.

This morning she was humming cheerfully as she moved through the house dusting the furniture and portraits on the walls. Near a corner in the dining room was a small portrait of her mother, Louisa, in a light-colored dress with crystal buttons and a white lace shawl around her shoulders. Her face was framed by curls. She had a long neck and full lips, which she had passed on to Tutney, whose reflection peered back at her from the glass. Tutney self-consciously reached up to smooth her dark hair toward the top of her head. Wispy curls fell at the nape of her neck. She wiped the sideboard with a cloth and ran gloved fingers over the surface to be sure she had left no dusty residue.

Tutney was a wiry woman but quite attractive. She preferred pleated blouses with high, starched collars and flat button-up shoes. She deliberately stepped toe first to quiet the sound of her walk. She stood as straight as an arrow. When she spoke her voice was mesmerizing and she possessed a quick, intimidating wit. The men in Marbleton noted her good looks but resigned that she was only for the most courageous of suitors. The one exception was Eldrin Booth, a recent widower. Today, he was meeting Tutney at the market and accompanying her to the drugstore for ice cream.

'I don't know why I put up with Eldrin,' she thought. 'He's such a nuisance really.'

When she finished her housecleaning, Tutney started toward the bedroom to dress, still humming. Addison came out of the bathroom, clean-shaven and smelling of lemon after-shave.

"Tutney, you want company today?" he asked. "Dr. Sullivan's leaving the clinic early and says I'm to lock the door promptly at noon, no matter what. I could meet you at the market. I want to look for jars to take back to the school lab."

"Can't do it today, Brother," Tutney replied as she disappeared into her room. Addison paused, waiting for an explanation but none came.

'As long as I'm not involved in her plans, I suppose I should be grateful,' he thought. He reached down to pull on his rain boots. It was dark and gray outside and he anticipated rain and didn't want to walk the muddy streets of Marbleton in his only good pair of shoes. When he walked out, Tutney was still getting dressed so he didn't bother to say good-bye.

There was already a light mist falling. The Christmas wreath on the Bagby's door was covered with dew and its velvet ribbons hung straight and limp to the floor. Ephraim Bagby was the town banker and rather standoffish, but Mrs. Bagby was quite friendly. She waved from the porch as Addison walked up the hill carrying his medicine bag. Addison's derby hat was keeping him reasonably dry and it would only take another two to three minutes to reach the clinic. Dr. Sullivan had said since he would be there early it would be all right for Addison to be a little later arriving. Soon he reached the stoop and opened the door. A heavyset young nurse greeted him.

"Good day, Dr. Blair," she said kindly. "Poor weather we have today, huh?"

Addison was beginning to like being called 'Dr. Blair.'

"Good morning, Alice," he replied. "Has Dr. Sullivan started seeing patients yet?"

"He's in with Mr. McGaughey now....gout in his right foot," she said matter-of-factly.

"Dr. Sullivan wants you to see Mrs. Andrews and Millie in the back room," she added, pointing down the hall. "Mrs. Andrews says Millie had a couple of faintin' spells this week and may be in a family way. She's worried Gus won't have the money to pay for Millie's care and wants Dr. Sullivan to trade his services for a few canned goods and a couple of young roosters until Gus can earn a few dollars."

"It will be a challenge to confront him with that request," said Addison rather sarcastically and Alice nodded in agreement. Addison knew Dr. Sullivan was a hard man and not apt to agree to such an arrangement. Taking the chart from Alice he walked down the hall and into the examining room.

"Good morning, Mrs. Andrews ... Millie." Addison took a seat at the desk. He immediately noticed the strained buttons at Millie's waist, which she had attempted to conceal with a large sash.

"How are you feeling, Millie?"

"Fine, Addison ... uh, Dr. Blair," Millie blushed.

"I'm afraid Gus has gone and gotten Millie sick," interjected Mrs. Andrews (good decent folks never used the word 'pregnant').

Addison put the stethoscope to Millie's chest and listened intently. He put the tongue depressor in her mouth.

"A-a-h-h-h." Millie complied.

Addison had Mrs. Andrews take a seat in the waiting room and asked Alice to come into the room while he examined Millie, who was somewhat embarrassed but managed to get through it.

"Have you been nauseated, Millie?" asked Addison.

"I've been so-o-o sick, Dr. Blair. I don't dare have my eggs in the mornin's no more. Gus says I got to quit vomitin' 'cause he can't eat when I'm like that."

"Well, tell Gus your nausea should subside in a few weeks."

Addison placed the stethoscope on Millie's lower abdomen, then took a look at her ankles.

"Have you had any bleeding?"

"Oh, no! My last monthly was the end of the summer. I'm healthy as a horse, 'cept for not bein' able to eat much. I been helpin' Gus deliver ice on the weekends."

"Well, Millie, it's better if you don't lift anything too heavy. I think you'd better tell Gus you can't help him anymore till after the baby comes."

"So, I am preg—" Millie looked excited but stopped herself.

"Yes, you're going to have a baby, Millie. I'd say about the middle of next May." It gave him a lot of satisfaction to be the bearer of this exciting news. He told Millie to dress and meet him in the office and had Alice bring Mrs. Andrews back so he could tell her of Millie's pregnancy.

"Well, it looks like you coulda waited," said Mrs. Andrews scoldingly to Millie. "It ain't easy havin' the two o' ya takin' up space, and Doc Barnes at the pharmacy will make ya quit, o' course. Now, we're 'bout to have anotha mouth to feed." Earlene Andrews was unkind. She turned to Addison.

"You think Dr. Sullivan'll take a couple o' roosters and some canned jelly for his services, Dr. Blair? Gus ain't got no money!"

Millie, quietly rose from her chair.

"I'm sorry to be so much trouble, Ma Andrews," she said. "I'll get back to work soon as the baby comes and start payin' you back for everything."

Addison hated seeing Millie humiliated. He knew how that felt after years of putting up with Tutney's stabbing remarks. He wished he could find a solution.

"Mrs. Andrews," started Addison. "I, uh ... " He tried desperately to think of the right way to say it.

"Dr. Sullivan has a lot of overhead trying to keep this office open on the weekends. Isn't there any way you can come up with the money for his services within the next month?"

"It's all I can do to keep me and Fred goin'," replied Mrs. Andrews, "And heaven knows it's been hard keepin' Gus and Millie up, too!" she added. "Surely you don't 'spect me to have any money today?"

Millie started to sob quietly.

"I'm sure we can work something out, Millie," Addison offered. "You think you and Gus can come up with enough to pay for today's visit? It'll be two dollars."

"Oh, I can do that, Dr. Blair," she said wiping her eyes. "I still got two dollars left from last week." She reached into her skirt pocket to pull out the money.

"Oh, no, you don't, Millie" said Ms. Andrews. "You promised to pay me back some of what you owe me and I'm countin' on it to pay our bills this month."

Addison reached into his pocket and pulled out two dollars.

"Here, Millie," said Addison putting the money into Millie's hand. Give it to Alice when you go out."

"Oh, I couldn't Dr. Blair."

"Just promise to come see me and Tutney at the house at the end of every month to be sure everything's all right with the baby. Make it the last Sunday morning in the month around nine and try not to be late. I have to leave for Louisville by noon. I'll plan on delivering the baby when it's time, and then you and Gus can talk with me about a trade." Addison wondered how Dr. Sullivan would feel about his taking one of his patients, although he suspected he'd be relieved when he learned of Millie's inability to pay.

Addison patted Millie on the shoulder.

"Now you take care of yourself and that baby! No more carrying ice!"

"All right," Dr. Blair. "If you say so."

"Yeah, thanks, Dr. Blair," said Earlene Andrews. "You're a real gentleman!" Addison wondered if Earlene Andrews knew what a gentleman was.

Addison followed them down the hall to the office. Millie handed Alice the two dollars and she and Earlene Andrews left.

"Tell Gus I said 'hello,'" Addison called to them, as he returned the chart to Alice.

Eldrin Booth spotted Tutney leaving the market and walking toward the pharmacy.

"Tut!" he called as he caught up to her. Her expression revealed how much she hated the nickname.

Eldrin was very handsome, tall and broad-shouldered. He had a plaid scarf around his neck and locks of his straight black hair hung into his dark eyes, which were very kind. He had a disarming smile.

"Notice anything different?" Eldrin said with a mischievous grin.

"Yes! You're late!"

"One of my most endearing qualities, no doubt, but that's not what I had in mind. Is there anything different about me?" he asked a second time.

"Eldrin," Tutney started, "You know how upset I get when my schedule's disrupted. I have to grade papers this afternoon ... and Brother will be coming in hungry from Dr. Sullivan's office and needing his clothes packed for his trip back to Louisville tomorrow."

"Sorry," said Eldrin. "Dad asked me to help him board up the stalls we're not using. I underestimated the time it would take." For a few minutes they walked in silence.

"I give up!" Eldrin said finally. "It's my mustache. It's gone!"

"I'm so tired of the holidays," she added. "I hate the clutter and décor. Things can't get back to normal soon enough!" She obviously was ignoring him.

Eldrin was becoming discouraged, but persisted.

"Remember, Tutney," he said. "You told me if I shaved off my mustache, you would marry me."

There was a long pause. Tutney looked at him in disbelief. She was surprised she hadn't noticed.

"Why, Eldrin Booth!" she exclaimed. "You look like a schoolboy! Surely you didn't take me seriously. I'd never marry a man so easily manipulated!"

Eldrin was speechless. He couldn't believe he'd been so naïve.

"Anyway," Tutney added, " What I said was 'I might marry you.' "

"Tutney," Eldrin said softly. "You know how I feel about you."

"Well, I guess you've projected those feelings onto me!" Tutney said, "And that was a mistake."

'That was a mistake!' Eldrin thought to himself as he wrapped his fingers tightly around the small box in his pocket. He'd had the ring for weeks but hadn't been able to get up the nerve to approach her.

When they reached the drugstore Eldrin opened the door for Tutney who walked toe-first across the checkered tile and took a seat at one of the parlor tables.

"Hello, Miss Blair," said Millie Andrews from behind the counter. "What will you have today?"

"Why, Millie, you're pregnant!" Tutney said emphatically as she stared at Millie's abdomen.

"Yes, Miss Blair," replied Millie. "Did Ad--, did Dr. Blair tell you? He's goin' to see me the last Sunday mornin' of every month till the baby comes, and he'll be doin' the delivery."

"He certainly did not tell me, Millie!"

"Well, I guess he'll be tellin' you this evenin'," Millie said as she placed two paper napkins on the table. "It's due in May. What'll you be havin', Eldrin?"

Tutney didn't like Millie calling Eldrin by his first name.

"*Mr. Booth and I* will have chocolate sodas, Millie," Tutney replied for them both.

Eldrin hung his coat and scarf on the coat tree and joined Tutney at the table. Tutney pulled off her coat and draped it over the back of her chair. When Millie returned with the sodas her eye caught sight of a beautiful gold brooch pinned to Tutney's coat collar, an onyx peacock with spreading sapphire wings and diamond eyes set in 14-carat gold filigree. Millie's mouth fell open.

"My, Miss Blair. That brooch is really special!"

"Mr. Booth gave it to me," Tutney responded with pride and turned to Eldrin who, apparently, was lost in thought.

"Eldrin!" she said indignantly.

"Sorry," said Eldrin.

"I was telling Millie you gave me this brooch," said Tutney, lifting the collar of her coat.

"Oh, yes, I ... "

"Brother!" interrupted Tutney as Addison walked through the door. "You're done at Dr. Sullivan's?"

Eldrin rose from the table and went to pay for the sodas.

"I told you this morning Dr. Sullivan wanted me to close the office early," said Addison, then looked in the direction of the counter.

"Hello again, Millie."

"Can I get somethin' for you, Dr. Blair?" Millie asked.

"I'll have a malt, Millie--vanilla--to go. I'll bring the glass back tomorrow."

By the time Eldrin returned to the table, Tutney had finished her soda and stood there waiting for Eldrin to help her with her coat.

"Eldrin," she said as he assisted, "I won't need you to show me home, now. I'll be walking home with Brother."

"Of course, Tutney," said Eldrin glancing at Addison. Good day, Addison." He hurriedly retrieved his coat and rushed out the door. His disappointment was obvious to Addison but seemed of no consequence at all to Tutney. She felt she couldn't discourage his attentions if she wanted to and, besides, he had to understand her brother would always come first.

Addison, embarrassed for Eldrin, ushered Tutney out the door toward home.

"If I were Eldrin Booth, I'd be very upset with you, Tutney. You didn't even thank him for the soda. I wonder if he knows he's the butt of a lot of jokes because of the way you treat him."

"H-m-m-m-ph! His own fault!"

On Christmas morning Addison got up to wrap the Victrola he had purchased for Tutney. He had found it at the dry goods store in Louisville. He was quite excited. He knew Tutney would never buy one for herself even though she loved music and often stayed late to play the Victrola at the schoolhouse. He carefully wrapped it in newsprint and tied it with the red velvet ribbon he had saved from the gift he'd been presented by the school for his service to the Anatomy Department in Dr. Equin's absence. When he finished wrapping the gift, he left it on the bed and followed the smell of frying bacon into the kitchen.

"Good morning, Tutney", he said cheerfully.

"Good morning, Brother," she replied. "I've served your plate," she added gesturing toward the table. Next to Addison's plate was a cup of coffee and a small gift wrapped in brown paper. Addison quickly returned to his bedroom to retrieve Tutney's gift and presented it to her as she sat down.

Tutney held the large box and looked at it blankly.

"What on earth is this, Brother?" she asked, obviously displeased. "I hope you haven't gone and spent some of the money I sent you for school."

"Open it," said Addison excitedly.

"I'll not open it," she said adamantly. "You must return it! When you have your own practice and your own money, I'll accept gifts from you."

Addison's enthusiasm quickly left him. He didn't feel like replying. He sat down beside Tutney and when the two of them finished eating Tutney cleared the table, washed and put away the dishes and left the room.

Addison, curious, reached for the package from Tutney and opened it. It was a picture of Walter in a small bubble glass frame. 'Does Tutney have a soft side, after all?' he mused. He would take it back with him to Louisville.

"Get your coat on!" Tutney shouted from the hall. "We're going to church."

"That will make me late for the train," Addison protested.

"It's Christmas!" she said walking toward the parlor. "A physician is expected to present himself at church on Christmas. We'll hurry!" Tutney didn't care about God, just about making good impressions. Addison pulled on his coat and met her at the front door.

The Marbleton Methodist Church was especially full that day. Lottie Thompson was singing the lead in Handel's Messiah along with the Marbleton Children's Choir. Tutney deliberately stopped at a pew near the back of the church across from Eldrin Booth who sat next to the aisle with Vivian Nelms, the postmaster's daughter. She and Addison took a seat near the middle, and when Tutney was settled she glanced back in Eldrin's direction to find him staring back at her.

When the service was over Tutney deliberately walked up to Eldrin and Vivian.

"Why, Eldrin!" she acted surprised. "How nice to see you!"

"Tutney," he nodded.

"Hello, Addison ... Miss Blair" said Vivian, adding "You look lovely."

"Oh, surely you jest, Vivian," Tutney replied. "I dressed in such a rush."

"Really, Miss Blair, you look absolutely breathtaking ... doesn't she Eldrin?"

"Yes ... she does." Said Eldrin politely.

"I trust you both had a nice Christmas?" said Tutney trying to sound interested.

"It was wonderful," Vivian answered enthusiastically, "and yours?"

"Mine was very busy," she replied. "Dr. and Mrs. Sullivan were our dinner guests Friday evening."

Addison detected a little jealousy in Tutney's voice and knew she was putting on airs.

"Well, I hate to rush off but Addison has to get back to Louisville this afternoon. Have a good day!" She didn't give them a chance to reply.

"Goodbye," said Addison following her down the steps.

When they reached home Addison went immediately to his room to pack his things. Tutney appeared in the room with several clean shirts, freshly starched and meticulously ironed.

"Thank you, Tutney, but I've told you all this work is unnecessary. I have to wear my suit and no one really sees the shirts."

"Nonsense! I won't have you looking like a vagabond!"

Tutney went to the kitchen, pulled out some leftover pork and greens and made a quick pitcher of tea. They had a quiet lunch together and then Addison left for the train station.

On Addison's return to school the classes seemed somewhat subdued. Some of the students had taken extended holidays and wouldn't be back till after New Years' Day. Henry Patterson was among them, as well as Bob Hamilton. Addison picked up his schedule next to the administrative office and went by the library to get the books he needed. It was going to seem strange to no longer be teaching, or even attending Anatomy, but he was sure advanced chemistry would be challenge enough to keep him busy and he was soon to start his residency at Louisville Hospital. That would make a big difference in his schedule.

A few weeks later on one of his weekends in Marbleton, Addison ran into Irene Sullivan. She was so cordial he thought about asking her to attend the Sunday morning services at Marbleton Methodist but failed to get up the courage. He read in the Sunday morning paper the announcement of her engagement to a Mr. Raleigh Saunders of Royston. He didn't know whether to be glad or sorry he hadn't acted on his impulse. Of course, Tutney was delighted. At least she wouldn't have to worry about Addison's attraction to Irene anymore.

Addison thought of Irene a lot over the next few weeks at school but finally settled into his studies. He became quite absorbed in the care of his patients at the hospital. He had learned not to call them "cases" after a patient expressed anger toward a fellow resident for referring to him as 'the cardiac'. Except for Dr. Sullivan's weekend patients and the end-of-the-month check on Millie whose pregnancy was coming along quite well, Addison dedicated himself to his new internship. He had true compassion and wanted to make a difference in the lives of his patients. He tried to equip himself with everything he needed to help them. He was a perfect candidate for this calling, which had come to him not only through his heritage and on Tutney's insistence, but through his own quiet spirit. There was more to learn than he realized and traveling back and forth from school to the hospital made the weeks seem long. Addison began making inquiries into various opportunities for physicians in Georgia and was leaning toward joining the practice in Athens he had mentioned earlier to Dr. Sullivan.

When spring came Addison returned to Marbleton for the holiday and found Millie in the throes of labor. He hurried to the Andrews' home just in time to deliver a wriggling infant boy that looked like a miniature of Gus. The nine-pound infant had left Millie very weak but she was ecstatic, and even Earline Andrews seemed pleased. When Addison presented Gus with his son, he beamed with a snaggled-tooth grin.

"Doc, you did it!" he exclaimed.

"No, Gus," Addison teased, "You did it!"

"Thanks, Doc," said Gus, "For ever'thing!"

"Now, don't you have Millie out there delivering ice with you, Gus ... understand!? She's too frail and you have to let her get her strength back."

"Don't worry, Doc. She's my treasure! She and this little 'un. I'll take care of 'em. You bettuh believe it!" he asserted.

"I'm counting on you, Gus," said Addison. He peeked into the room to see that Millie had fallen asleep with the new baby on her chest. Gus brought Millie and the baby to the Blair house later that afternoon and they both stayed in Addison's room for the rest of the week. Earlene Andrews sat with them during the day and Tutney checked on them during the night. The next Saturday Gus came by and he and Addison helped Millie and the baby into the Andrews' carriage, cushioning them with several blankets, and Gus took his family home.

51

CHAPTER FIVE

The last few weeks in Louisville were busy. Addison didn't make it back home because no one else wanted to take the weekend shifts, and since he wasn't thrilled with Tutney's company he volunteered to stay at school. It was the last month of the school year and Dr. Sullivan had agreed to Addison's being at school on the weekends.

Addison hadn't tried to have relationships with girls. His shyness was a part of his decision, but he also wanted to spend as much time as possible studying. He soon became an outstanding surgery resident.

The next year passed quickly and in the spring of 1905, his class was preparing for graduation. Tutney had been faithful to send money for tuition and expenses, and Addison was grateful and determined to find a way to repay her for her years of financial support. Unfortunately, Henry Patterson failed two classes and this contributed to his already dismal transcript and, to his father's dismay, he dropped out just before the end of the year. He was very nonchalant about it, assured Addison he would go onto better things and wished Addison the best with his career. Addison accompanied Henry to the train station and noticed Henry's sister Marilee seemed quite distressed when she met them but she managed to go along with Henry's pretense. Henry gave Addison a last, almost suffocating farewell hug, which Addison thought indicated some underlying despair, and boarded the train with the same big smile as always. He and pretty Marilee waved a whole-hearted good-bye. Henry's friendship had been good for Addison and it would be very hard to see him go.

The last week of school Addison went to the depository and purchased all the books he had used that year at a discount rather than turning them in. He wore his own suit for the graduation ceremony but used some of Tutney's money to purchase a cap and tassel. The school provided the sash that identified him as 'Summa Cum Laude'. Tutney's hopes had been realized. She managed to save enough money to buy a dress and a ticket to Louisville to attend the graduation. She beamed with pride, as if Addison were truly her own son. She put an article in The Marbleton Gazette about Addison's graduation from Louisville with highest honors. Dr. Sullivan wrote him a congratulatory letter, once again expressing his desire to have Addison join his practice. Addison didn't reply. He had confirmed a position on the Athens physician team, but there would be plenty of time to let Dr. Sullivan know.

On Tutney's last night in Louisville Addison took her to a special dinner at Bingham Hall given in honor of the graduates and once again presented her with the Victrola he'd failed to return as she'd requested. This time she accepted it and the next morning she and the new Victrola boarded the train for home. Addison wound things up at school and a few days later hitched another carriage ride with George Payne to the station and took the train to Marbleton.

Eldrin Booth was on the way to the post office when he spotted Addison at the train depot with two large suitcases.

"Good morning, 'Doctor' Blair," he said warmly, reaching down to take one of the bags. "It's good to see you. I hear you're about to make healthy specimens of us all."

"Thanks, Eldrin! It's good to see you again ... but I'm afraid you're misinformed. I'm joining a medical practice in Athens."

"Is that right?" he asked surprised. "I was so sure Dr. Sullivan would want you with him."

"He did offer," said Addison, "But as much as I admire him I didn't think it was a good idea. Dr. Sullivan can be rather abrupt, and more and more of his patients were asking for me. I just didn't want to be in that situation.

"Oh."

"What have you been doing with yourself, Eldrin? You and your father still raisin' horses?"

"No, Addison," Eldrin said pensively. "Dad passed away this spring and I sold the farm and moved into Marbleton Inn. I'm the new postmaster. Vivian's father retired several months ago."

"I'm sorry, Eldrin. I didn't know." It angered him that Tutney hadn't told him about Eldrin's father, but he wasn't surprised. When someone disappointed Tutney they no longer existed.

"It's not so bad, Addison. I get three meals a day if I want. Usually, I eat breakfast at the Inn, grab a sandwich at the drugstore for lunch and Vivian makes supper for me every evening."

"So, you're still seeing Vivian?"

"Oh, yes. She's talking of marriage, but I'm not ready just yet."

Addison wondered if Eldrin still hoped time would somehow miraculously put him and Tutney together again. If he did he was a hopeless optimist. Tutney blamed Eldrin for the rift between them. She never considered it might have anything to do with her presuming upon his good nature, much less realized things could be different with just a word from her.

"How is Tutney?"

'So you are still smitten!' thought Addison.

"She was fine last week," said Addison. "She came to Louisville for my graduation. She's very excited about my becoming a medical doctor..... almost more so than I am. I'll try not to disappoint her but I'm sure I will. It's hard to live up to Tutney's expectations."

Eldrin couldn't help but smile at that. He walked with Addison all the way home discussing the changes in the town that had taken place during Addison's college years. When Tutney opened the front door Eldrin deposited the suitcase on the porch and turned to walk back toward town. He didn't speak.

"How rude!" said Tutney immediately. "What's Eldrin Booth doing with you anyway?"

"I ran into him as I was leaving the depot and he graciously offered to help me with my suitcases."

"Eldrin never did anything graciously," said Tutney harshly. Addison didn't reply, though he wondered how deep was the well of bitterness in his sister's soul. Tutney took one of his suitcases then turned to him.

"Aren't you going to give me a kiss, Brother? I've waited patiently for your return to Marbleton as a physician and done everything I could to help make it happen." She offered her cheek and Addison gave her a quick kiss.

"I'm eternally grateful, Tutney," he said, knowing it was vain hope to believe he would ever be able to show sufficient gratitude.

"When you get your things put up, come to the kitchen," said Tutney. "I knew you'd be hungry and I made stew and biscuits."

"Good!" said Addison. Whatever else his sister was, as Dr. Sullivan had commented, she was a 'wonderful cook'.

The next morning Addison went to the drugstore to see Millie. When he walked in she was scolding her son Nathan at the soda fountain. He had climbed up on one of the stools and helped himself to a jar of peppermints, spilling most of them on the floor. Addison couldn't believe how he had grown.

"I see you have your hands full, Millie," said Addison.

"Dr. Blair!" Millie shrieked, throwing her arms around him. Nathan looked up at them with wide eyes.

"Doc Barnes lets me bring Nathan to work in the mornin's" said Millie, "till Gus gets through with his deliveries. Nathan, this is Dr. Blair! He brought you into the world."

"Where was I?" asked the toddler.

"Can I fix you a soda, Dr. Blair?" asked Millie.

"You big!" said Nathan interrupting. Addison bent to the floor and gave Nathan a shiny dime.

"I'm not so very big now am I, Nathan?" Nathan grabbed the coin.

"You big!" he repeated.

"I guess I am at that," said Addison rising to his feet. "How's Gus, Millie?"

"He's doin' fine, Dr. Blair. He was promoted to manager and has a couple o' guys workin' under him deliverin' ice. We bought the Wilder farm on the edge of town. It needed a lot of work but we got it lookin' nice."

"I'll have to come by to see it before I leave."

"What do ya mean, Dr. Blair? You ain't stayin' in Marbleton?"

"No, I think Dr. Sullivan pretty much has this town wrapped up," Addison replied. "I'm joining a group of doctors in Athens. The town's growing and there's a need for physicians there."

"I'm so disappointed. I was hopin' you'd take care of me and Gus and little Nathan when you got back."

"Well, I'll be here occasionally," assured Addison, "And you know if you need me I'll find a way to help you."

"Sure I do!" said Millie trying to hide her despair. "I'll get your soda."

"No thanks, Millie. I need to be on my way ... but I did want to speak to Doc Barnes. Is he here?"

"Back there in the pharmacy. He'll be so glad to see you."

Doc Barnes was getting up in age and even with his thick glasses he had to get right up to the shelves and strain to read the labels. He was rearranging shelves and didn't notice Addison.

"Doc Barnes!" said Addison. "How are you?"

"Why, Addison!" he exclaimed. "You're back!" I guess you'll be giving me some business now."

"Maybe occasionally, Doc, when I'm home, but I'm leaving for Athens next week to join a practice there?"

"You don't say! Do I know 'em?"

"You might. It's Dr. David Hargrove's group. I'll be one of three new physicians starting there this summer. I think the other two are from up North somewhere."

"No-o, don't believe I know them ... but I wish you luck. I'm highly disappointed you and I won't be doing business together. Of course, I'm going to have to retire soon. Can't read the medicine labels very well anymore. I have to get Millie to check them last thing before I get them ready to go out."

"I'm sorry to hear that, but I hope retirement will be good."

"Oh, it's all right. That's life, you know. The only thing we can be sure of is change. How's Tutney going to take your leaving? You're all she has now that Walter's gone."

"You know Tutney, Doc. She's a survivor!"

"You know," he mused, "We have quite a few little Tutneys runnin' around now. Some of her students have named their children after her ... boys and girls!"

"Well, if those children get her determination they'll do all right in life, won't they, Doc Barnes?"

"That's for sure!"

"Well, I have to get home. I have a lot to do to get ready for my move." Addison shook Doc Barnes' hand heartily.

"Good-bye, Boy" said Doc Barnes with moist eyes. "You take care of yourself!"

Addison's last stop that day was Dr. Sullivan's office. Alice greeted him warmly and fixed him a cup of hot coffee.

"I'm going to miss you so, Dr. Blair," said Alice. Addison remembered she was the first to call him that. Now, it was official but he didn't feel any different, just a lot more overwhelmed with trying to live up to everyone's expectations.

"Is Dr. Sullivan busy, Alice?" asked Addison. "I'm trying to say my good-byes today. Tutney has her list of things for me to do before I leave."

"I'll bet she does," confirmed Alice. "Don't let her take advantage of you, Dr. Blair. She's a pretty demanding woman!"

"Actually, I have her to thank for my medical degree."

"Oh, there's a lot to admire in her. We all know that. But don't sell yourself short. Your intellect and hard work are what got you through medical school."

"Thank you, Alice," said Addison smiling. "I like to think I had a little to do with it."

"Dr. Sullivan's in his office with Amy. She married Jerome Stacks, an attorney from Jeffersonville. She's expecting a baby in September and she told me if it's a boy she's going to name him Walter."

"How does her husband feel about that?"

"He knows all about Walter, Dr. Blair. Everyone who knows Amy knows about Walter. She loved him very much."

"I know," said Addison.

Dr. Sullivan walked into the room with Amy by his side.

"Who is this handsome young physician?" he asked.

"You're looking good yourself!" said Addison.

"Addison!" Amy put her hand on Addison's shoulder and leaned up to put her cheek against his. "You look taller than ever."

"Apparently," laughed Addison. Little Nathan Andrews just told me I was 'big'.

"I have to agree," said Dr. Sullivan. Then added, "I'm going to be a grandfather, Addison—sometime in September."

"I heard! Congratulations, to both of you!"

"Thank you, Addison," said Amy. "I'm going to name him Walter."

"She's made up her mind it's going to be a boy," said Dr. Sullivan.

"Knowing Amy, I'm sure it will!" said Addison. "Walter would be honored."

"Take care of yourself, Father," said Amy, kissing Dr. Sullivan good-bye. "I have to get home. Addison, Tutney told me you're going to be practicing in Athens. Good luck!"

"Thank you, Amy. Please let me know when the baby comes."

"I will, Addison. Good-bye."

"Good-bye." As she left Addison noticed how petite and fragile Amy was. He hoped everything would go well.

"So you're joining the Athens group. Is there any chance of changing your mind?" inquired Dr. Sullivan.

"I'm afraid not," said Addison. "You do well for the folks in Marbleton, and there are too many good years left in you for me to hope to fill your shoes."

"Well, thank you, Addison. If I have my way, I'll die in this lab coat! Now, I'm going to take you to lunch, and don't argue!" He turned to Alice.

"Alice, take care of things here for about an hour. If you need us, we'll be at Marbleton Inn."

Alice watched the two of them as they left, Dr. Sullivan puffing constantly on his pipe, his arm around Addison's shoulders. She turned and went to the exam room to get it ready for the next patient.

"Irene's married and living in Royston," said Dr. Sullivan. "She has no children, but I expect to hear that news soon. She wants several of them."

"She'll be a good mother, Dr. Sullivan. I admire her very much."

"I didn't know that, Addison. I don't think Irene knew that."

"I'm hoping you'll help me make a list of the basics I need for setting up my office," said Addison changing the subject.

"I'll be glad to, son. Now, let's see what they have good to eat today." Dr. Sullivan insisted Addison order the most expensive meal on the menu. They sat there an hour eating and discussing Addison's plans for his future practice.

"How's Tutney?" asked Dr. Sullivan. "I know she hates to see you leave."

"She's just fine, Dr. Sullivan. She won't miss me much. She's too active in her own right."

"Yes," said Dr. Sullivan. "She's a beautiful, strong woman."

When the two of them finished lunch they parted but before he left for home Addison had to promise Dr. Sullivan he would correspond to keep him informed of his new practice.

CHAPTER SIX

Addison's first few weeks in Athens were overwhelming. He worked diligently on his curriculum vitae for the position on the medical staff at Athens Regional. The practice was called the Prince Avenue Clinic. He would be a junior member. The senior member was David Hargrove, who was from Connecticut and had graduated from Harvard Medical School. Dr. Hargrove had married the daughter of Dr. Albert Rogers of Savannah, Georgia, and moved from New England to open his practice in Athens. The two other junior members, Virgil Herron and Michael Balfour, were both graduates of Medical College of Georgia in Augusta.

Addison was going to room with Michael Balfour at Johnson's Boarding House in Athens. Old Mrs. Johnson had given them strict instructions. Fortunately, her cooking was easier to swallow than her attitude, which took them aback.

"I don't care if'n yore doctors. Ya'll get the same treatment as my otha boarders. Dinner's right at six o'clock ever' day, so if'n yore workin' overtime ya don't get fed, not by me anyways!" Mrs. Johnson had a round face, wide eyes and a very large nose.

"An' by the way, you do yore own laundry so you'll have to work out a sched'l with my otha boarders ... or there's Mrs. Duffy on Berle Street who'll do it fur ya for two dollars a month."

Addison promptly got in touch with Mrs. Duffy and made arrangements to deliver his dirty laundry every Friday at seven p.m. and pick it up on Monday afternoons.

The beds were not the best in the world, but he and Michael were getting the place for eight dollars a month so they felt they shouldn't be too choosy. Michael was a pleasant chap, a bit chubby but nonetheless meticulous, so he worked himself into the laundry schedule so he could take care of his own clothes.

Michael was the only child of a widowed father, Armistead Balfour, who owned a clothing store in Chicago. He had helped his father in the store in the afternoons after school. but after graduating he had come to live with relatives in Augusta and eventually enrolled in the medical college there. He had a high-pitched voice and was very articulate. Even Addison's vocabulary was lame in comparison. Addison couldn't figure out why Michael wanted to be a physician. He was more enthusiastic about art and had shown Addison some of his paintings. His method was much like that of Rembrandt, the characters all in bright-colored frocks and coats with very expressive faces. Michael was a perfect companion for Addison. He loved to talk and Addison was a good listener.

Virgil Herron was tall like Addison, much more business-like and a bit too sure of himself for most people's liking. His father was a New York banker and he constantly reminded others his family lived on New York's Upper East Side. He hated everything about the South and treated colored folks with a contempt that far outweighed that of most southerners. Addison didn't care for him at all and wondered why Dr. Hargrove, who seemed so discerning, would have made him a choice. At any rate, Addison would manage to work with him.

The first morning in the office Dr. Hargrove told Addison he wanted him to see all the elderly patients. His first was a Mrs. Cunard of Watkinsville. She was approaching her ninety-sixth birthday and had been living in Atlanta when Sherman made his famous 'march to the sea.' She was highly respected in Athens because she belonged to the Daughters of the American Revolution. Her great-great-grandfather had been one of the original English to come over with James Oglethorpe to Georgia. She made it her business to inform everyone she met that Georgia was not founded by debtors but by noblemen of England sent by the King to help govern the southern colony.

Addison opened the door to the examining room with chart in hand.

"Good morning, Mrs. Cunard. I'm Dr. Blair. I'll be caring for you this morning."

The old lady was severely bent, her rounded shoulders wrapped in a gray shawl. She sat in a wheelchair.

"Dr. Blair, you say! As in Dr. Addison Cambridge Blair of Harrison, Georgia?"

"Dr. Cambridge Blair is my uncle, Mrs. Cunard, and his son Jeffrey Clark is my cousin," said Addison, though he knew very little of these wealthy relatives.

"Well, I'll say!" she muttered, her voice fading slowly.

"What seems to be bothering you today, Mrs. Cunard?" Addison asked politely.

"Nothin' more'n usual. That Dr. Hargrove just has me come back every month for no reason 't all. I keep tellin' him it's foolish, but he won't listen."

"Well, since you're here, let's check your heart and lungs," said Addison placing the stethoscope on her chest. He heard a bothersome irregularity in her heartbeat but he reassured her.

"Young lady!" he said. "You're in good health for a matriarch! Still, I'd like to do a few tests this week for good measure. I'll have the nurse arrange it."

Addison took her hands and stroked the gnarled arthritic joints of all her fingers.

"Do you have any pain in your hands?" he asked.

"Lan' sakes, everything hurts when you're my age!" she laughed.

"Well, a good soak in Epsom salts will help your hands and feet a little."

"I'll try to do that Dr. Blair," she answered, "if you'll do something for me!"

"What's that?"

"Come have Sunday dinner with me," she said. "I need to tell you all about Athens ... who you need to know, and who you need to avoid!"

"What time should I be there?" Addison asked enthusiastically.

"Be there at noon, of course," she said. "That's when respectable folks have Sunday dinner."

"I'll be there!" Addison asserted.

"Promise?!" she demanded more than asked.

"Promise!" said Addison as he wheeled her back to the front office. He handed her chart to the waiting nurse to schedule the tests he ordered.

"Good-bye, Mrs. Cunard. Let me know if you need anything," Addison said as he finished up her chart.

As fate would have it Addison didn't keep that appointment for dinner. He learned Mrs. Cunard had a fainting spell that turned out to be a heart attack and was taken to Athens Regional. Addison met her family there--Grace Bailey, her oldest daughter, her husband Kenneth and her two brothers, Herb and Gil Cunard. Addison also met his own wealthy uncle, Dr. Cambridge Blair, who was a long-time family friend of the Cunards and came to the hospital when he heard of Mrs. Cunard's admission.

Addison quietly walked into Mrs. Cunard's room. She seemed to sense his presence and opened her eyes.

"Dr. Blair," she said weakly, "I must tell you something."

"What is that, Mrs. Cunard?" Addison asked.

"There's something about you," she said with quiet authority. She paused to catch her breath.

"There is healing in those big hands of yours!" she added. "I could feel it when you were stroking these old ugly bones of mine ... and you have diagnostic insight. I saw your expression when you listened to my chest. You knew this was coming."

"Mrs. Cunard," Addison began.

"No, I mean it! You listen to me. I've earned it!" she said strongly. "Don't take your gifts for granted ... and don't withhold them from anyone, no matter what their station in life."

"I won't, Mrs. Cunard," said Addison. "Now, you get some rest." He tucked the covers around her shoulders and quietly left.

An hour later he was urgently summoned and rushed to her room but by the time he arrived she had died. He didn't look forward to informing her family.

"Mrs. Bailey," said Addison as he approached the waiting area. "I'm afraid I have some bad news. Your mother has just passed away." None of the family looked surprised or even sad ... just resigned.

"I know Mother was ready to die," said Grace, "and that makes it easier. I've said my good-byes, Dr. Blair."

A young girl, probably a great-granddaughter, began to sob. Grace Bailey caressed her.

"Mother Cunard is with Jesus, darling," she assured.

Addison went home that night with a heavy heart. Later that week he visited Mrs. Cunard's home and met the rest of her family. He knew he would probably face the death of several patients in the ensuing years and it was a part of medicine he didn't like. He wrote in despair to Tutney.

Dear Sister,

I experienced my first patient death tonight. Though she was elderly, the inevitability of it was not at all comforting. I had examined her this morning and I felt so responsible, in spite of the fact I believe such things are in God's hands. I do not look forward to this aspect of the practice of medicine.

Love,

Addison

In the fall Addison decided to make a trip to Marbleton and sent a message ahead to Tutney. He purchased two mares from the livery in Athens for twenty dollars each, a bay named Mag and a sorrel named Mae, and bought a buggy from Athens Coach Company. That Friday he set out for home. There was a light mist so he put on his derby hoping he wouldn't run into heavy rain.

After several hours and within five miles of Marbleton the bottom fell out and in minutes the buggy was full of water and the horses were bogging down in the mud and moving at a snail's pace. It was getting dark and Addison began to look for somewhere to stop. Through the lightning he caught glimpse of a small church away from the road. He turned in and drove the horses up to the front steps.

He hopped out and pulled his rig under a big tree to shield it from most of the rain, then ran up the stairs into the chapel. With the bursts of lightning from the storm coming through the stained-glass windows Addison could see the pulpit at the front. As the storm moved closer the steady roar of the thunder grew louder. He instinctively made his way to the altar and prayed for a hasty end to the storm and for good weather for the rest of his trip home. He felt a cold chill sweep over him.

He pulled his coat collar further together tightly. Suddenly something fell on his back. He reached up to grasp a pair of bony hands. Long fingernails dug into his neck. He flung his unknown assailant away from him with all his might. He turned and ran up the aisle and through the door without looking back. He jumped into the buggy and with a shake of the reins took off at breakneck speed up the muddy road. He wasn't sure how long he'd been driving the horses when he noticed a glimmer of light from a small house by the side of the roadway.

"Whoa, ponies," he said as he stopped his team. He hopped down and hurried up to the door, pounding on it like a frightened school girl. Finally, after what seemed an eternity, it slowly opened.

"Bless Patty!" said a stocky old woman with a lantern in her hand. "You look like you've seen a ghost! Come on in."

"Dr. Addison Blair of Athens," said Addison hurriedly. He felt foolish to be so flustered by what had happened.

"I'm sorry, Ma'am," said Addison, "I'm soaked. I probably should take these off." He tugged at his boots.

"I'm Minnie Hanks," she said politely. "What in the world?"

"I just had a very strange encounter," Addison said breathlessly. "I'm on my way to Marbleton and when the heavy storm came up I decided to stop at the church just up the road and wait until it slacked off. I went in and walked down to the altar and after a few minutes someone grabbed me from behind and seemed to be trying to choke me. I couldn't see but I pushed whoever it was away and got out of there as quickly as I could."

By this time the woman's husband had joined them at the front door.

"Caleb Hanks," said the gruff old man as he ushered Addison to a chair in the parlor. He hurriedly kindled a fire and looking a bit disheveled motioned for Addison to take a seat and asked him what had happened. Addison again related his experience. The old gentleman began to chuckle.

"I'm sorry, Dr. Blair," he said as he composed himself. "I don't mean no disrespect, but I b'lieve you've just met Miss Edmonds, our pastor's old-maid sister."

"Your pastor's sister?" Addison repeated incredibly.

"She ain't quite right in the head, Dr. Blair. Pastor lets her live in the church and she stays in her room while we have service. I never really thought about it but I guess she has the run of the place at night." Addison wasn't sure he felt relieved.

"I may have hurt the woman!" he said. "I'm a pretty big man and I threw her off of me as hard as I could."

"I think she's too crazy to get hurt, Dr. Blair," said Mr. Hanks, "but if it'll make you feel better, when the rain stops we'll take a lantern and go back up to the church."

"I'd appreciate it, Mr. Hanks," said Addison. "I'd like to know if she's all right." Minnie Hanks left for the kitchen and returned with a hoe cake and molasses and some very strong coffee. Addison hadn't eaten since early morning and didn't realize how hungry he was.

"This is very good, Mrs. Hanks," he said politely as he took his last bite. Mr. Hanks went to the door and opened it.

"I think the rain's 'bout as good as it's gonna be," he said. "You ready to go?"

Addison nodded and the three of them pulled on their coats and went out the door. They climbed into Addison's wet buggy and headed back down the road. When they got there the scene was far less menacing than Addison remembered. The rain had stopped and the moon had come out. The soft subtle light of dawn had begun creeping through the colorful windows and now gave the old church a nostalgic charm it had been missing before. Mr. Hanks approached the altar holding his lantern high and there at the altar lay the pastor's sister, apparently just as Addison had left her. She was completely naked and out cold. She looked to be in her fifties and Addison was touched by how thin and frail she was. He reached down to lift her up and she suddenly opened her eyes. She was very frightened.

"It's all right," said Addison softly. "I didn't mean to hurt you. You gave me quite a scare." It was plain to see she didn't understand.

"Miss April," said old man Hanks, giving her his hand. "You know you oughtn't be 'bout the church like a varmit at night. Let's get you back to your room so Minnie can get you dressed 'fore yore brother comes by this mornin'." Pastor Edmonds made a habit of bringing provisions to his sister every Saturday.

Minnie Hanks took the woman's hand and escorted her to her room at the side of the foyer near the front door of the church.

"Let's have a seat," said Mr. Hanks motioning for Addison to join him on one of the pews.

"Say you're from Athens?"

"Yes," said Addison. "I'm part of a medical practice there. I'd be glad to see you and Ms. Hanks if you should ever need me."

"Thanks, Dr. Blair," the old man replied with a grin, "but Minnie and I ain't never been to no doctor, and we don't plan on needin' one any time soon."

"Well, I hope not," replied Addison. The old gentleman had a way about him and after what seemed like hours Addison realized he'd shared quite a lot with Mr. Hanks about his schooling, Tutney, and even Walter's death ... in fact, his whole life's story. They were both beginning to show their fatigue and the conversation had begun to ebb when Minnie Hanks came waddling down the aisle.

"I finally got her settled, Caleb," she said. "She was so scared. I think she'll be all right, though, till Pastor Edmonds gets here in the mornin'."

"Shucks, it is mornin', Minnie." The first glimpse of the sun had appeared on the horizon and was shining into the old church.

"Well, I think it's time I get back on the road to Marbleton," Addison said as he rose. He walked toward the door and out to the buggy, the Hanks following close behind him.

"I'll take you back home and then I'll be on my way," said Addison, taking an old blanket from the back of the buggy and drying off the seat a bit.

"Oh, no, that won't be necessary," protested Caleb Hanks. "Pastor Edmonds will be here in an hour or so and we need to let 'im know what happened. He'll give us a ride home."

"Are you sure?'

"I'm certain."

"Then, I'll just say good-bye and thank you! I don't know how I would have coped with this without your help."

"Our pleasure, Doctor Blair. Glad to meet you! Stop and see us when you're down this way again." The old couple watched as Addison's buggy slowly disappeared from view.

Tutney had been anxiously awaiting Addison's arrival. She was relieved but puzzled when he finally drove up.

"I went to the depot to see if you arrived on the nine o'clock train. Where'd you get that rig?" she asked.

"I bought it in Athens," said Addison. I'll tell you all about it later."

"I'll put the horses away," said Tutney. "You go get a warm bath. I've got the water already hot on the stove."

Baby, Tutney's cow, mooed her disdain at the two equines that were going to be occupying some of her space. When Tutney got the horses unharnessed and settled in the barn, she went back to the house and found Addison sitting by the fire warming himself. She listened intently to his grim tale of Miss Edmonds and the old church.

She told Addison it had been a difficult term for her at school. One of the female students had gotten pregnant and been shipped off by her father to relatives in Tennessee. Tutney had also gotten into a fray with the county school supervisor for giving his approval for some of the students to leave school early to practice for Marbleton's Fall Choir Concert. She had nearly been fired over the incident.

"Brother," she sighed. "How I've missed you. I can't wait to hear about your practice in Athens. I was sorry to hear about the old lady who died, but you'll have to harden your heart. It's better if people don't outlive their usefulness. I don't want to be around too long for my good."

"Do you remember Dr. Cambridge Blair, Tutney? Did you ever know him?"

"Our uncle?" she quipped. "Of course I know him. You're his namesake. He's Dr. *Addison* Cambridge Blair. He came to see Sally when you were born. I've never met his son, but I understand he's also a physician and the two of them are quite wealthy."

"I met him in Athens," Addison mused. "He was a good friend of Mrs. Cunard, the patient I wrote you about. I didn't speak to him at length, though."

"You're going to surpass him, Addison. You're going to surpass them all. You're tall and imposing and have a superior intellect."

"That's funny," said Addison. "I thought I had 'diagnostic insight ... and healing in my hands.'"

"What?" Tutney looked curious.

"That's what Mrs. Cunard told me," he explained. "She told me not to withhold my medical skills from anyone, no matter what station in life."

"Do that and you'll be poor, Brother. You can't give away your livelihood."

"Is anything happening in Marbleton I need to know about, Tutney?" asked Addison in an attempt to divert her attention to something less serious.

"Nothing life-threatening. That fool Eldrin Booth is still running around with Vivian Nelms."

It struck Addison that Eldrin was the first name Tutney mentioned.

"You didn't think him a fool when he was running around with you," he said.

"He wasn't 'running around' with me. I was just humoring him ... but he's always been a fool, just the same."

"Irene Sullivan is expecting a baby in January," said Tutney, hoping to strike a nerve.

"Irene Sullivan Saunders," corrected Addison. "Pregnancy usually follows marriage, Tutney. Dr. Sullivan told me she was hoping for a family soon."

"I thought you might be upset about her getting married," Tutney said. "You were taken with her."

"I respected her," he replied.

"Amy had her baby," Tutney suddenly remembered. "It was a boy and she named him Walter."

"Walter!" said Addison. He smiled to think how that would have pleased his brother whom, he was sure, would be watching over that boy.

Addison decided he'd do some visiting while he was home, but first he had to have some rest. He planned to spend Sunday morning at home. Friday evening's rain and the long vigil at the little church had been exhausting and cut his visit short, but he still hoped to look up Dr. Sullivan and go by the Pharmacy. He didn't ever want to be totally out of touch with Marbleton.

Early that afternoon after a good nap he got up and headed toward the drugstore. Eldrin Booth was there buying liniment for Vivian's father who was nearly disabled from bad joints.

"Well, we meet again Doc," Eldrin said heartily.

"Hey, there, Eldrin," Addison replied. "You doing all right? How are Vivian and her father?"

"Mr. Nelms has arthritis pretty bad, but otherwise he's all right," said Eldrin, "and I guess Vivian's the best thing that ever happened to me. She takes good care of me."

"Not married yet?"

"No," said Eldrin, and then trying to show only a passing interest asked the inevitable. "How's Tutney?"

"She's fine, Eldrin. Just fine."

"I hear she may quit teaching to become Dr. Sullivan's nurse," said Eldrin not knowing Addison had heard nothing of this.

"Well, I can't imagine why she'd do that! She hasn't mentioned it to me ... and surely she would if it were true."

"Ah, Addison," said Eldrin with a grin, "You know you can't be sure of anything when it comes to Tutney. I hope I haven't spoken out of turn."

"Oh, no. She'll eventually tell me. She shares what she pleases of her affairs in her own good time."

"I can believe that, Addison. Well, I'll see you again soon, I hope."

"Me, too," said Addison.

Addison visited with Millie and Doc Barnes for about an hour, then went by to see Dr. Sullivan whose waiting room was full of patients. Addison decided to go home and spend the rest of the day with Tutney. The next morning he asked her about what he'd heard from Eldrin.

"Eldrin doesn't know enough to mind his own business," she said defensively.

"Well, is it true, Tutney?" asked Addison. "I have to learn about my sister through the grapevine, but you've always expected me to answer to you."

"Brother, you're getting upset over nothing. I assure you I would tell you first, if I made that kind of decision."

"Tutney, you know Eldrin is still in love with you."

"I'm not in love with him."

Addison knew there was no getting through to Tutney once she made up her mind. He went to his room and began to pack.

Michael greeted Addison with some disturbing news on his arrival back to Athens. David and Mrs. Hargrove were moving back to New Hampshire. Virgil Herron's father had paid a substantial sum for the practice and Virgil was to be the new proprietor and senior member. Working *with* Virgil had been difficult enough for Addison. He didn't know if he would be able to work *under* him, but he would try. Michael felt he and Addison would both have more autonomy, but only time would prove whether the change was a good thing.

Addison went by Ms. Duffy's to pick up his laundry and left his rain-stained suit.

"I'll try to git it to the drycleaners," said Ms. Duffy. "I ain't got the proper stuff to clean it without' shrinkin' it."

When he reached the apartment he sat down and composed a letter to Reverend Travis Edmonds concerning his sister in an attempt to persuade him to admit her to the Indigents' Home in Athens for a trial period. Addison was delighted when two weeks later he received an answer from the reverend that he would agree to the arrangement. There was no doubt Miss Edmonds would be well taken care of physically but they would have to see whether the home's staff could handle her strange behavior. Addison saw to it Reverend Edmonds was sent the appropriate papers to fill out and together they planned for Miss Edmonds to be admitted.

At the first of the month Reverend Edmonds and his wife, Rebecca, brought their charge to Athens with some medical records and quite a few clothes, which they would have to take back, as the patients were not allowed to keep their own clothing. They found it difficult to leave her. She had no experience with anyone but family and while they hoped this arrangement would give them a more normal life, they feared the unknown for themselves and for their timid and confused sister.

"Do you remember me, Miss Edmonds," Addison asked her. She didn't answer but Addison thought he detected a glint of recognition in her large eyes.

"This is going to be your new home."

"Mrs. Appley," said Addison turning to the charge nurse, "This is Miss April Edmonds. Will you kindly take her records and prepare a chart while I walk her back to her room?" Mrs. Appley was a brute of a woman, six feet tall with an iron-willed constitution. She was middle-aged and top heavy but in beautifully starched white from hat to shoes.

"Miss Edmonds, I'd like you to meet our charge nurse, Mrs. Appley. She's here to help you. If you need anything, just ask her." Addison took April Edmonds back to the last room on the hall. It was rather stark but much warmer than the cold room she had lived in at the back of the old church sanctuary.

"Won't you have a seat, Miss Edmonds." She took a seat in an overstuffed chair in the corner.

"Do you have any questions?" Miss Edmonds gave him a stoic stare and said nothing.

"Well, if you should need anything tell Mrs. Appley, and I'll get back to you as soon as I can. Meanwhile, enjoy your new home." He hated leaving her almost as much as the Edmonds had. She was more of a child than a woman and he hoped this would prove to be a good experience for her but that remained to be seen.

After six months at the Indigents' Home Miss Edmonds seemed to be doing well. Addison tried to visit at least twice a month. She always got up to meet him when he came in but she still hadn't spoken. Mrs. Appley had reported she was really no problem, but she continued to refuse to participate in any activities and had nothing to do with the other patients. When Addison arrived for his next visit, Mrs. Appley was quite distressed.

"Dr. Blair!" she announced, "Miss Edmonds has been crying all day! A-l-l-l da-a-y!" she added for emphasis.

"What's wrong?" he asked.

"'What's wrong?'" Mrs. Appley mimicked, obviously exasperated.

"Pardon me, Dr. Blair, but only the good Lord knows! She absolutely refuses to communicate, though I know she can speak ... I've heard her singin' from the room when she thinks no one's around."

"Yes, singin!" she repeated when Addison looked surprised.

"Where is she?" asked Addison.

"Sittin' in the corner there in the receivin' room," said Mrs. Appley, "all curled up like a baby!"

Addison found her just as Mrs. Appley had said, cowling in the chair in the far corner of the room, her head in her hands and her knees drawn up into a fetal position. He walked up slowly, not wanting to startle her.

"Miss Edmonds," he said quietly.

She unfolded at the sound of his voice, letting down her hands and lifting her head, her eyes full of tears.

"Come, Miss Edmonds," said Addison, "Nothing can be that bad. Walk with me out into the garden. It's a beautiful day!"

The two of them made a strange pair, Addison with his arm around her shoulders and Miss Edmonds, half his height, walking beside him and clinging frantically with both hands to his sleeve.

"What's upset you?" Addison asked, not knowing whether she would answer.

She reached down to grasp the hem of her gray muslin skirt. It was torn in several places.

"You've torn you're dress," said Addison. "How did that happen?"

April Edmonds grabbed his hand and led him back into the receiving parlor to the fireplace on the back wall. He could see where gray threads had caught on the old fire screen.

"Goodness, Miss Edmonds. Have you been sitting that close to the fire?" She didn't answer him, just pointed again to the hem of her skirt.

"I see. Well, we can fix that. We'll just have to get you a new dress!" he assured. "Do you like flowers?"

Miss Edmonds shook her head with a faint smile, the first one he had seen.

"Then, flowers it is!" he said, "Blue ones to match your eyes." He took her hand and led her back to the lobby and up to Mrs. Appley's desk.

"Mrs. Appley," he said kindly, "I need a favor. It seems Miss Edmonds has torn her dress and is in need of a new one. You're the only person I trust to select a proper replacement." April Edmonds lifted up the hem to show Mrs. Appley.

"So she has!" Mrs. Appley noted. "Well, she could have told me, but you have only to ask, Dr. Blair! I'll see to it right away!"

"Thank you, Mrs. Appley. Oh ... and find something with blue flowers."

"Why, that wouldn't be appropriate, Dr. Blair."

"It would in this case," Addison replied.

"As you say, Doctor."

"What would I do without you?!" Addison praised. The large woman swelled with pride.

"One more thing! See to it that old fire screen is replaced and watch for patients getting too close to the hearth."

"Yes, Dr. Blair."

"Well, Miss Edmonds," Addison began. "Now, let's resume our walk."

Behind the old farmhouse was a quaint garden. The hollyhocks and gladiolas were beginning to fade. Chained to an old stump was a black and tan coon hound with a ring of gold hair around his neck.

"This fella's name is Ring," said Addison. "Someone feeds him every morning but he loves to be sung to, and there's no one here willing to do that for him. Do you think you could take on the task of singing to old Ring a few minutes every day?" Miss Edmonds nodded in agreement.

"I knew I could depend on you." He walked her up to the porch and back inside and told Mrs. Appley at the desk about their "arrangement".

"Will you see to it she accomplishes this task every day, Mrs. Appley?"

"Consider it done, Dr. Blair," she paused, "But it's a strange order!"

"Strange orders are sometimes necessary," he said, patting her on the shoulder.

He escorted Miss Edmonds back to the receiving room and she sat back down in the corner. She watched intently as he walked out of the room.

Virgil Herron was waiting for Addison when he got back to the clinic.

"Where have you been?" he asked impatiently.

"I stopped by the Indigents' Home to see a patient," said Addison. "Why?"

"We've had two emergencies, Addison, and certainly could have used your help. In the future be sure you keep us informed of your whereabouts at all times."

Addison wasn't surprised at Virgil's impertinence but he was a little surprised he actually managed to hold his own tongue.

"How do things stand now?" Addison asked.

"There is a boy in Room Three who needs stitches in his knee. He ran his bike into someone's carriage. You can handle that, can't you?" he asked patronizingly.

"I'll certainly give it a try," said Addison, determined to address Virgil's rudeness later.

The boy's name was Sammy Reisdale. He was sandy-haired and small for his age of twelve but had no problem with words. A ragged little sack of marbles sat beside him on the cot.

"Hello, Doc!" he grinned. "You gonna fix me up?"

"Well, I'll do my best," said Addison. "Is your bike in bad shape?"

"Mr. Saltzman offered to take it to Vinnie's Bicycle Shop. Dr. Saltzman's the guy I ran into. He knows my uncle and he said he'd square things with 'im."

"Well, you must be a man of influence, Sammy!"

"Yeah," Sammy agreed. "Everybody in Falkirk kinda depends on me ... you know, for deliveries, yard work, you name it!"

"Is that right?" asked Addison. "So you live in Falkirk!"

"Well, right now I'm visitin' my uncle in Athens. Mama's real sick and Mary Blanche says with her sick and all, she just cain't handle me during the summer when I'm not in school."

"Who's Mary Blanche?" asked Addison.

"She's my sister," replied Sammy. He clinched his teeth and winced when Addison started to insert a needle. The Procaine the nurse had applied had only slightly numbed the knee, so Addison applied more and waited a few minutes longer.

"Mary Blanche, says I get my cleverness from my uncle. I'm named after 'im," Sammy added with pride.

"Is that right?" asked Addison beginning to suture the wound. Sammy didn't seem to notice.

"I'm pretty broke this summer. This is when I make my best money in Falkirk. It's hard to get around to everything when a man's in school. Somehow I just ain't been able to break into business in Athens yet." He added.

Addison was focused on the wound and was catching only bits of Sammy's lively conversation.

"You should see my sister, Doc. She's as purty as I am smart!" Sammy said with authority. "Are you married, Doc?"

"No, I'm not Sam," Addison replied, "But I will be one day." Addison loved children and he loved Sammy's confident ways.

"Well, Mary Blanche is too young for you, anyway, Doc. She's only fifteen. But maybe she'd be right for your son!"

Addison was amused.

"I'll have to check her out I guess ... when Junior comes along." He laughed.

"Well, there you are, Sam," said Addison as he covered the gauze over Sammy's knee with the last bit of adhesive tape. "You're good as new."

"Thanks, Doc!"

"Sure, Sammy. Now, be sure your uncle brings you back in next Tuesday to get those stitches out," he instructed.

"I will, Doc," answered Sammy, "Just charge this to Uncle Samuel's account, and let me know if you have any yard work you want done."

"You're a good man, Sam," said Addison, "I don't have a yard. I live in a boarding house but if anything comes up I'll be sure to find you!"

"I'm your man!" Sammy asserted, as he grabbed his sack of marbles and ran out the door.

Addison saw eleven patients that afternoon and was quite tired when Virgil Herron walked into his office.

"The thing is," said Virgil, "This isn't going to work unless everybody pulls his own weight." Addison didn't reply.

"I have the responsibility of overhead ... paying for the nurse, keeping the premises in repair, buying the medicine and supplies. I have to be able to depend on you and Mike to see as many patients as possible. Now I've figured if you spend fifteen minutes with each case you can see at least twenty-five to thirty patients a day and still have an hour at noon for your lunch and a bit of a rest."

"Well, that's an interesting proposal," replied Addison. He paused for a moment. "But you must know some patients require more than fifteen minutes or you compromise, if not their care, their diagnosis."

"Compromise their diagnosis?" asked Virgil incredulously.

"The most important task a physician has is making a correct diagnosis," said Addison. "To do that you have to listen to your patients or you'll miss the very clue that reveals the cause of their illness. That may take more than fifteen minutes."

"Are you saying you refuse to cooperate for the good of our practice?" Virgil asked rather haughtily.

"I'm saying I'll do all I can to contribute to your clinic except compromise the care of my patients," said Addison matter-of-factly.

"If you don't put the practice first, there won't be any patients," Virgil reasoned.

"There is a balance, Virgil. One that keeps the patients and the practice healthy. If you neglect either it will be a disaster, and if you make profit the most important component of your practice you'll miss your calling."

"Calling?" replied Virgil sarcastically. "This is not a calling for me, Addison. It's a profession."

"It seems we have two opposing philosophies, doesn't it?"

"I have a cousin who's interested in coming into the practice," Virgil began and after a long pause, "I think that's the way we need to go." Addison stood and extended his hand.

"It's been an experience, Virgil," he said.

"What does that mean?" he asked.

"It means," said Addison, "you've made your point. I'll start looking for something else right away." He walked out leaving Virgil flabbergasted and already scheming as to how he could get his cousin into place and force Addison's early departure.

Michael was devastated to learn Addison was leaving.

"You haven't really given it a chance," he said doing his best to make Addison feel guilty. "I mean, anyone should try something for at least a year before giving up on it."

"Michael," Addison assured, "everything will be all right. Virgil's cousin is coming, from New York I believe, to take over my office and my patients."

"Aren't you going to take your patients with you?" asked Michael.

"I don't think that would be right, Michael," said Addison. "Besides, I'm not sure where I'll end up. It might be impossible for them to follow me."

"Well, I don't think you're going to find anything better than this," Michael offered.

"Perhaps not, but I told you it would be difficult for me to work for Virgil ... and as it turns out, it's impossible."

"Don't worry, Michael," Addison said seeing Michael was visibly shaken. "Virgil will be very successful, and if you stay you can be a part of that."

"Now you're putting me in the same category with him," said Michael, "and I resent it."

"That isn't what I meant," said Addison.

"I know," said Michael apologetically, "I just wish I could talk you into staying."

"Virgil and I are on a different page," said Addison. "You're more accommodating and less opinionated than I am, and you and Virgil don't seem to have a problem getting along. He has a lot of ambition but he can depend on you and he'll reward you for that."

Michael didn't have what it took to stand up for his convictions and, actually, did not give a lot of thought to what they were. For someone like Michael, Virgil was a necessary evil, if not a godsend.

When Virgil learned his cousin wouldn't be coming he told Addison he needed the space for supplies and requested Addison vacate his office as quickly as possible.

"Of course, you can stay long enough to see your followup appointments," Virgil had added. Addison told Michael he might need to stay in the apartment for awhile.

"I don't know how long I'll be able to pay but I promise you won't have to keep me up for long. When I find something else I'll be sure and make up for it."

"Stop, Addison," said Michael. "You know you can stay as long as you want. It's going to be hard for me to see you go, but I have no doubt clinics will be competing for you when they hear you're available."

"I hope you're right," said Addison. "Now, let's go to Capps' Cafe for a sandwich before thoughts of Virgil start to spoil my appetite."

Michael went to get his coat while Addison finished up his notes and closed his office door. They walked up the sidewalk. Stripes of light and shadow were created on the walk by the bright afternoon sun beaming through buildings and posts along the way. Toward the west, trees were silhouetted in black against an orange sky turning to shades of pink when it touched the low clouds above. Summer was about to be over and autumn would be upon them with winter soon to follow. Addison hated the thought of another long, rainy Georgia winter. He hoped he'd be settled in another practice before December.

Sammy came in for removal of his stitches and Addison was glad he got a chance to say good-bye.

"Hey, it would be great if you came to Falkirk!" Sammy had said excitedly.

Tutney arrived by train to Athens unexpectedly that weekend to tell Addison she had taken a position as a teacher at another school and would not be working with Dr. Sullivan in Marbleton.

"It's in a little town called Falkirk," she said. "I'm not sure if it's incorporated." This made Addison wonder if Sammy's suggestion had been some kind of omen concerning his future.

Michael stayed at the hotel so Tutney could have his bed. She brought a trunk full of clothes and announced she would be staying a week to visit the University campus, check out the congregation at the local church and see Addison's medical office and Athens Regional Hospital. She was dismayed to hear her brother was without a position.

"Brother, you should have given it more thought. You didn't struggle to get through medical school so you could make impulsive decisions."

"Tutney, sometimes decisions are made because they're inevitable," Addison said defensively. "There's no point in trying to be a part of something that's contrary to everything you believe and offends your conscience."

"Conscience won't put food on the table, Brother." Tutney said emphatically. "Or shelter you, clothe you and give you prestige."

"Prestige doesn't feed one's soul, Tutney," said Addison. "No matter how good it may make him feel about himself."

"There's no point talking about it, Brother. You've always been a dreamer and I guess you always will be. If it hadn't been for me you wouldn't have gotten this far!"

"And how far is that?" asked Addison. "I'm an unemployed physician with no patients."

"Walter wouldn't have squelched an education like yours!" said Tutney meanly.

"No, Tutney. He wouldn't have, and neither will I ... for his sake!"

"Are you going to show me the campus?" asked Tutney. "I'd also like to attend church with you."

"Actually, Tutney, I haven't been going to church. I work late on Saturdays and take Sundays to rest and read."

"Well, you must find a church," said Tutney, "for the sake of your career."

"It's a little late for finding a church here, don't you think?" Addison replied. "Now, tell me about your new teaching position in Falkirk."

"I've rented two rooms on the top floor of a boarding house in Falkirk. Belgrove School is about five miles from there. There's only one other teacher, but we will each have our own classroom, teaching supplies and blackboard. I start in two weeks. I've rented the house in Marbleton to Jerome and Amy Stacks - you know - Amy Sullivan. Jerome and Amy want to stay in Marbleton until he decides where to open his law practice. Our house will be perfect for them and the new baby, since it's so close to Dr. and Mrs. Sullivan. I guess that's all right with you, Brother?"

"You don't need my approval, Tutney," said Addison.

"Well, it is legally your property, Brother. You're the oldest son."

"The only son now," Addison muttered. Thoughts of Walter were still painful.

"What did you say?"

"Nothing important," said Addison. "Of course, it's all right with me if it helps you."

"Why don't you go to Falkirk with me next week, Brother," Tutney said excitedly. "You don't have a schedule to keep and I'd like for you to know where I'm going to be."

"Don't you think I need to be looking?" Addison asked. "For a new practice, I mean?"

"You never want to be with me," she said accusingly. "You know I never get to see you anymore."

"I guess it would be easier to go now before I get established with another practice." He paused. "All right, I'll go!"

Dr. Blair with Mag and Mae

CHAPTER SEVEN

Tutney took Addison's clothes to Mrs. Duffy to get them ready for the trip while Addison explored opportunities around Athens that week. She bought him a new suit and new pair of shoes and packed all his things. She also picked up some current newspapers so she could peruse them for physicians' opportunities.

They left for Falkirk Thursday afternoon in Addison's buggy. The air was cool and Tutney was glad she'd worn her heavy wrap. She pulled the hood over her head and toward her face and kept her hands in her pockets. Addison decided to ride up the Harrison Highway and through Harrison, so he and Tutney could see the homes of their Uncle Cambridge and his son, Jeffrey Clark, which were built side-by-side in an upscale area of Harrison near the Mayor's house. After about three hours they reached the quaint little town. They flagged down a man driving a dairy wagon and he pointed them toward Main Street, saying they had only a few blocks to go. Finally they came to two large Victorian homes occupying three grassy acres surrounded by hedges and a wrought iron fence.

"Let's go in!" said Tutney. "After all, we're family. I'm sure they'll be glad to see us." Addison hesitated.

"You may not get the reception you expect, Tutney," he warned her. "We're 'poor relations.' "

"No one has ever made me feel inferior and no one shall," she asserted. "I can associate with the best of them."

"I know you can, Tutney," Addison said, "but you have a brother who's somewhat uncomfortable around the upper echelon. I may embarrass you."

"You could never embarrass me! You're brilliant, articulate and a gentleman!"

"How can I argue with that!" chuckled Addison, and he turned the rig into the drive.

He tied the horses to a post beside the carriage house and together he and Tutney walked along a winding path of stepping stones to the porch of the larger home and up the steps to the front door. There were three large maple rockers on the porch and a heavy white-washed urn of English ivy beside each of four tall columns supporting the enormous porch roof. Squirrels were burying acorns that had fallen underneath large oak trees that graced the front lawn and massive ferns planted around their trunks had begun to brown from the fall air.

Addison reached for the heavy brass lion's head and knocked several times. After a few moments, the huge door opened and there stood Dr. Cambridge Blair in a white suit holding a large carved bamboo cane.

"Yes," said the distinguished white-haired gentleman. "Can I help you?"

"Uncle Cambridge!" said Tutney. The old man looked uncertain.

"Dr. Cambridge Blair," he replied. "Do I know you?"

"It's Tutney Key, your niece," explained Tutney, "and this is Addison." His expression altered and a smile began to broaden across his face.

"Addison," he said nostalgically. "My goodness, Addison. Last time I saw you, you wore an organdy dress and bonnet and cried every time I looked at you!" He laughed loudly.

"Come on in, children. Would you like some hot coffee?" He asked, taking their coats.

"Abigail!" he shouted, "We have guests. Bring some coffee to the library."

He led them into a large room with very high ceilings and elaborate crown moldings. A brass chandelier hung from a gaudy plaster medallion. The walls were lined with bookshelves loaded with thick medical volumes, literary sets, encyclopedias and novels. A picture of Cambridge Blair hung ostentatiously over the mantle of pink Georgia marble and two large porcelain greyhounds guarded the hearth.

He directed Tutney and Addison to an oversized tan leather divan and took a seat in a chair by the fireplace.

"Tell me all about yourself, Addison," he said.

"I met you recently," said Addison, "at Athens Regional when Mrs. Cunard died."

"That's right!" he said astonished. "I'm sorry I didn't realize who you were, Addison. I'm getting to be an old man, you know!"

"And you, Tutney," Cambridge continued. "You were a teenager the last time I saw you--somewhat of a tomboy. You certainly turned out to be a striking young woman."

Tutney didn't know how to take compliments. She pretended to find beauty totally irrelevant.

"I suppose I should say thank you, Uncle," she responded without much enthusiasm.

A woman walked in with a server of coffee and a plate of lemon scones. She was very short and pale with thick dark hair and black eyes. She was quite pretty but terribly thin. She placed the refreshments on a marble side table and gave each of her guests a neatly folded, linen napkin.

"Children, my wife Abigail," said Cambridge. "Abigail, this is my niece Tutney and my nephew Addison Blair. We visited Lycurgeus once when they were children. Addison is a physician with David Hargrove's practice in Athens."

"Why, Tutney," she offered, "You're lovely!"

"Thank you," said Tutney with somewhat of a sigh.

"Weren't you Mrs. Cunard's physician?" Abigail inquired of Addison.

"That's right, Abigail!" said Uncle Cambridge. "At least one of us remembered."

"I was with her at the end," Addison replied.

"Grace Bailey certainly sang your praises. I spoke with her shortly after her mother died."

"Mrs. Cunard was a special lady," replied Addison.

"She certainly was! I miss her. Grace is having a tough time adjusting. She's trying to take over her mother's involvement with the DAR but she's not near the socialite her mother was."

"She manages," offered Cambridge. "She enjoys prestige, all right!"

"Do you have a beau, Tutney?" Abigail asked.

Tutney's face turned beet red. She thought of Eldrin and the very thought made her angry. 'Why?' she wondered 'must people always attempt to pair a woman up with some man right away.'

"No, Aunt Abigail," she said holding her temper. "At present I'm focusing on teaching. I'll be starting at Belgrove School in Falkirk in the spring, and Addison and I are on our way there now."

"That's wonderful, Tutney. I know the other teacher there, Mrs. Cleo Bynum. Is she leaving?"

"No," answered Tutney. "We'll each have our own classroom."

"How about you, Addison?" interjected Cambridge. "How is the Hargrove practice going?"

"I'm no longer with the practice," said Addison. Cambridge looked surprised.

"I didn't expect that," he said. "What happened?"

Addison explained that the Hargroves had moved back to Connecticut and Virgil Herron's father had purchased the practice. He didn't mention his enmity toward Virgil, but said the practice didn't fit his particular medical mission.

"I'm investigating opportunities," he added.

"Well, you know," said Cambridge. "The mention of Belgrove School brings to mind that Falkirk's desperate for a physician. The new mayor, Shelton Cole, is a friend of mine. Most Falkirk folks travel to Macon or Atlanta for medical care and it's very expensive for them, as well as inconvenient. You might look that town over while you're there. I might be interested in helping you open a practice. We have to make a success of you. You're my namesake, you know." He winked.

"Thank you, Uncle Cambridge," said Addison. "If anything turns up there, I'll let you know."

"Would you like another scone?" asked Abigail.

"No thank you," answered Tutney. "We'd best be on our way. We hope to reach Falkirk before dark. I want Addison to see where I'll be living."

"And where is that?" asked Abigail.

"I've found a two-room upstairs apartment," said Tutney. "The building is granite, of course, somewhat ominous-looking from the outside but quite cozy."

"Wonderful!" said Abigail. "We'll have to come by to see you when you get settled in."

"That would be nice," said Tutney then turned to Addison. "We really do need to get on our way, Brother. Thank you, Aunt Abigail, for your hospitality!"

"My pleasure, children. I hope you'll visit again soon."

"Anytime, Tutney, anytime," said Cambridge. "Addison, you keep in touch, you hear! I'd like you and Tutney to come back in the spring and meet Jeffrey. He lives next door but he's away today."

"We'll plan on doing that," said Addison.

Abigail retrieved their coats and handed them two jars of her orange marmalade and everyone said their goodbyes. Addison and Tutney climbed up into the buggy and Cambridge grabbed the reins and pulled the horses to the back of the house for water. He told Addison where the livery was so he could stop by and get his buggy tires checked.

CHAPTER EIGHT

They reached Falkirk about eight and it was already dark. They stopped by the home of Joe Malone, Tutney's new landlord, who gave them the key and told them to make themselves comfortable for the weekend. Addison had to leave his rig in Joe Malone's barn, as there was no carriage house for the boarders. It became increasingly cold after the sun went down and by the time he and Tutney walked across the lot to the boarding house they were chilled through. Addison wasn't too impressed with the stark granite structure and the plain wooden four-by-fours that held up the porch roof. There were two or three empty buckets strewn close to the front door. Just inside the door on each side of the hall, were doors leading to two one-room apartments, and stairs straight ahead that led up to what was to be Tutney's quarters on the second floor.

The stairs creaked with their steps and ended at a small landing. Tutney turned the key in the door and slowly opened it. There was one large bedroom to the left that also served as a kitchen with a sink, small stove and cupboard in the corner. A small rectangular table with two chairs sat beside a window on the back wall. On the right side of the apartment was a larger bedroom where a small chair sat under a window beside a full-sized canopy bed. On a little round table on the other side of the bed was a rose vase and an oil lamp. Above the table was another small window framed by white organza curtains pulled back and tied on each side with a satin bow. Addison immediately spied a bookshelf containing several books, including a complete set of commentaries on the English bible.

Tired from their journey Tutney and Addison didn't talk at all. Tutney took the room with the kitchen, as she'd be the first one up the next morning, and Addison took the other room. Addison got in bed, took a book from the shelf and read awhile, then looked at the newspapers. Nothing looked promising.

A dog was barking somewhere far away and occasionally Addison heard a train whistle in the distance. He thought about the offer his Uncle Cambridge had made. He determined to rise early and walk through town in hopes of meeting a few people and learning from hearsay if Cambridge were right about Falkirk's needing a doctor. Finally, he fell asleep.

The next day Tutney decided to stay in Falkirk and wrote to her Marbleton neighbor, Bryce Stoddard, asking if he would pack the remainder of her clothes and bring them to her. He responded by mail that he would try to bring her things by the middle of the month. She told him she wouldn't need her rig, now that she and Addison were together, and promised it to him for compensation.

She and Addison took the entire day to get familiar with the community. They walked up and down Main Street and out Athens Road to an old granite quarry. They visited the drugstore and the library, brought some turnip greens from a colored lady in the courtyard at Town Hall, and rode in the buggy up to Belgrove School. They rested in a small park called Calder Mountain Park. They had a few conversations with townsfolk they met, but nothing was said regarding physicians in the area. On the way back Tutney bought a quilt from an elderly lady who lived just up the road from the Malone boarding house.

Bryce Stoddard showed up with Tutney's belongings that weekend. Two weeks later school started. Tutney awoke very early one morning and walked to Sully's Market about a mile away in the center of town. She bought a few groceries and a small coffee pot. She stopped by The Falkirk Star for a local newspaper. When she returned Addison was dressed and waiting.

"Brother," said Tutney, "Give me a few minutes and I'll have some good hot coffee for you. I've bought us each a homemade peach pie from Sully's made by the women of the DAR. They look just like Sally's pies."

While she heated up a little butter in the iron skillet, Addison turned to the classifieds in The Falkirk Star. There were a few business opportunities, but there was no mention of any medical prospects. There was an article about the new mayor, Shelton Cole, who was about to begin his first term after gaining the overwhelming support of Falkirk's townspeople. He was having a council meeting at the Town Hall that morning and everyone in the city was invited. Addison decided it would be a good idea for him to attend and see if he could get a moment with the Mayor. Falkirk was a great deal like Marbleton, but seemed less prosperous. Many of its citizens made their living in the quarries. Most of the buildings were granite, some very crude, some Greek Revival. The colored part of town was run down, with rows of shabby-looking houses and stores, which sold mostly liquor and cigarettes and little of the staples and food its community actually needed. There were many two-story Victorian homes along the railroad tracks in the main part of town needing a lot of care. Addison spotted a little house just beyond the railroad tracks where Main Street became St. Andrews Chapel Road. It was at the top of a hill graced with gum trees, sycamores and a flock of sheep. A 'For Sale' sign had been nailed to a small tree beside the walkway. He planned to inquire about it.

Tutney served Addison a fried pie and coffee and they sat down together at the little table. She had covered it with a tablecloth to hide the nicks in the porcelain top.

"This is good pie!" asserted Addison. "I knew there was a reason for the DAR."

"It's not as good as Sally's," commented Tutney.

"I'm going to the council meeting at Town Hall to try to talk to the mayor about medical care in Falkirk," Addison said as he finished his coffee. "Would you like to go?"

"I have to get to school," said Tutney, as she gathered her things. She was quickly out the door. She was to meet Mrs. Cleo Bynum down at the corner for a ride.

Addison reached for his coat. The bright sun caused him to sneeze as he stepped out on the porch and down into the street. Two large gray mules came clopping by pulling a wagon, and in the back were three barefoot colored boys in overalls sitting on top of a large pile of hay. An older colored gentleman sat in the front holding the reins. Frothy drool clung to the mouths of the gray mules pulling the wagon. Worn, heavy collars hung round their necks and they wore blinders. Addison walked past three colored women standing on the corner holding parasols to shield themselves from the sun. They, apparently, hoped to find a day's work for one of the white folk passing by. A few small colored girls played hopscotch in the sand by the side of the road. Addison wondered why they weren't in school.

Addison joined a stream of people on the sidewalk, mostly men, headed for the mayor's meeting. He was beginning to feel a kinship with this town and some real excitement over the possibility of permanently locating here. When he arrived at the town hall all the seats were taken, so he slipped in the door and went to stand in a back corner.

Mayor Cole had a personable, friendly way about him. There was a lot of applause and frequent laughter as he recounted his ascent to office and his plans for the town. Occasionally, he would reach into his left pocket, pull out a handkerchief and wipe his brow, as the temperature in the room was stifling. The mayor spoke of plans for an expansion of the library and talked about building a school for the Negro children.

'Ah, that explains it,' thought Addison remembering the girls playing hopscotch. 'The colored have no school'.

The mayor's words caused a few scowls and a rumble through the crowd. One rather nasty gentleman advised the mayor that educating the colored would cause problems, because they would no longer want to labor in the fields or become house servants. He got a roar of support from the crowd, and Mayor Cole changed the subject. The discussions that followed were informative for Addison who learned all sorts of things about the town--when it was founded, who ran the drugstore, who shipped the most goods by railroad, and that the post office was located in the kitchen of the Sprayberry House, and its owner, Mrs. Ida Sprayberry, served as postmaster.

About twenty minutes into the mayor's talk there was some sort of commotion near the back of the room but Addison couldn't see well enough to figure out what was going on.

"Someone help!" A young man in a dark suit shouted anxiously. A man had fainted and people were trying to hold back the crowd to give the man more air. Addison pushed his way through and there on the floor was an elderly gentleman--thin, pale and unconscious. He was clutching at his throat as if struggling for breath.

"I'm a physician," said Addison to the young man. "Get his tie and collar off." The young man removed the gentleman's tie and began to unbutton the high starched collar. Addison got down on the floor and put an ear to the man's chest. His heartbeat was weak.

"Do you have a side room?" asked Addison.

"Follow me," said the sandy-haired man as Addison reached down and lifted the ailing gentleman into his arms. They went down a long hall decked with pictures of Confederate heroes and came to a large room with several partitions along the walls on each side. Addison laid the man down on a small green couch near the door of the room. He removed his own coat, rolled it up and lifted the man's head placing it underneath.

"Can you get me a damp cloth?" he asked.

The young man left and returned with a cloth, as requested. Addison bathed the man's face and he awakened.

"What is your name?" asked Addison.

"Beecham Cole," said the man. "Are you a doctor?"

"I am, and you've given me quite a scare! Are you feeling better?"

"I feel fine," he said. "Would you help me up?"

Addison and the young man helped get Beecham to his feet. When he seemed stable Addison recommended someone take him home and instruct his family he should take it easy for a few days.

"He's the mayor's uncle," said one of the men, "and he lives alone. We'd better let the mayor know what happened."

"Don't bother him!" said Beecham. "I'm all right. Let him finish his speech. Just ask him to come by to see me when he's done."

"All right, Beecham," said the man. "In the meantime, you let these boys get you home."

After those present had introduced themselves to Addison he went back to the main hall but by that time Mayor Cole had ended his talk and everyone had started to leave. Addison thought he'd missed his chance to speak with the Mayor but as he walked out someone shouted after him.

"Young man!" Addison stopped near the door.

"I'm Mayor Shelton Cole," the man said catching up to offer his hand. "The gentleman you took care of today is my uncle. I didn't realize it at the time or I wouldn't have been able to get through my speech. I can't tell you how grateful I am."

Addison took his hand. "Dr. Addison Blair. Glad I could be of help."

"Are you related to Dr. Cambridge Blair of Harrison?" asked the Mayor.

"I'm his nephew," answered Addison.

"He's a good friend of mine!" offered the Mayor. "You'll have to say 'hello' for me."

"Uncle Cambridge told me about you, mayor. I'll be certain to mention you next time I see him," Addison assured him. "There is something I'd like to discuss with you when you have some time."

"Well, I have time for you right now!" he affirmed. "Why don't you come along with me to check on Uncle Beecham and then we'll walk to Sully's market for a sandwich and I'll buy you lunch." They walked together to a large old two-story house on Third Street painted ecru with a large wrap-around porch. A stout black woman greeted them at the door.

"Aftahnoon, Mistah Cole," said the lady. "Mr. Beecham waitin' fo' ya' in the liberry."

"Uncle Beecham, you all right?" asked the Mayor as they entered the room.

"I'm fine, son. Your young companion took very good care of me! I believe in guardian angels and today he was mine! Good to see you again, Dr. Blair. Ella, bring us some lemonade to the library."

"Yessuh," the black woman replied.

"Don't be botherin' about us, Uncle Beecham," said the mayor. "Just take it easy. Are you sure you're all right?"

"I said I'm fine, Shelton!"

"Well, I'm going to stop the lemonade," said the Mayor as he walked toward the kitchen. Beecham Cole rose from his chair and took a volume from the bookshelves.

"I want you to have this," he said, presenting a small book to Addison.

"The Power of the Master Physician," read Addison aloud.

"I've had it a long time," said Beecham. "The Master is the best teacher."

"I agree with you, Mr. Cole," said Addison. "Thank you."

"Call me, Beecham."

At that point Mayor Cole returned to the room.

"Take this young man and show him Falkirk, Shelton," said Beecham. "We want to be sure and keep him!"

"I will, Uncle Beecham," said Mayor Cole condescendingly. "Now you be sure Ella sends someone to find me if you start feeling ill, you hear?"

"Yeah, yeah, Shelton ... if you insist ... but I'm fine!"

Ella escorted them both out the front door and they walked together to Sully's Market. The Mayor greeted several people along the way. The colored women Addison had seen were gone, but the small girls still played along the street. There was a green and white striped awning over the door to Sully's Market. Brooms and mops were tied in bundles on the sidewalk and just inside the store was a barrel of pickles, bushel baskets of potatoes and a table loaded with large jars of licorice and peppermint. The Mayor led Addison to a small table and motioned for the proprietor. He didn't ask Addison what he'd like -- just ordered two corned beef and cabbage sandwiches and iced tea.

"Are you from Harrison, too?" the Mayor asked.

"No," said Addison, "I'm originally from Marbleton. I was part of a medical practice in Athens for a while, but I'm hoping to start my own practice."

"Marbleton," echoed the mayor. "Another granite town."

"Yes," said Addison. "I guess that's why I feel a connection to Falkirk. In fact, that's why I need to speak with you. Uncle Cambridge has offered to help me set up a private practice and suggested I might speak with you about it."

"He's a good man ... not many like him! How would you feel about a practice here?"

"Well, what do you think about it, Mayor?" asked Addison.

"I think it'd be great!" the Mayor said enthusiastically. "Have you looked for a place?"

"Well, I don't know a lot about this town, but I did see a house on St. Andrews Chapel Road about two-hundred yards beyond the railroad tracks. Apparently, it's for sale. I thought possibly I could buy it. I'd live in the back and set up my medical practice in the front."

"That's a good location," the Mayor confirmed, "And I know the man who owns that property--Dan Riley. I don't know what he's asking but he's a reasonable man and it's probably a decent buy. I'll find out if you'd like."

"I'd appreciate it, Mayor. My sister's teaching at the Belgrove School and has rented an apartment here. I don't have any other close family so I guess if I'm going to settle down it might as well be in Falkirk."

"Well, I hope so!" said the Mayor. "I'll try to do some scouting this afternoon and let you know something. I'm sure glad you came along today, for a lot of reasons. This town needs a good physician, as you discovered this morning."

He rose from the table and Addison followed his lead.

"You don't know what good news that is for me," said Addison. "I'll come by and see you at Town Hall tomorrow, if that's all right."

"That'll be fine, Dr. Blair. In fact, we can have breakfast here and go over the details. I might want to lend you a little support myself."

"Thanks, Mayor," said Addison, "and thanks for the lunch."

"Call me Shelton," said the Mayor, "I haven't been mayor that long."

"All right, Shelton." Addison watched the mayor walk up the street. It was early afternoon and had begun to get cool. Addison started walking back toward Tutney's apartment. The small girls had vanished. He soaked in the scenery on both sides, from the garden at Town Hall to the blacksmith's shop, to the Sprayberry house.

The next morning Joe Malone showed up at Tutney's door for the rent. Addison handed him the envelope Tutney had given him as she left for school. He poured Joe a cup of coffee and told him he would probably be living with Tutney in the apartment, which seemed to be fine with Joe. They both took a seat at the table.

"I'm supposed to meet Mayor Cole this morning at Sully's to see what he found out about a house I'm thinking of buying for my medical practice," Addison replied.

"Where is it?" asked Joe.

"It's on St. Andrews Chapel Road just past the railroad tracks," answered Addison.

"Oh, you mean the Riley's old place," Joe said. "I grew up with Eddie Riley. Boy, did he and I stay in a lot of trouble."

"Does he still live there?" inquired Addison.

"Oh, no," Joe responded. "He never got over his mother dying. He joined the armed forces and was killed in the Spanish-American war. His young wife Joan and their two girls moved back to Tupelo, Mississippi, to be with her family. Old man Riley married a wealthy woman from Atlanta and moved into her home. His place has been for sale for two years."

"I met the mayor yesterday and he said he knew Mr. Riley and could find out what he's asking."

"He'll have to talk to his brother, Howard," offered Joe. "Howard's in charge of the place and brought a herd of sheep and took 'em there. He goes by every day to feed 'em and check on the house. Does a little gardenin' there, too."

"The mayor didn't mention him," said Addison. "I hope he's been able to speak to him. I'm meeting the mayor this morning. You want to walk with me and have breakfast?"

"'Preciate it Addison," said Joe, "But I promised the wife I'd clean out that carriage house today. We need to make more room for your rig!" Joe put on his hat and left.

Addison was amused by the mayor's unshaven face when he approached Town Hall. He wore a green and tan flannel shirt and overalls and had a tackle bag slung over his shoulders. He peered out from under the brim of a beat-up straw hat and was wearing his brogans.

"Good day, Dr. Blair!" he exclaimed.

"Good morning, Shelton."

"Let's go get a good breakfast and talk business."

They began to walk the few hundred yards toward Sully's Market.

"You look like you're goin' fishin'," said Addison.

"I am," Shelton affirmed. "I'm meetin' Howard Riley down by South River Shoals and we're gon' see if we can catch a few bream. Howard is Dan Riley's brother."

"Yes, Joe Malone told me about him."

"I sent word to him yesterday. His guess is Dan'll take twenty-five hundred dollars, five-hundred down and the rest on a five-year note. Would that be something you could do?"

"I'll have to talk to my sister," said Addison. "Most of the money's hers. I was giving her everything I made toward reimbursing her for my schooling."

"Well, I just need to have an idea in case Howard asks me what you're willing to pay," he said. "I'm goin' to see if I can close the deal for you today." Addison was very excited about the prospect of starting a practice.

"It'll be hard to be patient, Shelton," he said. "Could you come by to see us as soon as you know something? Tutney'll want all the details before this becomes a reality."

"Just as quick as I accomplish my task," said Shelton. "Now, let's sit down and get to the real business -- eating!" On the red checked tablecloth were some white camellias in a canning jar filled with water, along with a large pitcher of Alaga syrup. Together the two of them sat down to a breakfast of eggs and pancakes and discussed Falkirk, Marbleton, the future and politics.

Sunday morning came and Addison hadn't heard from the mayor all week. He and Tutney decided to walk up to St. Andrews Chapel Methodist Church for the morning service and when they got there several carriages were lined up along the street beside the white frame building. Inside the small chapel there were long narrow windows along each wall with shutters for the mornings when the sunlight was too bright. There were two sections of wooden pews separated by an aisle between. At the end near the pulpit on each side of the aisle were two large white columns standing twelve feet high from floor to ceiling, framing the entrance to the pulpit. There was a step up to the oval-shaped pulpit area, which was circled by a hand rail of maple spindles with kneeling benches all along the congregation side. The floors were of heartwood pine, the walls of white bead board, and there were three chandeliers hanging above the aisle with one above the pulpit area. There was a beautiful heavy oak altar table graced by a potted fern decorated with scarlet branches.

The pastor's name was Clayton Reisdale. He was an insipid old gentleman, thin and pale, with long white hair on the sides and none on the top of his head. He had a bushy white mustache and wore spectacles and a long green robe. The choir section was in the right corner by the pulpit, and a slender man with a black goatee sat at a grand piano before the choir.

Addison recognized some of the men from the Town Hall meeting. He nodded at Shelton and his wife, who sat together near the back of the church. The sanctuary was full and on the left side of the aisle near the front sat four or five young girls with large-brimmed hats. Addison found himself staring at one of the girls and she caught his eye. Her green eyes peered inquisitively back from under a hat adorned with a long pheasant feather. She blushed and turned away, tossing her long chestnut curls. Everyone took their Bibles in hand and stood to read along with Pastor Reisdale.

'Trust in the Lord with all thine heart and lean not to thine own understanding. In all thy ways acknowledge Him and He will direct thy paths.'

'Who's directing my path?' wondered Addison. 'I'd planned to have my own practice in Athens near the university so I could stay abreast of the latest therapies. I determined to temper my skills with compassion and hoped one day my research would lead to some life-saving discovery on which I could author an article that would revolutionize modern day medicine.'

A matronly lady in a high-collared black dress stood and began to sing 'I come to the garden alone while the dew is still on the roses.' It was one of Addison's favorites but her shrill falsetto made it sound pretentious. When she finished the pastor stood and began his sermon. For the next 30 minutes he raised and lowered his voice for emphasis. When the service was over several of the congregation introduced themselves to Tutney and Addison and suggested they return for the evening service. Addison couldn't get out the door fast enough. In his haste he bumped shoulders with someone and turned to apologize. It was the chestnut-haired girl in the green dress.

"Excuse me," he said politely.

"Of course, Sir!" She replied. Again, she flashed her bright green eyes, then turned away. The scent of lilac floated behind her. Tutney put her arm in Addison's and quickly propelled him down the steps. That afternoon the Mayor came by Tutney's apartment with news about the property.

"Tutney, this is Mayor Shelton Cole," said Addison.

"So happy to meet you, Miss Blair."

"Glad to meet you," said Tutney.

"Well, are you ready to sign a contract?" Shelton asked.

"What contract?" asked Tutney.

"Do you have good news?" asked Addison as he pulled out a chair for Shelton and sat down with him at the kitchen table. He attempted to ignore Tutney's question.

"Well, I think it's good news," said Shelton. "Dan'll take the twenty-five hundred dollars for the house as I expected, five-hundred down and twenty-five dollars a month for five years."

"So my biggest hurdle is the five-hundred dollars down," said Addison. Tutney interjected herself into the conversation.

"Five hundred dollars for what?" she asked. "Addison, what have you done now?"

"For the little house on St. Andrews Chapel Road with all the sheep on the hill -- I told you about it." Addison replied.

"I didn't think you were serious!" said Tutney.

"Well, I was!" replied Addison. He turned to Shelton. "How many acres of land are there?"

"Ten acres, mostly in pasture, with three acres of hardwoods at the back."

"That would be ideal," said Addison enthusiastically. "I might even want to build a hospital there one day."

"You'd better be planning on working hard, then," said Tutney, "because I won't be able to help you."

"Uncle Cambridge will be willing to help," said Addison defensively.

"Well, I can see you two have a lot to discuss," said the Mayor uncomfortably. "I'll leave you for now." He picked up his hat and coat.

"Let me know when you want me to speak to Howard."

"Thank you, Shelton," said Addison. "Hopefully, this is the beginning of many things I'll be able to do for Falkirk."

"I believe you will, Addison," he affirmed.

Tutney waited until the Mayor had left to start in on Addison.

"Don't you think you're getting the cart before the horse?" she asked. "You could practice here until you had the money to buy the place outright, instead of going into debt before you get your feet wet."

"Tutney," said Addison, "Falkirk needs a physician and by the grace of God, I am one."

"By the grace of Tutney, you mean!"

"That's never going to change, is it? You'll always remind me I didn't do it on my own."

"Oh, don't be dramatic, Brother. You know everything I did was for you!"

"And you know this place isn't large enough for a decent medical practice!" said Addison. "Besides, many elderly patients can't climb stairs ... and where would you put your things? If I can get the house on St. Andrews Chapel I can live in the back of the house and have my practice in the two front rooms."

"You're so headstrong! I'll tell you right now, Brother," railed Tutney. "If it doesn't work out, don't expect me to come to your rescue! I've done all I can."

"Yes, you have, Tutney," Addison agreed. "Now let me use what you've done and make some decisions for myself for a change—for both our sakes!"

Tutney didn't answer.

"I'll go to see Uncle Cambridge tomorrow and talk to him about the down payment." His statement seemed to stun Tutney. She stood there speechless for several seconds. Finally, she put her hand over Addison's.

"Not so fast," she said. "I have the money."

"No," said Addison. "I'll handle this myself."

"Don't let pride make a fool of you, Addison," she said. "You can use my money for the down payment and sign a five-year note to me." Addison hesitated. He was unsure about becoming further indebted to his sister. He knew the more she did in his behalf the more she wanted to maintain control over his life.

"My money's as good as Uncle Cambridge's," Tutney persisted.

"I suppose it is, Tutney," he said finally. "I'll go to see the Mayor tomorrow. I'm going mad if I don't get started doing something besides wandering around Falkirk. It will be good to be working again."

Two days later the Rileys met Addison at the Mayor's office to sign the contract and Addison signed the note on the property. After they left the Mayor wasted no time advising Addison that Harley Anglin was the best contractor in town. Addison wrote Michael Balfour of his plans informing him he would send a check for the rent he owed as soon as possible, and asking him to pack up the rest of his things and send them to Falkirk. He quickly spoke with Mr. Anglin and hired him for the work needed to turn the front rooms of the house into a medical practice. He told Mr. Anglin he wanted him to grade a flat area of ground at the side of the house so his future patients would have somewhere to park their rigs ... or perhaps an occasional horseless carriage. There was a barn behind the house with room for Addison's buggy and a couple of stalls for Mag and Mae with a loft full of sweet hay. A few days later Harley Anglin met Addison at the house and for the first week he worked on the grading. The following week he got started on the renovation inside. He brought along some colored men to help carry building supplies and load trash from any demolition into a large wagon to be hauled away.

Addison's new neighbor who lived one house closer to the railroad tracks came over to see what was going on. He was a little rough around the edges and wore old gray flannel pants, a CSA (Confederate States of America) belt buckle and shiny cowboy boots. He poked around a bit outside, then came up on the porch and peeked in the front door.

"Hey neighbor!" he shouted to see if anyone would respond.

Addison appeared from the back of the house where Harley was putting in a new wall and door to the kitchen so it could be used as a laboratory.

"Slye Campbell," the man said offering his hand. "I live right next door. I wanted to see who my new neighbor wuz."

"Glad to meet you, Mr. Campbell," said Addison. "I'm Dr. Addison Blair. I'm trying to get ready to open up a medical practice here in a month or so."

"Sure 'nuff," said Slye. "Well, I guess I can get sick now. Never could afford to before. You have to be too rich to see them doctors in Athens." Slye paused to spit tobacco juice beside the porch.

"Is that right?" said Addison, feeling it was best not to mention he had been part of a practice there.

"At's right," confirmed Slye. "If you got younguns you jest hafta let 'em be sick and say yore prayers."

"Do you have children, Mr. Campbell?" asked Addison.

"Hell, no!" exclaimed Slye. "But my sister's got a passel of 'em. She and that no good brother-in-law o' mine don' know when to quit."

"Well, I'm partial to children myself," said Addison, "So be sure and let your sister know I'd be glad to see hers once I get started in my practice."

"I'll sho' tell ... " Slye stopped short when one of the colored men who was working for Harley brushed by and accidentally scuffed his boot with a piece of molding.

"Watch it, Boy!" shouted Slye nastily. "You'll be buyin' me a new pair o' shoes."

"Yessuh," Mistah Campbell, "I's sorry, Mistah Campbell."

"You bettah be, Boy!" Slye said angrily.

"Yes, Suh!" said the colored man. "I sho' is." As the apologetic man walked off Slye muttered something about 'niggers' under his breath.

"They know they place!" said Slye. "They sca'ed of the Klan. They know the Klan don' put up with no nigger foolishness."

Addison winced.

"Well, I really need to get back to work."

"Sure, Doc! You have to keep an eye on 'em niggers. They won't work when you turn yo back."

Slye stopped to brush off his shoe and started home.

"Damn sorry niggers," he mumbled.

After a few minutes, he turned around.

"I'm a purty good mason m'self if you have any brickin' to do. Thass what I do for a livin'."

"I'll remember, Mr. Campbell."

The house was gray and brown fieldstone. After the remodeling was finished Addison had Harley paint the wooden trim on the house a dark brown. There wasn't much, just a little around the windows and doors.

Tutney came over with an old wind chime she'd brought from their place in Marbleton and hung it on the small gabled front porch. She also placed a large concrete urn for ferns in the spring, and sat a large ceramic brown and white dog at the side of the porch to welcome visitors. Harley helped Addison design a sign, on which Tutney painted in fancy lettering, 'Jeffrey Addison Blair, M.D., Thirty-four St. Andrews Chapel Road'.

Harley hung the sign on a sturdy post out by the road.

'Now, the only things missing are the patients!' thought Addison. He put an advertisement in The Falkirk Star and Tutney prepared a few bulletins. 'Dr. Jeffrey A. Blair, Family Physician, Office at Thirty-four St. Andrews Chapel Road, Opening October 15, 1907.' She distributed these at several small establishments in town including the Falkirk Inn, Sully's Market, the Library and post office. With the help of his Uncle Cambridge, Addison furnished the two examining rooms with all the necessary medical equipment and supplies. Tutney managed to round up a few old straight back chairs, a small couch, and a couple of corner tables from neighbors for Addison's waiting room. Most of them were very excited about having a doctor in their town. She sanded, painted, polished and refurbished the furniture and arranged it tastefully, placing an old rug she had brought from Marbleton on the floor and hanging photographs of Lycurgeus and Sally, along with a photograph of her and Addison made when he graduated from medical school. Addison hung his certificates and medical degree in the first examining room. When he refused to let Tutney hang the 'Anatomy Class' photograph she strongly protested, but was finally convinced the patients might see it as gruesome rather than academic.

Finally, Addison was ready for his first day of practice. He was glad Tutney had to be at school and wouldn't be around to critique his performance. Shelton volunteered to help in the office the first morning, and when he arrived, there were already five patients waiting -- an elderly woman on crutches, two women with sick children and two expectant mothers.

"Who's first?" asked the mayor.

They all looked quizzically at each other and finally a young woman stood up with a toddler in her arms.

"I think I am," she said. "Ethan has been very ill, doctor," she informed him.

"I'm not Dr. Blair, Ma'am," said the mayor. "I'm Shelton Cole."

"Oh, of course," the lady said. "I recognize you, Mayor."

"I'm helping the doctor out this morning." he said. "Can you give me your boy's name?"

"Ethan Cobb," she said rather proudly, "and I'm Mrs. Russell Cobb." He wrote her name and address in the chart, along with her husband's name and place of employment.

"Mrs. Cobb," said the Mayor, "Be sure and tell Dr. Blair everything that's been going on with little Ethan." She followed the mayor to the examining room with the boy in her arms.

"Good morning, Mrs. Cobb," said Addison. "I'm Dr. Blair."

"Hello, doctor," she began. "I'm so glad you're here! Poor Ethan was burning up yesterday, and he's hardly eaten for the last three days. He's pulling terribly at his ears! Not quite as bad today as yesterday though, so I think he's a little better."

"Let's have a look, Ethan," said Addison, but the toddler began to cry and cling to his mother.

"Look here, young man, at what I have!" said Addison, holding up his stethoscope. Ethan stared at Addison, then at the instrument, then back at Addison again. He finally got the nerve to grab the dangling object and put it in his mouth. Dr. Blair pulled the stethoscope back, at which little Ethan jerked the whole thing from Addison's neck, heartily shaking it up and down like a rag doll.

"Mine," he said. "Mine!"

"I'll bet you'll like this even better!" said Addison. He handed Ethan the metal top off a jar of cotton balls. Ethan grabbed the metal top, unaware Addison was gently removing the stethoscope from his other hand.

Addison said softly, "I'm going to have a look at your ears, Ethan! Do they hurt?"

"Hut," said Ethan looking up at Addison. Addison took a look at Ethan's throat.

"Open wide. Good boy!" said Addison and then sat down opposite Ethan's mother.

"Ethan has pharyngitis, Mrs. Cobb -- and a pretty bad ear infection."

"He's not getting better? 'Cause he seems to feel so much better than yesterday."

"Well, an ear infection usually hurts more when it first comes on. As it worsens the drum may rupture. That relieves pressure and the ear actually hurts less." He picked up a bottle and scratched some instructions on the label.

"These are ear drops. Place them in hot water and when they're slightly warmed, put two drops in each ear in the morning when he first gets up, and again when he goes to bed at night. Get him to drink lots of water. Don't worry too much about any fever unless it gets really high."

"If it does, then what?" asked Mrs. Cobb.

"Bring him back in. If I'm not here, come find me at home. I live at the top of the hill at Malone House. If he seems all right, just bring him back Monday morning for a check. There won't be any charge for that visit." Addison wrote out a bill and handed it to Mrs. Cobb.

"Thank you, Dr. Blair. I was just frantic!"

"Well, I think he's going to be fine," reassured Addison, then he took a piece of paper and folded a butterfly.

"Ethan, my boy, how about trading me that top for this butterfly," he said as he set it to flight through the air. When it fell back on the table Addison picked it up and showed it to Ethan, and as he grabbed it Addison gently took the metal top, wiped it with alcohol and returned it to the jar.

"You're very good with him, you know," said Mrs. Cobb.

"He's a cute fellow," said Addison.

"Thank you again," she said as she turned down the hall. Addison then cleaned his stethoscope with alcohol. It was already plain he was going to need a nurse.

Shelton had another patient ready, the elderly lady with crutches. Addison took her chart and told Shelton to go on to Town Hall. He thanked him for his help and proceeded to take the elderly woman into the examining room.

Addison saw several patients that day including Beecham Cole who came in unexpectedly just before five o'clock. Addison was pleased to find he was doing so well. He'd been worried about his heart since the day at Town Hall, but he was stronger and his color was good so Addison sent him on his way. He then grabbed his own coat and hat and started home. When he got there he was famished and glad Tutney had a big bowl of soup and hot cornbread for his supper, and another peach pie from Sully's.

"Well, how was your practice today?" she asked him excitedly.

"Thirteen people," said Addison.

"Why, that's good for the first day, isn't it, Brother?"

"It's too good, Tutney. I'm going to need a nurse. Examining the patients and building their charts, plus trying to write out bills and make followup appointments is too much for one person."

"Nonsense!" said Tutney harshly. "You don't need a nurse. You're not going to have that many patients every day. It's bound to be worse on Mondays, and I can help you on Friday afternoons." Addison didn't refute what Tutney was saying. He decided to wait and see before he went rubbing her the wrong way. If he had to accept her help it would have to be worth it.

"Excellent supper" said Addison.

"Thank you, Brother," Tutney replied.

Addison went right to his room. He was exhausted. He took a medical journal from the shelf and read another article about lockjaw. He had a great interest in the disease and possible treatments. He read for a few hours and then returned it to the shelf, picking up a commentary and reading a few chapters on the Book of Revelation. The more he read, the harder it was to comprehend the symbolism and chronology of the apocalyptic horses, the vials, the two women, the bowls of wrath and the trumpets. It all proved too taxing so he lay the commentary on the nightstand and got into bed.

Over the next two weeks Addison furnished his new living quarters. The Mayor's wife had given him an old iron bed and Tutney had enough linens to furnish him with two sets of bed clothes and some towels. He purchased coffee and sugar from Sully's Market and bought an ironing board, broom and mop from the dry goods store. Joe Malone had sold him a kitchen table, chairs, an old couch with matching ottoman and an occasional table from one of the apartments because his new tenant had brought his own furnishings. On the last day of September, Addison moved his clothes to the St. Andrews Chapel house and spent his first night there.

It wasn't easy to leave Tutney behind. She didn't say anything, but he knew in her own way she loved him. Everything she had lived for had walked out the door that day. She didn't brood over him, it was not her nature; but she took an almost ferocious approach to everything she did in order to deny the anxiety she felt over losing control of her brother's life. She bought a new roll-top desk for the bedroom that had been Addison's and purchased some used books from the school to add to the shelves. She added another single bed and adorned it with the blue plaid blanket that had belonged to Walter and hung photographs of Walter and Addison when they were small. It was as if she believed filling the room with 'memories' would take away the emptiness she felt. For the next few months she poured herself into her students, teaching them things she had taught her little brothers and trying to inspire them to do their best to turn opportunities into achievements. On Saturdays she went to the park at Town Hall and read, and on Sundays she attended the First Baptist Church hoping to meet new people.

One of the young men in the church, John Parker, had introduced himself and was trying hard to get into Tutney's good graces. He would show up at Sully's Market offering to carry her groceries and would sometimes stop his carriage and offer a ride when she was on her way to the park or to the library. She refused to visit Addison at St. Andrews Chapel Road but she did occasionally have him over for Sunday dinner. At one of these times she invited John to come. He and Addison got along well and seemed to have a lot in common. He was a big man like Addison, somewhat reserved, and very smart. He parted his blonde hair in the middle and had a mustache. He had an openness about him and he was obviously addled by Tutney. His blue Irish eyes followed her as she moved about the room. Addison noticed Tutney really seemed to enjoy John's company but he feared she'd never allow anyone to get close enough to break down the wall she had built around her innermost feelings.

CHAPTER NINE

Addison's practice was growing and by November, he was seeing around ten patients every morning, and spending every afternoon going out into the highways and byways of Falkirk making house calls to patients who were too ill to come to the office or had no transportation. He and the Mayor opened a new pharmacy together located on the opposite side of the railroad tracks and he hired Andrew Ross, a young pharmacist from Decatur, as manager. Andrew and Addison became great friends and the last Sunday in November Addison asked Andrew to ride with him on a house call to the home of George Samuel Reisdale, the brother of Pastor Clayton Reisdale of St. Andrews Chapel Church. George's wife, Ara Olivia, was desperately ill and George had come by the practice the day before to request Addison's assistance. It was almost four o'clock and Addison hoped this visit wouldn't take long, and he and Andrew would be back home by dark.

When they arrived Addison got down from the buggy to tie up the horses. The Reisdale home was a large two-story pine board farmhouse with an adjacent one-level wing for the kitchen and parlor, and a large front porch running the entire length of the house. Addison reached for his medical bag in the back of the buggy, and he and Andrew walked together toward the house. Just as they topped the porch steps the door slowly opened.

"Gentlemen, come in," said a sweet voice as a young girl offered to take their hats.

Addison immediately recognized the young lady from St. Andrews Chapel Church, but she looked much more like a school girl now than

Mary Blanche

a woman. He thought she was the prettiest thing he had ever seen. She stood in her bare feet, barely five feet tall, wearing a plain yellow skirt and white blouse with a high collar. Her chestnut brown hair was pulled back and tied with a large yellow bow and her eyes were friendly.

"I'm Mary Blanche," the girl offered. "Papa's back in the bedroom with Mama." Her words stirred something in Addison's memory. *'You should see my sister, Doc ... she's as purty as I am smart' ... well, she's too young for you anyway, Doc ... '*

'Sammy Reisdale!' Addison almost said aloud. 'Of course!'

"Dr. Blair!" said Andy, noticing Addison was preoccupied.

"As I was sayin', Mama took a turn for the worse last night and Papa was afraid to leave her. We're sure hopin' you can get her on her feet again!"

"I'll do my best, Miss."

Andrew took a seat in the parlor and the young girl led Addison back to her parents' bedroom. Mrs. Reisdale was a very large woman and lay on a high canopy bed. She had strewn the quilts in every direction and her legs and feet were uncovered but she didn't seem aware of her surroundings. George Reisdale got up and let Addison have his chair. Addison checked her chest and heard a lot of fluid around her heart. He found her temperature to be one-hundred-three degrees.

"Ara's been sick for quite some time, Dr. Blair, but she's always been able to do what she had to do. These last few days, though, Mary Blanche has done everything for her. We've tried to get her to eat but she refuses. I don't think she's said a word for two days."

"Can your daughter sit with her mother for awhile so we can talk, Mr. Reisdale?"

"Of course," he said. Mary Blanche obediently took her father's place by her mother's bedside while Addison and her father retired to the parlor.

"Your wife is very sick, Mr. Reisdale."

Mr. Reisdale at first said nothing. He just stared out into space, shaking his head.

"Will she get well, Dr. Blair?" he asked finally.

"The problem, Mr. Reisdale, is her kidneys. They're worn out and they're just not working."

"But she always gets up so often during the night to relieve herself," protested Mr. Reisdale.

"That's probably her diabetes," said Addison. "At this point, there's little to be done. It has taken its toll on her kidneys and her organs are paying the price. As fluid builds up around her heart she'll begin to have a lot of difficulty breathing."

"How long does she have?" asked Mr. Reisdale. Addison tried to find a way to tell him what he was waiting but dreading to hear.

"Mr. Reisdale," he said, "for her sake we'd better hope it won't be long. If God is merciful, she will probably pass this weekend."

Mr. Reisdale wept softly. Addison wished there were something he could say -- something encouraging -- but he knew at a time like this silence was best.

Mr. Reisdale composed himself and stood. He offered Addison his hand.

"Thank you, Dr. Blair. What can we do to make her more comfortable?"

"Bathe her with a tepid cloth, Mr. Reisdale, unless she protests. Just your presence will be comforting, even if she doesn't seem to notice or respond. Talk with your children. Be honest with them."

Mr. Reisdale returned to his wife's bedside and Mary Blanche led Addison and Andrew back down the hall to the front door and retrieved their hats.

"How is Mama?" she asked.

"I'm sorry Miss Reisdale," said Addison. "Your mother is not doing well at all. She may not live but a few more days. Your father is going to need you."

"I won't leave his side," she said sobbing. "Not for a moment."

"Do you have a brother named Sammy, Miss Reisdale?" Addison asked.

"Why, yes I do!" she said. "Do you know Sammy?"

"I stitched up his knee for him when I was in Athens," answered Addison.

"Oh, yes ... he told me about you!" she said smiling. "That's where he is today, Dr. Blair, with his Uncle Samuel." Her smile faded.

"It will be hard to tell him about Mama ... "

"Let me know if there is anything else I can do," Addison said tipping his hat.

"Certainly, Dr. Blair. Thank you for coming."

Andrew joined Addison at the door and they walked back to the buggy. When they were seated, Addison turned to him.

"That girl is built from the ground up. I'm going to marry her!"

"You can't turn a moment of weakness into a marriage so easily," said Andrew. "Besides, she's practically a child."

"She'll grow up."

After they were back on the road awhile, Andrew quizzed Addison.

"How do you discover what's wrong with your patients?" he asked.

"Remembering and listening," said Addison. "You remember all the patients you've seen before and the symptoms they had, then, you listen to the patient as he describes his own symptoms, and if you listen long enough it will usually come to you."

"Yeah?"

'That's right, Andrew. And you pray a lot."

As Addison predicted, Mrs. Reisdale passed away the next evening. Sammy's uncle brought him home to see his mother one last time but she never spoke again, either to Mr. Reisdale or to her children.

CHAPTER TEN

Addison had determined to attend the funerals of his patients who died, so he canceled his appointments for Monday afternoon and left a sign on the door he would be out. He once again put on his gray pin-striped suit, which seemed to have become his funeral attire. He put on his derby and left in his buggy for St. Andrews Chapel Church. There was quite a crowd already there when he arrived. Ara Olivia and George Reisdale had been first cousins and both had the Reisdale name. Apparently, this was a large, well-known family in Falkirk. The body of Mrs. Reisdale lay in state at the front of the chapel and immediate family was seated in the first few pews on the left side. George Reisdale sat beside his daughter, Mary Blanche, who was dressed in black mourning. His brother, Pastor Reisdale, and his wife were seated next to them and George's other three children--Darby, Claire and Sammy--were at the other end of the pew. On the following pews were seated other uncles, aunts, and cousins and the Mayor and his wife sat on the very last pew. Addison extended his hand and took a seat beside Shelton.

George Reisdale had asked Pastor Stephens of the First Baptist Church to handle the service, as Clayton was simply too grief-stricken to speak. Pastor Stephens introduced himself and addressed the family and friends present. He gave a stirring appeal for belief in the promises of God and His Son in times of grief and loss. He pointed out the sanctity of life in every phase and how God protects those who love Him and blesses them in ways far more precious than worldly prosperity. He gave examples from the Bible of God's divine providence, and then examples from his own life of how God had intervened when he had

115

troubling circumstances. He then spoke of Mrs. Reisdale and of the many pregnancies she had lost and how she had persisted to conceive and give birth to four loving children in spite of her predisposition to ill health.

Lastly, he spoke of God's plan to purchase redemption for man with the death of His Only Son, so he could place in men's hearts a love like Christ's and make them fellow heirs and sons and daughters of God forever. 'Brothers of Christ with God as our Father,' thought Addison. He had heard all about belief and salvation, but it was obvious Pastor Stephens had an intimate acquaintance with God and was speaking from personal experience. He spoke of the abiding peace God's children can know at the death of a loved one who has gone on to his eternal home, and the anticipation he feels about seeing his loved one again and one day understanding the glorious purpose for the things that have transpired in his own life. It hit Addison hard. For three years he had bitterly blamed God for the death of his brother. He had been unable to let go of his resentment and had begun to truly believe Satan's lie that he was on his own in the world to survive or be beaten down by it. Tears welled up and with them came a sweet release from the abandonment he had been feeling for so long. 'Father,' he found himself saying, 'I've so misjudged you. Forgive me.'

When the service was over everyone filed out of the pews and followed the pallbearers down the aisle and out into the cool blue November day. Addison walked through the soft sod of the cemetery by several graves dating back to the early 1800's, even a few from the late 1700's. He intently watched Mary Blanche as he walked. She was attentive to her father who was quite broken, but she also kept an eye on Sammy whose energy was always a potential problem, although he had managed to keep still for the Pastor's remarks. People made their way to the Reisdale's to offer their support and then began breaking up and leaving.

"Sammy!" said Addison when he got close enough to speak without disturbing the rest of the family.

"Doc!" acknowledged Sammy excitedly, throwing his arms around him like he was greeting an old friend. Then he began to cry. Addison didn't try to speak. He just reciprocated with a hug and held him tightly for several minutes.

"How's that knee?" he said finally as Sammy pulled back.

"Oh, it's grand!" said Sammy displaying his scar. "It looks like a golf club."

"So, it does!" said Addison.

"Come and meet my sister, Doc," he said grabbing Addison's hand.

"I've already met her," replied Addison.

"You met Mary Blanche?"

"I certainly did, when I came to see your mother on Friday."

"Isn't she something, Doc?"

"Yes she is, Sammy."

"Sorry, Doc. I gotta go!" Sammy announced abruptly as he hurried to join a friend who was walking along the tops of the rock walls that bordered the cemetery lots.

Addison spoke to George Reisdale and made an attempt to speak to Mary Blanche but she was surrounded by friends so he decided to leave. Just as he reached the buggy, he heard her soft voice.

"Dr. Blair," said Mary Blanche. "Thank you for coming and for being so kind to my mother and father. I won't forget it." Addison turned around.

"It was an honor, Miss Reisdale," replied Addison. "Again, let me know if there's anything I can do -- to help your father."

"Of course, Dr. Blair. Good-bye."

"Good-bye," said Addison, noticing again how very young she was and hoping for his sake the next few years would pass swiftly. He didn't see her again for two full years. George Reisdale sent her off to Athens to the State Normal School to prepare to become a teacher.

CHAPTER ELEVEN

One mid-November morning Addison had breakfast at Sully's and when he got back to his office, there was a colored woman waiting by the front steps. He walked up to her and asked if he could help.

"You da doc'?" she asked.

"I'm afraid so," said Addison. "What do you need?"

"I ain't got no money, Doc'."

"Well, let's talk about what you need before we talk about money," Addison replied.

"My man sick," she said. "He pukin' up ever'thin' he try to eat. Lawd knows what da matta."

"How long has that been going on?" asked Addison.

"Three days," the woman asserted. "An' he ain't et nothin', so I dunno how he'd have anythin' to be throwin' up."

"Is he drinking anything?" asked Addison.

"We's givin' him watta, but he ain't drinkin' much," she said worriedly.

"Where do you live?" asked Addison.

"Out on the Stoneville Road, Doc, 'bout fo' miles."

"How did you get here?"

"I walked!" the woman said, laughing at his naïve question.

"Let me go in and get my medical bag," said Addison, "And you get up in the buggy. I probably need to have a look at him."

He had no upcoming appointments but left a note he'd be out for the rest of the afternoon. He helped the woman up into his buggy and

119

the two of them began the ride toward the Stoneville Road. It was a dirt road and their clothes were covered in dust by the time they reached her house. It was a two-room tenement badly in need of a new roof, and there was an outhouse behind and a small woodshed. A young colored boy was carefully sweeping the yard with a broom of bundled sticks and in the middle of the yard was a black kettle full of boiling fat for lye soap.

"What yo' name, Doc?" asked the old woman as she climbed down from the buggy.

"I'm Doctor Blair," Addison answered. "Yours?"

"Mattie Banks."

She led him to one of the bedrooms.

"Dis my husband, Doc'. Dis heah Otis Banks."

"Hello, Otis," said Addison. "Are you hurting anywhere?"

"My belly sho' actin' up," said Otis as he rubbed his hands over his lower abdomen.

Otis' forehead was very hot. Addison requested cold water and a washcloth and the woman returned with a dishpan full of water.

"This is awfully warm, Mrs. Banks."

"Yessuh, it is," she said, "but I ain't got no ice, Docta, and dat de best I can do!"

Addison began to bathe Otis' brow but his patient suddenly began to vomit, so Addison held the dishpan under his chin. It was yellow bile.

"His nausea is from the fever," said Addison to Mrs. Banks. Turning to Otis he asked, "Have you noticed any insect bites?"

"Yessuh. I's got two in my groin," he replied. He showed Addison two swollen and very warm areas, each with a head of pus surrounded by tight skin.

" I need to drain those, Mr. Banks," said Addison.

"Yessuh," said Otis.

Addison anesthetized the areas with Procaine and took a clean needle from his case along with a soft clean gauze. He pricked the skin and lanced the boils with a small blade and pressed against them until they emitted quite a bit of dark yellow pus, which he wiped away with gauze and alcohol. Addison poured hydrogen peroxide over the gaping holes left in each wound after its aspiration and covered the sites with clean gauze and adhesive tape. He went to the washstand and washed his hands, drying them with a flour sack hung by the side of the sink.

"We've got to get your fever down, Mr. Banks. Bring me some more water, Mrs. Banks." Addison commanded.

In a few moments she returned.

Addison pulled away the blanket and alternately bathed and covered Mr. Banks' face, neck, arms and legs faithfully every twenty minutes for about two hours, but the fever continued to burn, so he decided to stay the night. He dozed off and on, checking his patient frequently and bathing him. For fourteen hours he fought the fever and finally around 700 a.m. his patient began to cool down. Addison instructed Mrs. Banks not to give Otis anything but water and clear broth every three to four hours if he could keep it down. Mrs. Banks sent her son Dudley to kill one of her chickens, which she plucked and set on the wood stove to boil for fresh chicken broth to feed Otis, as instructed.

Mr. Banks seemed better but Addison wanted to make sure the fever didn't return. He knew if it were Rocky Mountain Spotted Fever it could flare on and off for days, and even be fatal. He told Mrs. Banks to continue the bedside bathing ritual.

"If the fever returns, don't give him anything but water," he told Mrs. Banks, "and send for me immediately."

He packed up his medical bag and headed for home, telling Mrs. Banks they would "settle up" later.

"Just call me, Mattie, Docta!"

"Yes, Mattie," said Addison.

Addison reached home and had just enough time to wash his face, relieve himself and change clothes when he heard a knock at the front door. It was Evelyn Cobb. Ethan seemed to have another ear infection. He gave her some more ear drops and asked her to bring the toddler back for another check in a week.

He saw patients the rest of the day until about seven o'clock when Otis Banks' son, Dudley, arrived with the news that Otis was again feverish and vomiting. Addison finished up with his last patient and once more rode along with Dudley out the Stoneville Road to the Banks' house.

Addison was disappointed to find Otis with a one-hundnred-four-degree fever and vomiting again. He started the cooling-down process and kept another night's vigil by his bedside. Again, the fever abated by morning and he left Mattie Banks in charge and headed back to Falkirk to his practice.

For three more days, Addison kept up this routine of seeing patients until late afternoon, going to the Banks' place for another night, and returning to his clinic the next morning. By Friday night he was exhausted and, fortunately, didn't get called back to the Banks' home. Apparently, Otis was finally progressing toward wellness. Addison would wait until Monday to check on him unless he heard from Mattie.

Addison attended the First Baptist Church that Sunday to hear Pastor Stephens again. Tutney was there with John Parker, sitting near the front. Pastor Stephens preached on the resurrection and talked about several theories Christ's opponents had championed during the two millennia since that miraculous event. He related that some of the Jews in Jesus' time believed the Christians had stolen His body and buried it in another location so they could claim He had risen and ascended to His Father. Still others believed He had never actually died and his disciples had nursed him back to health before he disappeared, for fear of ramifications. Pastor Stephens emphasized the resurrection was the absolute basis for our belief that Christ had conquered death and thereby paid the price for eternal life for believers.

When church was over Tutney and John hurried up to Addison to ask him to join them for a picnic at South River Shoals, a popular summer bathing site about five miles down the Stoneville Road where the South River cascaded over the rocks. Tutney had packed a basket of chicken sandwiches, stuffed eggs and pickles, and even managed to fry her own peach pies to persuade Addison. He agreed to go and went home to change clothes. He brought his buggy by to pick John and Tutney up for the trip. It was a lazy day, too cool to swim, but warm enough to enjoy the soft breezes and blue skies. They found a spot in the sand near the shoals, and Tutney spread an old tablecloth and furnished plates, napkins, sandwiches and goodies for the three of them. Tutney decided to brave the cold and took off her stockings and shoes to go wading. John followed suit, of course, pretending not to be bothered by the extreme temperature of the water. Addison had eaten heartily, bragged on Tutney's peach pies and then lain back to look up at the clear sky and feel the warmth of the autumn sun on his face. Stalks of yellow golden rod blew back and forth and a few maple leaves clung to seedlings that swayed in the soft breeze. There were sparrows flitting around to discover leftover tidbits of picnic food in the sand, and a few ravens gathered and cawed in the tops of the trees. He could hear the rippling water making its way around large stones and into deep pools in the middle of the river.

'What a wonderful place,' he thought. 'It would be nice to have a cabin on those banks looking out over the water. I'm going to see if I can buy a piece of this land so when Mary Blanche and I get married ... ' He stopped to laugh at himself. 'What an optimist I am'.

At seven o'clock the sun had set and it was almost dark so the three of them decided it was time to leave. Tutney sang some old songs as they rode home in the dusky twilight. Addison had noticed that John watched her and treated her as if she were made of china. Addison wondered how Tutney could sometimes seem so feminine and fragile, and at other times be as stingingly cruel as anyone he had ever known.

The following Friday Addison rode out to the Banks' place to check on Otis one more time. When he got there he found Otis sitting out on the front porch in an old rocking chair, fanning himself with a dried palmetto branch, while Mattie beside him shelled peas and swatted at flies with an old newspaper.

"Evening, folks!" said Addison.

"Evenin' Docta Blair," said Mattie.

"Doc," said Otis. "Yo' patient doin' jes' fine."

"Dudley told me you were better when I saw him in town today," said Addison, "and I was sure glad to hear it."

Addison took Otis' temperature and it was normal. He left some ointment for Mattie to put on her hands, which were terribly dry and crusty from washing clothes and bathing Otis' for days.

"What we owe ya, Docta?" Mattie asked.

"Don't worry about it, Mattie. Maybe you and Otis can do something for me sometime."

"Oh, Lawdy, Docta Blair, you cain't go treatin' folks free! We's got to give you sumpin'. "

"Just take care of Otis, Mattie. That'll be enough for me!"

"Docta Blair," said Mattie. "You know what you is? You is a white angel"

Addison left the Banks' house as night fell and pulled up to the barn right at dark.

"Well, Mag, Mae," he said, "We had a good day today, didn't we?"

He removed the bridles and hung them on the wall, then led the horses to their stalls. He refilled the water pails and gave them both some hay, then went up to the house.

The next morning he was ready to see patients by seven but the first patient didn't arrive until nine. A young colored girl who was obviously pregnant was dragged into the office by a very disgruntled father.

"What's your name, young lady?" asked Addison.

"Annie Ruth Sims," replied the girl.

"How long have you been pregnant, Annie, do you know?"

"I think about two munts," she answered. "I's been bleedin' and Mama got sca'ed so Papa brung me to the docta."

"Well, let's have a look at you," said Addison, ushering her back to the examining room.

After examining her he had her sit up on the exam table.

"There's not a lot of blood, Annie ... but you're going to have to stay off your feet for awhile!"

"Dat not possible, Docta. My Papa say I got to wuk to hep pay for dis baby. He ain't gone let me be sittin' roun'."

"Well, maybe I can speak to him for you, Annie. You've got to take it easy, and I'm sure he doesn't want a sick girl."

"I dunno, Docta. He sho' mad at me. I's tol' 'im I ain't been wid no man, but he don' b'lieve me. He say I's lyin' and he don' wanna heah no mo'."

Addison told Annie to get dressed and go wait in the parlor while he talked to her father.

"I'm Dr. Blair," said Addison offering his hand to the man.

"Henry Sims," answered the man introducing himself.

He was a big man, very dark, with graying hair and bent over by years of hard work.

"Henry, you're daughter can probably carry this baby to term if she stays off her feet most of the day. Are you and your wife able to look after her?"

"I s'pose," said Henry, "But we depends on huh to help wid our bodas."

"You run a boarding house, Henry?"

"Yessuh. We got three young mens dat live wid us. Dat help us make a livin'," he added.

"Henry," started Addison. "Do you think Annie could help with something she can do while sitting, like ironing or preparing food, so she can stay off her feet at least till the bleeding stops?"

"Well, we try to hep huh do dat somehow," answered Henry.

"That's good, Henry. Now you bring her back if she has any further problems."

Henry gave Addison one dollar, "I get da rest fo' ya nex' week, Docta."

"This will be fine, Henry." Said Addison.

Addison wasn't sure what to make of Annie's story about celibacy but somehow he was inclined to believe her.

After Henry and Annie left, a young mother came in with three young children covered with chicken pox. Addison prescribed some calamine lotion and sent them on their way. Another lady brought her elderly mother who had fallen at home. He wrapped her sprained ankle and told her to try to get by with aspirin for the pain and come back if the swelling had not gone by the weekend. For the next two hours no one arrived so Addison decided to close up for the day. As he was locking the door there was a loud knock. Addison opened it to find Dudley Banks standing there with a watermelon in one hand and a plucked chicken in the other, as payment for Addison's services. He took them to Tutney.

It was December and everyone was getting ready for the holidays. It was Saturday and Tutney had already finished grading papers so she was taking time to make a wreath for the front door out of some grapevines she had found in the woods behind Belgrove School. She added native holly and pine boughs, a little bit of bittersweet and a bundle of cinnamon sticks tied up in a red bow, and hung the wreath on the door to the apartment.

'No one's going to see it,' she thought, 'except maybe Addison or John.'

For her little table Tutney pulled out her favorite tablecloth, one Sally had embroidered. She placed a large bouquet of fresh pine and holly in the center of the table. She took out some favorite photos of family and placed them in frames she had made of sticks and painted gold and silver, gluing a small red bow at the top of each frame. These were to hang on the tree when she got one. John was coming by with a pine tree from his father's farm.

Tutney really missed Addison and couldn't understand why he didn't keep her posted as to what was going on in his life. She had picked up the mail at Sprayberry House earlier in the day and began to sort it out. There were a few things she would have to give Addison when she saw him again. Among the letters she noticed a parchment envelope addressed to 'Miss Tutney Key Blair and Doctor Jeffrey Addison Blair'. It was from Marbleton.

'What in the world can this be?' she wondered. 'No one ever writes us from Marbleton except that disgusting little Millie Andrews who designated herself as a family friend after Addison delivered her baby.' Most of the time, Tutney just threw Millie's letters away. She despised her, as she despised anyone who received special attention from her brother.

She tore open the fancy envelope and opened the folded invitation inside.

Mr. and Mrs. Harold Jordan Nelms
Request the honour of your presence
At the marriage of their daughter,

Vivian Elizabeth Nelms

To

Eldrin Kirkpatrick Booth

Saturday, December 23, 1907
First Baptist Church
One-hundred-seventy Main Street,
Marbleton, Georgia

'Incredible!' thought Tutney. 'Eldrin is getting married to that mousy Vivian. I always knew he was a fool. Well, there's no way I'll be there. I wouldn't dignify either of them with my presence ... but I suppose I'll have to give this to Addison.'

She put the invitation back into the envelope. Disappointment by disappointment she was getting more bitter because she denied her feelings when they were uncomfortable for her. This was how she had become so cynical and the harder her heart became the less chance there was of anyone being able to get close to her, which was what she really needed.

Tutney decided she would visit Addison, telling herself it was to take the invitation to him and decorate his office for Christmas while she was there. In truth, she just wanted to vent her bitterness one more time. She put on her coat and scarf, put the envelope in her pocket and headed for Addison's office. On the way John passed by in his carriage.

"Hi, Tutney! Where are you going?"

"Is everything I do your business?" asked Tutney harshly.

"Why, no, Tutney, ... I just have the tree you wanted ... "

Tutney was in denial about what had really put her in such a foul mood ... 'could it be the invitation?'

'Absurd!' she thought quickly dismissing it.

"Can I give you a ride?" John asked.

"No, thank you. I have to go and see Addison. Just leave the tree on the porch. I'm in the mood for walking."

"Is everything all right?"

"Of course, everything's all right, John. Stop hassling me!"

"I'm sorry," said John. He felt rejected but resigned himself to her wishes and headed for her apartment to drop off the tree, still wondering why Tutney had seemed so agitated.

'He's just like Eldrin Booth!' thought Tutney.

When Tutney arrived Addison was going over Annie Sims' chart.

"Do you think it's possible for a woman to get pregnant without knowing a man ... intimately, I mean?" he asked Tutney.

"Why not?" she quipped. "The Virgin Mary did!"

"That's uncalled for," said Addison.

"Have you no sense of humor, Brother?"

"Some humor is inappropriate."

"Well, why on earth would you ask a question like that anyway?" said Tutney.

"I have a patient, a young colored girl who's three months pregnant and swears she has never known a man."

"And you believe it?" asked Tutney. "I certainly wasted a lot of money on medical school."

"I do believe it, Tutney. Her father takes in boarders, three young men. I think she may have come into contact with a towel one of them had soiled. You know how hot it is in the summer in a shanty. I think it would have been warm enough for sperm to survive for hours."

"It sounds rather far-fetched to me," said Tutney, "but I suppose anything is possible. What difference does it make? She's just a colored, everybody knows they multiply like rabbits, in or out of wedlock."

"It would make a good deal of difference to her father," said Addison, "if he could only believe it. Unfortunately, I don't think he could, so I'm not going to mention it."

"Well, thank goodness!" said Tutney. "Next you'll be offering to raise the bastard!"

"Is there some special reason for your visit, Tutney?" Addison asked impatiently.

"Yes, there is, Brother." She pulled the envelope out of her pocket and handed it to him.

"What's this?" he asked.

"An invitation," she announced. Addison opened the card.

"So Eldrin Booth's getting married, is he? That explains your hostility."

"Don't be silly," said Tutney. "You know I never really cared for Eldrin. He was always making a fool of himself over me and it was ... amusing!"

"Sometimes, I think you don't know yourself very well, Tutney. At least, I hope that's what it is!"

"What do you mean?"

"I mean no one could intentionally be as cruel as you are at times."

Tutney changed the subject.

"I came to decorate the office for you, Brother. I've got ribbons, holly and pine, white candles and a few sprigs of mistletoe. I even have a chain of bells I found at Sully's Market for the front door."

"Help yourself!" said Addison. "I'm going to fix a sandwich--turkey from Sully's. Would you like one?"

"No thank you, Brother," said Tutney as she began her task.

In a few minutes, he returned with sandwiches and iced tea. He'd fixed Tutney a sandwich anyway.

"Do you know any Reisdale's?" he asked.

"Reisdale's?" Tutney paused. "I teach a Sammy Reisdale. He's one of my sixth graders. Why?"

"Sammy was one of my patients in Athens when he spent the summer there. I met his sister, Mary Blanche, when their mother died. She's attending State Normal School and is to become a teacher. I'm thinking of asking her out when she comes home for the holidays."

CHAPTER TWELVE

Mary Blanche was getting lonely for home. She had made a lot of friends including her roommate Grace Chapman from Carrollton, Eileen Burton from Harrison and Sissy and Mannie Filbert from Albany. Friends, however, didn't make up for her being away from her father, and especially Darby, Claire and Sammy, who had become like her own children since her mother died.

One of the boys from the University of Georgia, Jim Watkins, had spied her in a coffee shop in Athens and started a conversation. He had pretty much been her shadow ever since. His father was a wealthy Athens attorney with a charming wife who had entertained her for dinner several times. Jim had a very winning way about him, gave Mary Blanche lots of attention when they were together, and always knew the right things to say. He made her feel like a princess. She loved his wide smile, his deep-set blue eyes and his curly blonde hair. In fact, she was beginning to like everything about him a little too much. Of course, she hadn't kissed him. She was very old-fashioned about such things, but she knew he was beginning to be a little impatient. He was coming to pick her up to have dinner at his home this very night, and she had put on her favorite dress. She pinched her cheeks and dabbed a little perfume behind her ears. It was six o'clock and he would be there soon. She decided she'd better let the house mother know she would be going out.

Mary Blanche walked down the hall to Mrs. Cox' room and knocked. Mrs. Cox opened the door with her chubby hand and asked Mary Blanche to come in. She was already in her nightgown and cap, cold cream all over her face, and hair tied up in curling strips.

"Come in, Mary Blanche," she said, "Sit with me awhile."

"I'm sorry, Mrs. Cox, I haven't time. Jim Watkins is picking me up to have dinner with his family again. I just wanted to let you know I'd be out until about eight-thirty."

"You're seeing a good bit of this young man, aren't you?" asked Mrs. Cox. "Does he respect you, Mary Blanche?"

"Very much, Mrs. Cox," said Mary Blanche. "He's quite the gentleman -- well-dressed, debonair, courteous, charming ... "

"I see," said Mrs. Cox cutting her short. "Well, just be sure you give yourself enough time to know all about him ... and be here by eight-thirty as promised!"

"I will, Mrs. Cox. Have a good evening."

Mary Blanche rushed back to her room to get her coat and gloves. Grace, her roommate, was back home from Carrollton where she had been visiting her family.

"Hi, Grace!" said Mary Blanche. "I'm so glad you're back. Did you have a good time?"

"Wonderful," said Grace. My brother and I went on a hayride with the junior choir to Stanley Gibbons' farm. We do it every year, and every year it gets bigger. I met a boy named Barry Reynolds!" she added triumphantly.

"Oh, how exciting! What did he look like?"

"He was shorter than I am, but so good-looking it didn't bother me-- sandy hair, big brown eyes and the cutest smile. We talked and talked. I think he's coming down next weekend." Grace could see Mary Blanche was dressed in her Sunday best. "Are you going out?"

"I'm waiting for Jim to pick me up. He should be here any minute now. We're going to his folks' house for dinner."

"Well, I'm going to get ready for bed. I'm exhausted. I hardly slept all weekend. My cousins came for a sleepover and we talked all night about school, boys, and how I'm going to marry Barry."

"You're too young to be talking about marriage, Grace."

"Speak for yourself, Mary Blanche," said Grace. "Have a good time!" she shouted as she headed down the hall to the bathroom.

When Grace came back into the room an hour later Mary Blanche was sitting on the bed.

"I guess he's running late," said Mary Blanche. Another hour passed and there was still no sign of Jim.

"Mary Blanche, I'm sure something important must have come up," said Grace, knowing how disappointed she must be. "Why don't you get ready for bed and we'll have a chocolate and some hot tea and just chat a bit."

"All right, Grace," said Mary Blanche. "Do you suppose he's all right?"

"I think someone would have gotten word to you if he were in serious trouble," suggested Grace. "It could be anything. I'm sure he'll have a good explanation."

As Mary Blanche was leaving class the next day she decided to stop by the library to look for the books she needed for her theme paper. She looked through the library cards and found "European History in the Middle Ages". She went to the 'History' section at the back of the room and as she neared the bookshelf she distinctly heard the voice of Jim Watkins.

"Jim!" she said excitedly as she turned the corner.

She was shocked to find Jim standing there beside Eileen Burton, his arm resting on her shoulder and the two of them obviously enthralled in conversation.

"Oh, Hi, Mary Blanche," said Eileen.

"Hi, Eileen."

"Hi!" said Jim awkwardly.

"Jim and I ran into each other yesterday evening and decided to attend the choral offering at St. Pius Cathedral. It was wonderful!" said Eileen. "He came to the library to walk me to the dorm this afternoon. Would you like to walk along with us?"

"I ... I'm sorry, I have to run. Grace is expecting me. We have ... something planned."

Mary Blanche hoped she was out of their sight when the tears started down her cheeks. 'Oh, God,' she cried to herself. 'How could Jim do this? How could he?'

She raced to her room and was glad Grace was home already. She ran into her arms and burst into tears.

When Mary Blanche finished sobbing, Grace asked, "What is it?"

"It's Jim."

"I was afraid of that," said Grace.

"He was with Eileen Burton last night. He just stood me up. He never intended to be with me." The two of them sat side by side at the end of the bed saying nothing for several minutes.

"Well, Mary Blanche," said Grace finally, "better you find this out now, than later."

"I know," said Mary Blanche, "but it hurts just the same."

The next afternoon as Mary Blanche left the dormitory, Jim ran up behind her gasping for breath.

"Mary Blanche," he panted, "I've been trying to catch up with you since you walked out on us at the library yesterday."

"Why?" she asked.

"Because I wanted to see you."

"If you wanted to see me so much, you should have shown up Sunday evening."

"Surely, you won't hold that against me?" said Jim desperately. "I got to talking with Eileen and the time got away ... and ..."

"A boy may stand me up once, Jim," said Mary Blanche, "but it will never happen twice."

Jim looked shocked.

"Now, if you'll excuse me, I'm meeting Grace Chapman." Jim had no choice but to let her go.

'She'll come around,' he thought. She didn't. Mary Blanche deliberately avoided Jim and when they saw each other by chance she managed to slip out of sight. In her mind it was over and even if she still had feelings for him they would eventually fade. She would see to that. She just had to keep herself together long enough to get out of Normal School.

CHAPTER THIRTEEN

Addison had been really busy since the holiday season had begun. It seemed everyone had colds or bronchitis and was passing it around at alarming rates. He had been working until eight every evening and was going to have to see some patients that Saturday for follow up of various flu maladies. He was up early Saturday morning making coffee and toast. The windows were fogged up from the cold and frost covered the bottom panes. Addison decided he wanted to get a newspaper before the patients started arriving, so he threw on his heavy overcoat and went for a walk up to Sully's Market. Abe Sully was busy making delicatessen sandwiches and slicing up Kosher dills when Addison walked in.

"Good mornin' Dr. Blair!" he greeted. "What on earth are you doin' out this early on a cold day like this?"

"Crazy, I guess," said Addison, "but I want to see the newspaper this morning. Isn't this the week Edward Chambers is supposed to address the City Council about a reservoir in South Albert County near Calder Mountain?"

"I think so," said Abe handing Addison a copy of the Falkirk Star.

Addison thanked Abe and ran out the door right into Mary Blanche Reisdale, knocking her down.

"Oh, excuse me, Miss Reisdale," he said, quite embarrassed. He could see Mr. Reisdale wrapped in blankets awaiting her in the carriage. She was more beautiful than ever in her white fur hat and muff. Her cheeks were red from the cold air.

"I was just … well, first, let's get you in out of this cold." He put his arm around her waist, escorted her up the steps and opened Sully's front door.

"You back already, Doc?" asked Sully. "Oh! You're not alone this time."

"Sully, you know Miss Reisdale. I almost ran her over going out the door. Do you have some warm coffee to offer her? I have to be on my way. Good-bye, Miss Reisdale," he said tipping his hat.

"Good-bye, Dr. Blair, and thank you again. You're always so kind." She smiled warmly and offered him her hand.

"It was hardly kind of me to knock you down. Forgive me! I was in a hurry to get back to the office to see patients this morning."

"That's perfectly all right, Dr. Blair. I understand." She turned to take the cup of hot coffee from Abe's hand as Addison walked out, this time a little more slowly. He spoke to George Reisdale briefly and then left toward home.

When he arrived there were no patients so he went in and warmed his coffee and read the paper. He kept thinking about Mary Blanche Reisdale. She was two years older and he was two years more anxious to get to know her better.

'If things go well today,' he thought, 'I'll visit St. Andrews Chapel Church tomorrow and get George Reisdale's permission to court her.'

Addison saw Annie Ruth Sims later that morning. She came in, already much bigger than at her last visit, but apparently doing well with no complications. Addison checked her abdomen for the baby's heartbeat. It was rather fast and he suspected she was carrying a girl.

"What are you going to name this baby?" he asked Annie Ruth.

"If it' a boy, 'Henry' after my Papa." She hesitated. "If it' a gul, I's gone name her 'Blair', aftah you, Docta."

"Well, that's mighty decent of you Annie. I believe I'm going to have a namesake."

"You mean it' a gul, Doc?"

"I think so, but don't put too much stock in that. There's really no sure way of knowing. Meanwhile, you'd better try to eat a little less. You're ankles are already swelling. Are you having to urinate a lot?"

"What dat mean, Docta?"

"You know, pee ... "

"Oh, you mean make watta ... yessuh, I's havin' to make watta every time I turns 'roun' seem like."

"Well, your sugar may be high, so try to leave off biscuits and cornbread and rich sweets for awhile.

"Whatever you say, Docta. I's wantin' to get 'dis ovah wid, and be jes' as hardy as evuh."

"You're doing fine, Annie."

He took her dollar and told her to come back in a month and to let him know of any unusual events.

Addison thought he'd never get through that Saturday. He wanted to try to find a new shirt to wear to church. He walked up to Nelson's Millenary and found one with a ruffled collar, and he picked out a new derby to replace his weather-beaten one. He even bought a new pair of shoes. He felt like a schoolboy meeting his teacher for the first time. He wondered if George Reisdale was going to be receptive to his seeing Mary Blanche. After all, he was ten years older, and not from Falkirk. He got into bed early that night, reading a few chapters of a commentary before going to sleep.

Roosters were crowing in Slye Campbell's barnyard next door when Addison got up Sunday morning. He had to have his coffee before he put on his new collar and shoes. He toasted a piece of bread and spread it with honey butter and a spoonful of his Aunt Abigail's orange marmalade. After dressing, he took a small oval mirror that had belonged to his mother down from the wall and looked at his attire in sections from head to toe. He liked his shoes. As for the rest of the reflection, he sighed, and put the mirror back on the wall.

It was nine-thirty, time to leave if he were going to be on time. It was still very cold outside, so he put on his overcoat and hat and headed for the church. There were quite a few people going into the chapel in their finery, the women in long taffeta dresses with feathery hats and white gloves. When he got inside the sanctuary he found a seat near the back at the very end of the pew. Soon Mary Blanche walked in with her father and sisters. They seated themselves near the front of the church. Sammy had preceded them and taken a seat on the first row. All three of the girls were in blue taffeta dresses that, apparently, Mary Blanche had made. Addison had been told she could sew and cook better than any of the other young women in Falkirk.

Clayton Reisdale was unusually wordy that day. He was praising

God, admonishing the congregation about every conceivable sin of omission or commission and ended by reciting a poem. Finally, he called on someone to bring the benediction and as quickly as Addison heard 'Amen' he was on his way down the aisle to George Reisdale's pew.

George saw him immediately and removed his hat.

"Good morning, Dr. Blair," he said.

"Good morning, Mr. Reisdale. How are you this morning?"

"I'm fine," said George, "getting ready to go home and enjoy a good Sunday meal. Won't you join us?"

"Oh, no, I'm afraid not, Mr. Reisdale. I have lab work to do this afternoon."

"I understand," he answered.

"There is something I'd like to ask you, if it's all right."

"Of course, go ahead."

Mary Blanche had left with the other children and now that Addison had Mr. Reisdale's attention, he wasn't sure how to phrase his request.

"I'd like to court your daughter, Mr. Reisdale," he finally blurted out.

"Mary Blanche?"

"Yes, Sir."

"Well, you certainly have my permission," said George. "But, of course, that will ultimately be Mary Blanche's decision. You're a good deal older, Dr. Blair ... and Mary Blanche is very special. She doesn't know much about men. Looking after the children has left her little time for boys."

"I'm aware of that, Mr. Reisdale. I assure you I'll treat her with the utmost respect."

"I believe you," said Mr. Reisdale, "Good day."

"Good day!" returned Addison. He walked back home whistling all the way. When he got there Tutney was waiting with two fruitcakes she had made for Addison to set out for his patients during the holidays.

"They're made from Aunt Abigail's recipe," said Tutney "and they've been soaked in bourbon for a full two weeks."

"You'll have my patients intoxicated, Tutney."

"Brother, you know most of the bourbon evaporates."

"Yes, I do, Tutney. I'm only teasing."

"Why are you in such a good mood today?" inquired Tutney.

Addison knew he would probably be sorry, but he was so happy he couldn't keep it to himself.

"Well, if you must know, I arranged with George Reisdale to court his daughter today."

"You mean Mary Blanche?" asked Tutney.

"Yes. Now, don't start by saying she's too young. I've waited two years for her to become of age and she's old enough now to be a respectable wife."

"A wife!" exclaimed Tutney. "She's too young for that!"

"She would be a wife any man would be proud to have."

"Have you lost your mind? Do you know how far you can go in this world with your background and education, Addison? A wife will simply tie you down to a house full of children."

"Do you expect me to remain a celibate, Tutney?"

"I'm not naïve," said Tutney. "I know a young man is driven by strong desire but you're about to jeopardize your career when you're just getting started. Besides, there are other ways to meet your needs."

"I prefer God's way, Tutney. I have no intention of being left to my own devices."

"That isn't what I meant!"

She considered for several minutes whether to make her proposal, not sure how Addison would react but willing to chance it for what she thought was his good.

"I'm an attractive woman, aren't I, Brother?"

"Reasonably attractive ... for a sister!" said Addison teasing.

"Well, Brother, I love you enough to--," she hesitated. 'Dare she say it?'

"Enough to make myself available when your urges are more than you can control ... " she feared she was about to say too much.

"And I know how to prevent children," she added before he could respond.

Addison face flushed beet red. What had he heard ... and from what misguided soul had it come? His sister in that moment repulsed him.

"Are you insane!" he said finally. "What about me made you think you could make such a suggestion!" He took her arm and angrily escorted her briskly to the front door and handed down her coat and hat.

"Don't ever speak to me like this again!" he commanded.

For the first time Addison could remember, Tutney turned her eyes away--those penetrating eyes that had always been so bold and had so many times driven him to shame. Then, very calmly, Tutney pulled on her coat and turned to him. There they were, those eyes, as steely as ever.

"You needn't be so self-righteous, Addison. I'm a woman but I know how men think. Are you better than Papa? When I was young he found my companionship quite desirable ... and mother? Mother was so pleased she no longer had to be bothered by his affections."

Addison was dumbfounded. He'd always sensed something in the past had made Tutney closed up and somewhat thwarted in her devotion toward him, but he had never suspected this. He suddenly felt overwhelming compassion and reached out to her.

"Tutney ... "

"Don't pity me, Addison. I've done nothing wrong. It's you who have no courage when it comes to anything the least bit unconventional. You're a slave to your 'biblical view.' "

"Tutney, you must forgive our father!" Addison persisted.

"There's nothing to forgive!" She snapped angrily. Then, her voice became eerily cool. "Papa was a pragmatist. So am I!"

With that she left and Addison watched as she crossed the yard.

'So this is what she has hidden ... what destroyed her trust!' he thought to himself. 'The betrayal of her father ... our father. Someone who should have protected her and loved her.'

Addison sat down and covered his face with his hands. How he wished someone were there ... Walter ... someone. Tutney's revelation was more than he felt he could bear.

As Tutney made her way toward home she came close to tears but she swallowed them down and composed herself.

'Come on, Louisa,' she heard her father say. 'Your mother will never know ... and you'll like it' and, incredibly, she had. It felt like love ... but the price had been too high ... self-loathing, loneliness, the complicity of her mother and the growing conviction love was a ruse. Yet, she had participated, loving and despising her father at the same time. His death had left her dead toward God for allowing it and angry at herself for giving in. She thought she had put it all behind her, but now she had inflicted this terrible abomination on her brother, the only one she'd ever truly loved. She felt sick. A fragile thread of shame, birthed by the girlhood innocence she had lost so many years before, taunted her. She had never seen Addison so angry, and yet so caring, but even in her pain the last thing she wanted was to let him see her weakness.

'I thought he knew there was nothing I wouldn't do for him,' she told herself. 'It wasn't my fault he had too much pride to accept me.' The emptiness that had once been her young girl's heart condemned her, but she was too proud to try to make amends. She could only hope time would be a friend and her brother would eventually forgive ... and forget.

PART II

CHAPTER FOURTEEN

Christmas came and went in a flurry. Addison had been too busy with patients to continue grieving over his sister's incredulous behavior. Unfortunately, he never got the chance to speak with Mary Blanche, who had already returned to State Normal School for her last term.

The next sixteen weeks seemed to pass slowly for Mary Blanche. She couldn't keep Jim Watkins off her mind no matter how hard she tried. When Graduation Day finally came her father and the children were there for the ceremony and reception afterwards. Sammy picked up on his sister's unhappiness.

"What's the matter with you, Mary Blanche?" he asked. "You ain't been near as much fun as you usually are!"

"I'm sorry, Sammy," she said. "I guess I'm thinking about how much I'll miss my friends at Normal School."

"Gotcha!" said Sammy with the wisdom of a fourteen-year-old.

Beecham Cole was ill with double pneumonia and Addison had been spending every evening by his bedside until about nine p.m. Shelton took over after that and did the best he could until morning when Addison returned to check on him and give Ella instructions for his care. Addison had already told Shelton there was a good possibility Beecham's diseased heart would not survive his illness.

Beecham asked if he were dying, assuring Addison, "I'm ready to go." Then he demanded that Addison tell him the truth.

"I'll be honest with you, Beecham. It's not good, but God's never going out of the miracle business."

145

"Miracles are for babies," said Beecham, "not for old men like me."

"It's best to leave things in God's hands," said Addison.

At the middle of the week when Addison reached the Cole's house he learned that Beecham had died around three that morning. Addison could not get used to death, especially when friends were involved, and in a small town like Falkirk almost everyone was a friend. The funeral was the following Saturday morning. It was raining but almost everyone in Falkirk was there. Reverend Stephens performed the service and Beecham was buried in the church cemetery. After the funeral Addison went home with Tutney for dinner. He had decided to put the terrible knowledge of his father's betrayal behind him and not to mention it to anyone for Tutney's sake.

Tutney heated up leftover meatloaf and rice and Addison ate his fill. She was crocheting hats to sell at the Belgrove School Bizarre and when she picked up her yarn, Addison sat at the table watching her.

"If I had known how much death I would see in this profession," he said, "I'd never have chosen it."

"Death is a part of life," said Tutney. "It's certainly been a part of ours. You and I are the only ones left."

"For us, life is just beginning Tutney. Don't you want to have a family of your own?"

"John Parker certainly would like that," said Tutney. "He's driving me crazy to marry him."

"Why don't you?" asked Addison. "You wouldn't have to live here all alone."

"It wouldn't be right for either of us."

"Are you ever going to be in love?" asked Addison. Tutney rolled her eyes, not bothering to answer.

"I'm going to St. Andrews Chapel Church Wednesday night, and I'm going to make a point to speak with Mary Blanche," he stated matter-of-factly. Tutney got quiet as always whenever Addison spoke of Miss Reisdale.

'She could never be good enough for him,' she thought.

On Wednesday night, as promised, he left for St. Andrews Chapel Church in his buggy. There weren't many in attendance but he was delighted to see Mary Blanche there with her father and the children. He walked to the front and sat on the pew behind them, nodding at

Mary Blanche when she turned to see who was there. Pastor Reisdale mentioned several in the community who were ill or needed special prayer and asked his brother, George, to pray. Addison was struck by the humble way Mr. Reisdale approached God, thanking him for life and simple necessities and asking His Holy Spirit to guide those present in their efforts to become more like Christ. Addison felt unworthy after such a prayer to approach Mary Blanche, whom he had definitely placed upon a pedestal.

Mary Blanche smiled at Addison as they got up to leave. He was awestruck when she stood. Her deep burgundy skirt fell softly around her hips and came up high in the front under her full bosom. She reached for her muff as she prepared for the cold outside.

'How will I ever do this?' he asked himself. 'But I must ... I must.'

"Miss Reisdale," he heard himself say.

"Dr. Blair," she responded, "How are you this evening?"

"Very fine, thank you."

Mary Blanche began to walk toward the door, Addison close behind. When they reached the steps outside, desperate to say his piece, he almost shouted.

"Miss Reisdale!"

"Mary Blanche," she instructed.

"Mary Blanche, I ... I have asked your father's permission to court you, and he said I should speak with you about it."

"I'm flattered, Dr. Blair. Of course, I'd be willing to see you occasionally." She was always so calm and poised.

"Then, perhaps you'll do me the honor of having supper with me and my sister Tutney at her home on Saturday." This wasn't good planning as he'd have to convince Tutney to prepare a meal for them and he knew she was averse to his seeing anyone.

"I'd love to, Dr. Blair."

"Then, it's settled. I'll pick you up in my buggy at five Saturday evening."

"I look forward to it!" she said. "Good evening."

"Yes, good evening, Miss Reisdale--Mary Blanche."

Addison worked with fervor that week, thinking only of Mary Blanche. He wondered if his patients could see he was preoccupied but no one made it apparent, so he went through the motions of being absorbed in their conversations. There was an outbreak of measles in Falkirk and he saw a child from almost every household with fever and rash. God was merciful and there were no serious complications but Addison learned from Tutney that school attendance had been off for two or three weeks.

Addison told Tutney of his plans and persuaded her to cook for him and Mary Blanche. He asked her to make a list of what she needed so he could pick up the groceries himself and pay for everything, even requesting that she plan a centerpiece for the table. Tutney knew how Addison looked forward to being with Mary Blanche, and she was even more convinced it wasn't what he needed, but she held her tongue hoping nothing permanent would become of his infatuation.

'The more I protest, the more enamored he will become,' she told herself.

On Saturday morning Addison got up and had his usual coffee and toast, then started out for Tutney's to pick up the food list. He almost fell when a sleek carriage rushed by him in a torrent. He got himself together and realized the young woman in the carriage was Mary Blanche Reisdale, seated next to a dashing young man, obviously wealthy. Who was this stranger in the navy suit and top hat? His heart sank. For some reason it hadn't occurred to him he might have competition, although he thought her the prettiest girl in the county.

'Of course, she's going to be pursued by other men,' he told himself.

The young man beside Mary Blanche was Jim Watkins. He had made amends for his faux pas at State Normal School and was courting her again. She was still quite taken with him but he would have to prove himself before she would trust him enough to show her feelings. Addison watched as the two of them got out of the carriage at Sully's Market and went in, apparently, for breakfast. There was no way he was going in to pick up groceries while they were there, so he stopped by the drug store and talked with Andrew for awhile. When he was sure Mary Blanche and her suitor had enough time to have finished their meal and leave, he put on his overcoat and started out, perhaps with a little less enthusiasm. He got everything Tutney had requested including flowers she had gone by and selected the evening before, and delivered it all to Tutney at her apartment. She had everything spotless in anticipation. She had gotten down her best china from the cupboard and polished the family silver.

She used a white tablecloth with a border of blue ribbons and yellow asters and designed a centerpiece with white daisies and yellow rosebuds. She became annoyed with Addison's fidgeting and suggested he go home and leave the preparations to her. Addison submitted, taking the Falkirk Star he had picked up at Sully's. He decided he would clean up his rig for Mary Blanche. He bathed and brushed Mag and Mae until they looked like circus steeds and washed and polished the buggy. It didn't look as uptown as the carriage of her dashing escort that morning, but it would do.

Addison had a few panicky thoughts of her canceling their dinner but he put them out of his mind.

'She wouldn't do that, even if she wished it. She's too much of a lady; and, besides, Mr. Reisdale is too much of a gentleman to allow it.'

Addison polished the new shoes he had bought a few weeks before, pressed his suit and brushed off his derby. He had saved a yellow rosebud from Tutney's bouquet and placed it in his lapel. He wore his ruffled collar and even splashed on some cologne he had gotten from the drugstore that morning. It was four-fifteen and time to leave if he were going to pick up Mary Blanche by five. Mag and Mae held their heads high as if they knew they were on a special mission. Mary Blanche was standing at the door watching for him when he arrived.

"Come in and speak to Papa," she told him leading the way down the hall to the library.

"Good evening, Mr. Reisdale," said Addison. "How are you?"

"I'm doing well, thank you, Dr. Blair."

"Please, call me Addison, Mr. Reisdale."

"All right, Addison."

"I promise to have Mary Blanche back by eight-thirty, Mr. Reisdale. Is there anything I may bring you from town when I come?"

"Just my daughter," Mr. Reisdale chuckled. "Be on your way and have a good evening."

Mary Blanche kissed her father good-bye as she always did. Addison helped her into the buggy, covering her knees and feet with a small blanket. They didn't converse much on the way. Mary Blanche seemed preoccupied and Addison was too nervous to speak. Finally, they arrived. Addison left Mary Blanche waiting at the door of Malone House and put the horses and buggy into Joe Malone's carriage house. He walked the trek back to the boarding house, took Mary Blanche's arm and walked her up the stairs to Tutney's apartment. Tutney greeted them pleasantly, determined not to fuel Addison's fire. She took their coats and told them to have a seat at the table.

Addison was again impressed with his sister's talents. She served a crown rib roast, mushrooms and onions in wine sauce and an elegant broccoli casserole topped with cheese and crushed pecans.

"Addison tells me you graduated from State Normal School, Mary Blanche," said Tutney. "Are you going to teach?"

"Right now I'm just focused on my sisters and brother," answered Mary Blanche. "My mother died two years ago."

"Yes, I remember."

"When the children are older, I may consider teaching for the county. I've heard *you're* an excellent teacher, Miss Blair!"

"I certainly enjoy it, but Belgrove School hardly has room for the students and almost every week a new one comes in. They'll have to do something soon to accommodate the growth." Tutney and Mary Blanche continued to converse during the meal. Addison found himself at a loss for words. Finally, he reached over to get the roast and held the plate for Mary Blanche.

"Would you like another serving?" he offered.

"Oh, no thank you, Dr. Blair," she said politely, "But everything was wonderful. You certainly are a good cook, Miss Blair!"

"Tell me what you'll have for dessert, Mary Blanche. I have fruitcake and a cobbler."

"I'd love some cobbler. May I help you serve?"

"No, I can manage," said Tutney.

"I'd like some cobbler, too," said Addison.

She brought them a bowl of hot blackberry cobbler with a slice of butter melting on top. By the time they finished it, Addison had just enough time to get Mary Blanche back home. Just before they left Tutney pointed out the picture of Addison in anatomy class, which she had hung by the door after Addison refused to allow it in his office.

"The other students seem quite awed by you, Dr. Blair."

"I liked that class," said Addison. "I learned a lot about the human body, thanks to this poor chap whose family couldn't afford a burial."

"Sometimes good comes from misfortune," offered Mary Blanche.

"Well, I'd better get you home," said Addison. "It's eight o'clock, and I did promise. I'll get your things."

"Thank you for a lovely meal, Miss Blair," said Mary Blanche. "I'll reciprocate soon!"

Addison returned and helped Mary Blanche with her cape and then went to get the buggy. He lifted her up onto the seat. As they rode along she talked, mostly of Claire, Darby and Sammy.

"I'm hoping to see you often," said Addison.

"We'll see," said Mary Blanche. She didn't want to completely close her mind about Dr. Blair. She knew what she felt in her heart about Jim, but she was unsure of his feelings for her.

George Reisdale was out on the porch smoking his cigar when they arrived.

"Thank you for a lovely evening!" said Mary Blanche. "Please thank Miss Blair again for the wonderful meal!"

"You can do that when we're together again, Mary Blanche," he said, surprised at his boldness.

"Goodnight, Dr. Blair."

"Goodnight, Mary Blanche. Goodnight, Mr. Reisdale," he said as he left."

The next Friday morning the Sims sent their son to summon Addison to their home where Annie Ruth was in labor. He arrived there about noon. Velma Sims was keeping water heated on the wood stove. Mattie Banks, who Addison had learned was Henry Sims' sister, had reportedly been by Annie's bedside for a couple of hours. It was obvious Annie was struggling. Her pelvis was narrow and the baby appeared to be quite large. He encouraged her in labor for hours, fearing both she and the baby would be in trouble if she didn't deliver soon. Finally, at about six that evening the baby was born.

"It's a girl," said Addison. The baby wasn't breathing. Addison quickly tied and cut the cord and Mattie and Annie watched terrified as he worked with the baby, suctioning her nose and mouth and lightly pounding her back with the flat of his hand. The infant finally gasped and started to spit up mucus. Addison turned her over and pummeled her back. She began to cough and cry, struggling at first, but then letting go and screaming at the top of her newborn lungs. Mattie, relieved, took the baby from Addison and wrapped her in a blanket. Addison turned his attention to Annie. He thoroughly swabbed her clean with alcohol and then washed and dried his hands. He then took the baby from Mattie and laid her on Annie Ruth's abdomen. She looked serene, as if there had never been any pain and uncertainty.

"Your new granddaughter!" said Addison turning to Mrs. Sims. "Take care of Annie. Don't let her get up for a week and when she does watch for heavy bleeding and let me know immediately if that happens."

"I sho will." said Mrs. Sims. "God bless you!"

"Dr. Blair", said Mattie. "God got his hands on you!"

"Babies are born everyday, Mattie!"

"But you special!" she praised.

"Everyone feels that way about the doctor when a baby arrives."

Annie sat her new daughter up on her chest and with her fingers wrapped around the tiny face, turned the infant toward Addison.

"Dis heah Blair," she said proudly.

"She's beautiful, Annie," said Addison. "Congratulations!"

CHAPTER FIFTEEN

Early in the week Jim Watkins stopped by the Reisdale home to invite Mary Blanche to a dance in Athens on Friday evening. She was surprised Addison hadn't called on her again but it was just as well, since Jim was becoming more and more important to her. His mother and father were throwing a ball in honor of the Governor. Everyone who was anyone in the state would be there and Mary Blanche was excited to accept with the blessings of her father.

"I'll be here in my carriage Friday afternoon around three," said Jim. "You'll share a room with my sister, Eloise. She's a lot of fun and she can lend you a dress for the ball if you'd like. She's just about your size."

"Oh, that sounds lovely, Jim. I'll be ready. I've asked my cousin Adelle from Juliette to help Papa with the children while I'm gone."

"Till then, sweetheart!" said Jim as he left in his carriage. He always called her 'Sweetheart' and the thought of it made her blush.

Mary Blanche worked hard during the week to make the time go by and to have everything in order when her cousin arrived. All of the children's clothes were clean and folded. She had shelled butter beans and cut off corn and put these in the icebox. She wrote down the time Adelle should get the children in bed.

Finally, Friday arrived and Mary Blanche had everything ready. Her suitcase was packed with all she'd need for the weekend. She was wearing a royal blue taffeta dress with leg of mutton sleeves and a bow at the back. She decided to wait for Jim by the road and took a seat on the stone wall that encircled the house. Darby and Claire sat beside her watching for Jim's carriage. An hour went by and as the sun lowered it began to get a little cool, so Mary Blanche took the cape she had laid across her suitcase and put it around her shoulders. Darby lost interest and went inside but Claire sat faithfully beside Mary Blanche, and Sammy and the dog chased each other around the yard. Mary Blanche guarded her thoughts but when the sky turned blazing orange her apprehension grew. Her anticipation soon evaporated with the certainty the object of her affection was disappointing her once again.

"He's not coming Claire," she said to her little sentry.

"Why?"

"Because something came up he'd rather do, I suppose," Mary Blanche said sighing. "You'd better go in. It's getting cold outside. I'll be right behind you."

Claire hopped down from the wall and ran into the house. Mary Blanche sat there in the dusk, quiet and disillusioned. This time she wasn't angry, just agonizingly wiser. It was almost dark when she heard the clopping of horses' hooves and looked up to see the silhouette of a buggy looming larger and larger as it approached. In the dim light, she barely recognized Dr. Addison Blair, looking very tired and a little disheveled.

"Whoa!" he said as he got to where she was sitting on the garden wall.

"Mary Blanche, what are you doing out here in the cold?"

"Enjoying the sunset," she answered deceptively.

"I just delivered a baby to Henry Sims' girl," Addison announced. "About 9 pounds, I suspect."

"That baby's illegitimate, you know!" said Mary Blanche. "Her father sometimes helps Papa in the garden and told him about it."

"She named the baby 'Blair', " Addison smiled.

"After you?" asked Mary Blanche.

"Yes," said Addison.

"I think that's sweet."

"I suppose." For a few moments neither of them said anything, then Addison broke the silence.

"I'd like to see you again."

"I think that can be arranged," answered Mary Blanche pensively.

"Good!" exclaimed Addison. "I'll call on you soon. Good evening." Addison tipped his hat.

"Good evening, Dr. Blair." As Mag and Mae pulled Dr. Blair and his buggy down the hill toward town she watched their silhouette fade.

Addison began to think more and more about Mary Blanche. He wanted to get past formality and tell her how he felt. Unbeknownst to her, he had been loving her since that first Sunday morning he saw her at St. Andrews Chapel Church. He wasn't getting any younger. He was several months away from being twenty-seven years old and was ready to start a family. Mary Blanche had the perfect build for motherhood and could give him healthy children and the love and warmth he'd been missing all his life. He determined to ask her to marry him.

A winter storm arrived in North Georgia in early January, bringing snow, ice and sleet. The trees looked mystical with their icy coating and the snow cover hid all the unsightly clumps of wild grass and underbrush and rendered the landscape smooth and white. Joe Malone pulled out a sleigh he hadn't used in years, hitched it up to one of his horses and gave rides to people all over the county. Everyone was delighted and seemed quite taken with this rare winter wonderland.

Addison had no patients. People, apparently, didn't want to weather the storm and were huddled around their fireplaces. He thought about asking Joe to take him out to see Mary Blanche but decided it might be a bad time for a visit. He had argued for days with Tutney after he told her he intended to ask Mary Blanche to marry him. She whined and pined, threatened and cajoled to no avail. John Parker was on Addison's side. He confided how disappointed he was that Tutney showed no interest in matrimony. The two of them spent some time together in the snow and at one point barraged Tutney with fresh snowballs as she walked toward the garden.

"You two have lost your minds!" she retorted angrily. "Marriage, indeed! Who would marry either of you? You'll never grow up!"

That night Tutney treated Addison and John to a dish of squash souffle, mashed potatoes and white turnips seasoned with bacon drippings and a little sugar, along with her buttermilk cornbread. This left Addison so stuffed he could hardly move. He had put on a few pounds and was somewhat bothered when Tutney called him 'hefty.'

"Do you think Mary Blanche would find me too heavy?" he asked Tutney sincerely. "I wouldn't want my weight to offend Mary Blanche."

"Mary Blanche, Mary Blanche," she retaliated. "Is that witch all you think about?"

"She's not a witch! She's a young woman of character and a charitable spirit."

"She's only eighteen." Tutney knew it was futile to dissent when it came to Mary Blanche, so she said nothing more.

At the end of the week Addison came by Tutney's apartment. They talked for a while about his patients and about Belgrove School, but Addison felt frustrated and restless and began pacing back and forth.

"For goodness sakes, Brother, stop your pacing."

She didn't know Addison was rehearsing over and over in his mind how he would go about asking the young Miss Reisdale to marry him. Suddenly, he stopped in his tracks.

'Enough!' he said to himself. 'While I'm thinking about it, that slick young man from Athens will be trying to push himself on her and he may have less than honest intentions. I have to declare my feelings.'

He grabbed his overcoat and told Tutney he was 'going home.' When he got there he quickly hitched up the horses, climbed into his rig and immediately set out for the Reisdale home. It was rough-going in the slush from the recent snowstorm, and he was having trouble being patient with Mag and Mae. He was thinking only of what he was about to do. Dusk turned the still somewhat white hills a soft shade of purple and as it grew colder the wind escalated and Addison pulled his overcoat tightly around his neck. In his haste he'd forgotten to get his derby and scarf and by the time he arrived at the Reisdale's his hair and scant mustache was wet and he felt half-frozen. He tied the horses to the steel post by the garden wall and walked up the slippery stone path to the front porch. He climbed the steps and knocked. He could see lights in the parlor and hear voices, but he didn't see Mary Blanche. After what seemed like an eternity George Reisdale opened the door and invited him in.

"I have to see Blanche!" Addison exclaimed urgently.

"Blanche?" said Mr. Reisdale inquisitively.

"I mean Mary Blanche, Sir."

"Come in, Addison."

"No thank you, Mr. Reisdale. My boots and coat are all wet. I'd just like to speak to her briefly at the door if I may, then I'll be on my way home before dark."

"Of course, Addison," said Mr. Reisdale. "I'll get her for you." After a few minutes, Mary Blanche came to the door.

"Dr. Blair!" she said with surprise.

"Mary Blanche," said Addison, "I need to say something to you."

"Well, come in from the cold, and ... " Before she could finish her sentence, Addison interrupted.

"Mary Blanche, I want you to become my wife!"

She knew Dr. Blair was a serious man, but she hadn't expected him to be this direct.

"I don't know what to say."

"The truth is, I'm a practical man, and I loved you the first time I saw you, and when you're sure there's no need for waiting."

"I don't know what to say, Dr. Blair," she repeated.

"Say 'yes', Mary Blanche," he whispered softly. "Just say 'yes'."

Mary Blanche's head was spinning. She was thinking about how kind and strong Dr. Blair was, and how terribly disappointing Jim Watkins had turned out to be. What could be more desirable than being wed to a physician, the only one in Falkirk, whom everyone respected and admired.

"Yes!" She said, finally, so emphatically it caught Addison off-guard. He smiled and stared at her without speaking until she became embarrassed.

"I'd like to call you Blanche," he said.

"Why?" she asked.

"Because it suits you," he answered. "It's French."

"I know," she said, hesitating. "All right."

"It is all right?"

"Yes ... I like it," she smiled. "Now, you'd better speak to my father." The two of them walked toward the library and after the somewhat tremorous presentation of his intentions, to Addison's surprise George Reisdale seemed delighted.

Addison turned toward Blanche and took her hands in his.

"I thank God for you," he said. Then he turned and ran out toward the buggy.

"Dr. Blair! Wait!" she shouted after him from the front door. "We have to make plans!"

"Plan exactly the wedding you want, Blanche," he shouted. "I'll pay for everything. It 'll be the happiest day of my life!"

After he left Mary Blanche felt somewhat uncertain. Had she done the right thing? She respected him tremendously, but would she ever love him?

CHAPTER SIXTEEN

For the next few weeks Falkirk was abuzz with the news that their young physician was marrying Mary Blanche Reisdale of St. Andrews Chapel Community. Everyone seemed personally enchanted with them ... everyone but Tutney. Addison had gone by her apartment to spring the news the very next morning after obtaining the consent of George Reisdale. Tutney was making coffee when he burst in, picked her up and flung her around the kitchen.

"She said yes!" he exclaimed.

"Who said yes?" asked Tutney, "And put me down for heaven's sake!"

"Blanche said yes!" he repeated.

"Mary Blanche said 'yes'? So you're betrothed, I suppose," she stated cynically.

"The prettiest girl in Falkirk is going to marry me!" he continued, as he buttered a piece of toast from Tutney's platter and took a bite.

"Brother, you are hopeless. I've tried to warn you not to get involved with a woman this early in your career, and you've not only gotten involved but you've asked her to marry you!"

"Tutney," said Addison patiently, "You needn't go off on a tangent. It won't do any good. She's what I want and, apparently, she wants me. That's a good start, don't you think?"

"You're hell-bent on this foolishness!" Tutney exclaimed.

"Tutney," he asked ignoring her remark, will you help Blanche if she needs you? I know she's going to want an elaborate wedding because she has so many friends. She'll want to invite everyone in Falkirk, which is fine with me. I want it to be all she desires."

"Brother, people get married every day. If you insist on this there is no need being excessive, but I'm sure you will despite my advice. As for helping 'Blanche', when did she change her name?"

"That was my idea," said Addison.

"Hmmph!" puffed Tutney. "Well, as for helping 'Blanche', you know I will if that's what you want. You know I'll do what's in your best interest." She didn't know how she'd manage something so distasteful but she did want Addison to have an appropriate wedding for the sake of his medical career.

The following week Addison went to the Reisdale home to discuss a date for the wedding with Mary Blanche, who was not too enthused over the help he promised from his sister. She had an uncanny feeling Tutney could be quite arrogant and overbearing. Still, she would be accommodating to her future husband's wishes. At Addison's insistence Mary Blanche agreed to marry by the middle of May. The ceremony would be performed by her Uncle Clayton at the St. Andrews Chapel church. She was excited about her plans and visited Grace to share them.

"I'm going to make the dresses for the entire wedding party. I'll buy white taffeta and organza from Sully's and create my gown. I want you to be my maid of honor and Dr. Blair's sister Tutney will be a bridesmaid. You and Tutney will wear pastel green. Claire, in yellow, will be my flower girl."

"Just imagine it!" she continued. "The three of you will carry a bouquet of yellow rosebuds tied with pastel green ribbons flowing to the floor, and Claire will sprinkle yellow rose petals from a basket lined in organza with a yellow bow."

"It all sounds beautiful, Mary Blanche," said Grace, "and, of course, I'll help you any way I can."

Clayton's wife, Madeline, offered to plan the reception. She was going to serve 'chicken Madeira' with potatoes au gratin and wax beans and she asked Evelyn Cobb to make the wedding cake in three tiers decorated in green leaves and yellow roses.

Blanche ordered tie and tails from Decatur for Addison and his best man, Shelton Cole. The ushers would be Dr. Blair's classmate, Henry Patterson from Charleston, and his former colleague from Athens, Michael Balfour.

Addison was busier than ever in his practice. Annie Ruth Sims came in for a visit and was doing fine. She brought baby Blair with her, who was already a chubby thirteen-pounder. Ethan Cobb had his usual change-of-season allergy and ear infection; Mayor Cole's daughter was pregnant and coming in for regular checkups, Tutney had caught a cold and developed bronchitis and Joe Malone had broken his leg below the knee when he fell while making repairs to his back steps.

Despite Addison's highly unpredictable itinerary and his feeling the day would never come, May 17, 1908, finally arrived and he found himself harnessing Mag and Mae to his buggy and helping to transport dishes, silverware, flowers, packages of cut-up chicken and potatoes to the kitchen of St. Andrews Chapel Church. Shelton came through, as usual, and rode by the Cobb's home to pick up the cake and jugs of lemonade.

It was four o'clock and Addison had to get home, dress, pick Tutney up and be back at the church by six. He had trouble with his starched collar and tie but finally succeeded in getting them right. He buttoned his gray vest and combed his curly dark hair as best he could, parting it on the left side, and shaved his dismally failed attempt at a mustache.

The weather cooperated and it was a sunny day with just a slight breeze tickling the trees. Addison went by to get Tutney who, except for a somewhat red nose from her cold, looked very stately in her green organza dress. When they arrived at the church she instructed Addison to pull to the back door and let her out so her heels wouldn't dig into the ground.

Addison noticed Mattie, Otis, and Henry, Velma and Annie Ruth Sims sitting on a concrete wall at the back of the church, adorned in their Sunday best.

"What are you doing out here?" he asked.

"Lawdy, Docta Blair," said Mattie. "We's got to see you get married, but it ain't right for us to be inside."

"You most certainly will come in," said Addison.

He led them into the church and had them sit in the choir area beside the pulpit and the altar. This attracted a lot of curious looks from the other guests, but no one said a word, although Slye Campbell showed up with his wife and promptly turned and left when he spotted them there.

But when you are invited, go and sit down in the lowest place,
so that when he who invited you comes he may say to you,
"Friend, go up higher". (Luke 14:10)

Pastor Reisdale came in a little after Addison arrived and laid out for Addison how the procession would go. Blanche was overwhelmed. She had personally arranged the ferns and flowers in the sanctuary, dressed Claire, her little flower girl, and helped Grace Chapman into her green organza. She had placed the bouquets and the floral basket for the flower girl on a table in the foyer so she and the attendants could pick them up just before walking down the aisle. She had scarcely donned her own gown and veil when Aunt Madeline summoned her and the three bridesmaids to the back of the church and handed them their bouquets.

Henry and Michael dutifully seated the wedding guests as the organist began to play. A few minutes later Darby began to sing 'When the dawn breaks through the night, I-I-I-I L-o-o-v-e Y-o-u-u'. When she finished the song and after a few bars of Lohengrin's wedding march Madeline directed Tutney down the aisle followed first by Grace and then by Claire who dutifully sprinkled her yellow petals along the white aisle cloth as she tiptoed toward the altar. Suddenly, the organ grew louder and Blanche appeared in a gown embroidered with hundreds of tiny seed pearls with a white organza ruffle round her shoulders and over her long puffed sleeves. The bodice bloused over her waist and a long, fluted skirt flared out at the hem. She was escorted by her proud father, George Reisdale. Her hair was up in curls and lace covered her crown and flowed over her shoulders to the floor. Addison was stunned as he watched her come down the aisle and tears welled up in his eyes.

When he began to repeat his vows looking into the face of his bride, Blanche realized he was trembling and held both his hands tightly in hers giving him a reassuring smile. She then repeated her vows and the rings were presented.

"I now pronounce you man and wife!" declared Pastor Clayton.

Addison kissed Blanche softly on her cheek for the very first time and the handsome couple marched out to the cheers of the crowd.

Not until the reception did they realize what enormous support Falkirk had shown them. Several students from Belgrove School came to see Tutney who to Addison's surprise had actually invited them. Michael

Balfour brought the Hargroves who were visiting from New Hampshire and Addison greeted them cordially. Addison's patients and their families had come, Mayor Cole and his wife, Joe Malone and his family, Abe and Naomi Sully and Andrew Ross and his fiance from Decatur. Millie and Gus were there with little Nathan.

Slye Campbell stood near the punch bowl drinking lemonade. Tutney whispered to Blanche, "Can you believe that!? Walking out of your wedding and then coming back for the reception? White trash!"

Blanche ignored her. She wasn't going to let anything spoil this special occasion. She got Madeline to fix up a box of food and some wedding cake and had Sammy take it to the colored folks who were uncomfortable staying for the reception and had started to leave. Madeline insisted Addison and Blanche change their clothes and get on to Addison's house to prepare to leave the next morning for their St. Augustine honeymoon. She promised to be sure the church was sparkling clean and all the dishes and serving pieces were returned to their owners. Blanche asked her Uncle Clayton to have some of the young boys put all the wedding flowers on her mother's grave. She gave Mr. Reisdale a hearty good-bye kiss and then gave big hugs to Darby, Claire and Sammy. Sammy offered Addison his hand.

"Congratulations, Doc! I told you Mary Blanche was special, didn't I?"

"You did, Sam!" said Addison. "I'm forever in your debt!"

When they had finally said their goodbyes he and Blanche left in the buggy under a shower of rice thrown by the guests.

On the ride home Addison's shoulders touched Blanche's and she was keenly aware of his closeness. Her heart jumped at the thought of what she was about to experience but her uncertainty was mingled with anticipation.

Addison stopped at the front steps. He helped his bride out of the buggy and unlocked the door. Sweeping her up into his arms he carried her over the threshold and set her down just inside. Blanche was a little unsure what to do next. Addison had never openly shown his affection but she could see intense yearning in his blue-gray eyes. Looking deeply into them she encountered a completely unaffected, gentle soul.

Addison put his hand on her shoulders and looked into her eyes, then bent to give her a warm, tender kiss. She felt weak and something within drew her to him and took her breath away. When he put his arms around her, his lips still on hers, she reached up to embrace his strong shoulders. He smiled, took her hand and led her to the bedroom.

There are three things which are too wonderful for me.
Yes, four which I do not understand:
The way of an eagle in the air,
The way of a serpent upon a rock,
The way of a ship in the midst of the sea,
And the way of a man with a virgin. (Prov. 30:18, paraphrased)

CHAPTER SEVENTEEN

Blanche mailed George Reisdale a picture postcard of she and Addison sitting in a wagon in St. Augustine, Blanche in a white blouse, black skirt with bustle and full-brimmed black straw hat. Addison wore his new suit and derby.

Sunny days followed with the two of them strolling on the beach barefoot and touring the first known schoolhouse in the 'New World'. Everything was more wonderful than she could have imagined. She felt privileged to have a husband with the means and thoughtfulness to provide this week for his new bride. They spent an afternoon on the beach watching the waves rush one by one to slap the shore, then slip discreetly back into the sea underneath the next approaching surge. It was the first time Blanche had seen the ocean. The expanse of the sky made her feel as if she were invincible and seeing the whole of the universe, but with it came a sense of terrible loneliness at the knowledge of one's accountability to God, which no one can share. It made her long to know more of the man beside her who had just become her life's companion.

"Tell me about Marbleton, Dr. Blair," she said, "And your family."

"My father was Lycurgeus Blair," said Addison, "Can you imagine such a name?"

"Is that Greek?" asked Blanche.

"It is. My grandmother was into Greek mythology and gave Greek names to all ten of her children."

"Marbleton's a lot like Falkirk," he continued. "It's just larger. It's a granite town. Our school was a one-room building of granite with a tin roof and Walter and I were in class together for most of our school years, but the county kept growing and after they built the new high school I attended there."

"Walter?" inquired Blanche.

"Yes," said Addison, "My younger brother."

When Addison said nothing further Blanche decided not to ask more, but after a few minutes he continued.

"Walter was great! Everybody loved him. He was as simple a person as I've ever known. He didn't care about having nice things or being somebody. He was happy just to be a farmer ... and a fisherman."

"What happened?" asked Blanche.

"He got sick while I was in medical school. I came home as soon as I heard but he was already severely ill. I think he had the will to get well but his body just couldn't keep up. He died of pneumonia."

"I'm sorry. How terrible for you."

"It's all right," said Addison, moving closer to Blanche. "I've come to terms with it now."

"Were you close to your father?" Blanche asked.

"Tutney's mother was Papa's first wife. When she died he married my mother, Sally Olivia. I was only eight years old when Papa died and he was always working on the farm, so I'm afraid I never really knew him."

"Tell me about your mother."

"After Papa died she remarried and left us with Tutney. After that she was never really part of our lives and she died when Walter and I were very young."

"Tutney reared you?"

"She did her best."

"That's very sad," said Blanche and for several minutes they said nothing.

"What made you want to become a physician?" asked Blanche.

"It really was more a matter of what Tutney wanted," Addison said with a smile. "There are a lot of physicians in our family. You've met Uncle Cambridge and his son. My mother's second husband was Dr. Jacob Blair, who was a first cousin to both she and my father. In the 1800's, almost every educated family encouraged their sons to be either physicians, clergymen or attorneys. Being a physician was a prestigious thing to be and many Blairs chose that path. Tutney chose it for me."

"Are you glad you let her do that?"

"I guess it's my destiny. There has to be some reason why she was so determined to make it happen. I do believe compassion, next to love, is the truest reflection of God. It's hard to explain the good feeling it gives me to see someone restored from illness."

"Tutney said you're a surgeon," said Blanche.

"I wouldn't call myself a surgeon, Blanche," Addison answered. "I'm a physician who performs surgery. I don't envy the physician who actually does surgery for a living. When things go awry and surgery is the only hope I want to be prepared, but I think for the most part God's design is better left alone." Addison turned to Blanche and took her face in his hands.

"You're a beautiful woman, Blanche. I wouldn't want some physician to modify you thinking he was somehow making your life easier or better. God created hormones in delicate balance and they're best left intact when possible. I'm afraid one day well-meaning surgeons will be diminishing women in response to their whim to be rid of menstruation. If that should happen, there will be a lot of bewildered husbands who won't understand why their wives are no longer the women they married. It doesn't always happen, but it's difficult for a couple when it does." The two of them sat talking, watching the sun paint the low-lying skies with endless hues of pink and orange as it sank toward the sea.

'We're really just getting to know each other,' Blanche thought.

Evening shadows slowly began to transform the clouds into the ominous-looking billows of an approaching storm. Occasionally, a silver lining would appear when the sun's rays momentarily broke through, but the opposing darkness triumphed as the sun disappeared on the horizon. When the glow of the day finally died, Addison and Blanche gathered up their towels and sunhats and walked through the sand toward their villa. Occasional waves swept over their feet and the rest of the world seemed very far away. At the end of the week Blanche felt a little sad as she packed up their belongings and prepared for the journey back to the new life that awaited them in Falkirk.

Tutney had stayed at the house while Addison was in Florida so she could refer any emergencies to Cambridge Blair in Harrison or to the Leslie Memorial Hospital in Decatur. While she was there she did some cleaning and reorganizing of his supplies and planted some flowers and shrubs around the front of the house. She always had to be busy at something.

Sammy and the girls were ecstatic when their 'Mary Blanche' returned, and they talked her into cooking a meal for them and Mr. Reisdale. She made turkey and dressing, candied yams by her favorite recipe and a strawberry cobbler. Mr. Reisdale was the most appreciative, because although he had never considered himself a cook he had made a tireless effort while Blanche was away. When everyone finished dinner, George Reisdale called his 'Mary Blanche' into the library for a chat. Blanche had no idea what he was about to say.

"Mary Blanche," he began, "You know I've done the best I can with the children this week, seen to their meals in my own inexperienced way, been sure they had their baths and tried to keep them out of trouble ... but the truth is, I'm too old to be the kind of father they need. It's a pity your mother was unable to carry a child to term until we were both in our 40's. They're more like grandchildren to me than children, which would be all right except that I seem to become more incapable of dealing with them every day."

"Papa," interrupted Blanche, "What in the world are you trying to say? You're not thinking of giving them up, are you? I couldn't bear it."

"No, Mary Blanche, I'm not going to give them up," he answered. "I'm thinking of assigning them to you and Addison!"

Blanche said nothing for a moment. She had to absorb what she was hearing. She had Addison to consider before she even discussed such an idea seriously.

"Papa, you're springing this on us, aren't you? I'm barely a bride and just starting housekeeping on my own and Dr. Blair is very busy in his practice and will be too easily taken advantage of, by me, if I'm not careful. He's far too giving." She knew no one could love her siblings more than she did. George Reisdale knew that too, which made it easier for him to impose them on her.

"I'm not saying 'no', Papa," she assured him. "I just need some time to work it all out ... I mean, the implications for me and the expense for Addison. Let me talk to him tonight and I'll try to let you know of our decision soon."

"I understand you can't jump in and take them right away," said Mr.

Reisdale. "If Dr. Blair does agree I would keep them from now until school starts in the fall. That will give you and Addison a chance to get used to each other. I can find someone to stay with them during the day and see to it they get their meals. If you decide to do it, of course I would see to it you had the money to handle their expenses until they're all through school."

Blanche went back to the kitchen to help Darby with the dishes. Meanwhile, Addison was playing word games with the other two children in the parlor. She could hear them giggling and wondered what in the world they found so amusing. Suddenly, she had an idea.

"Hey, children!" said Blanche as she walked into the parlor removing her apron. "What do you say to spending the weekend with Dr. Blair and me?"

The children went absolutely wild with delight.

"Yea!" said Sammy.

"We're going to Dr. Blair's house! We're going to Dr. Blair's house! We're going to Dr. Blair's house," they sang as they circled first into the parlor, then the library and back through the kitchen to the parlor again.

"Children!" shouted George Reisdale with frustration. Blanche could certainly see what he meant by being 'incapable' of dealing with them.

Blanche helped them get their things together and Addison suggested she tie them into bundles while he went to find some long branches.

"They'll love being hoboes," he suggested enthusiastically and Blanche wondered who was the biggest child.

The three of them respectfully kissed their Papa good-bye and holding their hobo sticks over their shoulders followed Addison out to the buggy. George Reisdale took some money and pushed it into Addison's hand refusing to take it back, though Addison tried. He didn't want to embarrass Blanche so he accepted it and put it into his watch pocket. The air was a little cool and Blanche had put sweaters on the children but failed to get one for herself, so Addison put one arm around her and held the reins with the other.

"Giddy-up!" he shouted to Mag and Mae, and the five of them were on their way. The horses clip-clopped down the silvery moonlit road as frogs croaked from cattail ponds along the way. They all sang together, "Aunt Dinah's Quiltin' Party" and "Old Black Joe", except for Sammy who had reached the end of his energy reserve and collapsed in the back of the buggy, snoring for most of the ride home. When they reached the house Addison carried Sammy in and laid him on the couch. Blanche covered him with a quilt and used more quilts and blankets to make a pallet on the parlor floor for the girls and it wasn't long before they were fast asleep.

Blanche went into the new kitchen, which Addison had asked Harley Anglin to close off from the practice rooms, and made some coffee. She brought it to the bedroom, sat down and summoned Addison to sit beside her at the foot of the bed. After responding to a few kisses she got to the subject at hand.

"Dr. Blair," she said softly, "I have to talk to you about something."

"What is it, Blanche?" he asked with concern, perhaps fearing a tirade like those he'd become accustomed to from Tutney.

"Papa asked me tonight if we could take the children." She waited for him to respond.

"For good I mean! At least until they graduate from school." She wondered anxiously what would be his reaction.

"Is he having that hard a time with them?" Addison asked finally.

"You know Papa," she said. "He loves them dearly, really ... but he's getting old and impatient and thinks it would be better for them."

Addison thought about the situation a long time before he said anything further.

"I love children, Blanche, I always have; and you can't possibly know how much I'm looking forward to ours. I'll do anything for you but I don't want you taking on something that's going to leave you so exhausted and nervous we won't be able to enjoy each other."

"That won't happen, Dr. Blair," she said sweetly, "I promise!"

Addison sat quietly for a few more minutes. Finally, he spoke.

"I don't remember much about my father, Blanche, and had to give my mother up to another man when I was only eight. I can't tell you how hard Tutney could be, although I know she sacrificed a great deal. I won't have those children grow up not knowing that someone is on their side. If you think you're up to it, I want to do it ... for them and for us!"

"Oh, Dr. Blair," she cried throwing her arms around his neck. "You are the kindest man, I know!"

"I appreciate your admiration, Darling, but do me a favor?"

"Anything!" she assured him.

"Would you call me Addison? I am your husband!"

"Of course ... Addison."

One afternoon while the children were visiting they hiked up to Tutney's with Addison. He decided to walk to the carriage house to talk with Joe Malone, so Tutney took the opportunity to tell the children a delightful story about one of her ancestors, 'Massah Billy' Blair and his thirteen slaves and thirteen bags of gold.' They hung onto every word as she described the heavy breathing of his massive horse as he 'raced the three hundred miles from Albemarle County, Virginia to Marbleton with gold in his saddlebag and the British redcoats on his tail all the way.' She was really in her element when she was with children.

Meanwhile, she had her own axe to grind with John Parker, who was threatening to leave Falkirk if she didn't marry him. She didn't know how to tell her brother she was thinking of letting him move in with her, hoping to pacify him for awhile. She knew Addison would prefer marriage to such unconventional behavior but it was her life, after all. He had chosen his and she was entitled to make her choices, whatever the consequences.

After a couple of hours Addison knew instinctively Blanche would be worried so he bade Joe good-bye and hurried down the hill to Tutney's to get the children. Together with his "three musketeers" he headed back. Tutney had no chance to tell him about her upcoming arrangement with John.

Blanche was working on supper when the four got home. She'd been boiling a ham and black-eyed peas all afternoon and cooked a skillet full of fresh corn. She'd baked cornbread and opened a jar of Madeline's tomato chili to go with the peas and had gotten Sally's recipe from Tutney and fried up some delicious peach pies.

"I'm destined to obesity if you keep this up," said Addison when he saw the spread on the table.

The children couldn't eat for watching Addison. They obviously adored him and were copying his every move – fork to meat, meat to mouth, hand to glass, glass to mouth, and back to the table. Blanche didn't know where he found all his patience. Once he shook his napkin out and the three of them happily concurred, but when he pretended to blow his nose on it, their adoration waned.

"That's disgusting!" exclaimed Darby.

"That's disgusting," echoed Claire and Sammy.

"That's enough!" said Blanche. "Stop playing and eat, children." Addison gave the children a wink and they dutifully started on the peas they'd left in preference for the ham and cornbread.

After cleaning up the dishes Blanche got the children ready for bed, and then the five of them gathered in the parlor, Sammy on the sofa and the girls on their pallets, while Addison read the Bible. This had been a family ritual for the Reisdales since Blanche was a small girl and she had indoctrinated Addison right away. The children asked a question about why God made man if He knew everything and, therefore, knew He was going to regret it and send the flood. The explanation took Addison so long that by the time he finished the children were asleep.

Blanche's day wasn't over. She had to press the children's clothes for church. Addison sat in the kitchen supposedly reading but mostly watching her. He was so in love with everything about her -- her face, her feminine ways and her industry.

'How in the world can a man be so lucky?' he asked himself.

A few weeks later Addison went to the Reisdale home with Blanche to pack up the children's things for permanent residence with them. Blanche had decided that since school would soon be upon them, the remainder of the summer would be a perfect time for everyone to get adjusted to his expanding family.

CHAPTER EIGHTEEN

Tutney had barely gotten John Parker moved in before it was time for the new school year. She had decided not to tell Addison. She knew he would find out from Joe Malone anyway and he wouldn't be any angrier about her keeping it from him than he would be about her allowing it. She would have Darby and Claire in her class this year, in addition to Sammy who had been her student since she came to Falkirk. She and Cleo Bynum had decided to divide the children by age, Cleo teaching the younger children and Tutney teaching the older ones. Tutney liked Cleo and had even considered trying to make her a close friend, but Cleo was married and apart from school the two of them had little in common.

The first morning of the new school year Addison decided to check on Tutney. He never had a doubt she could take care of herself, but he knew how conscientious she was about teaching and that her hands would be full of interesting items she had collected during the summer to show the children, along with new books she had found for them to read. He thought he would volunteer to take her to school in his buggy and see how things were going since John Parker had moved in with her.

Just about daybreak he arrived and as he reached up to knock on the door Tutney opened it and came out with a heavy load in her arms.

"Let me help you," said Addison reaching for the items.

"Hell must be about to freeze over," said Tutney as she handed him her load and puffed and pulled to tie a woolen hat at her chin.

"I thought you'd feel that way," said Addison smiling to himself. If

173

nothing else, Tutney's bad humor was predictable.

"I'm going to take you to school this morning. I haven't had a chance to see you much since Blanche and I married."

"And how am I supposed to get back home? I have to stay late!"

"I'll get Otis to pick you up when school's over." He took the items from her arms and walked down the stairs to put them in the back of his buggy, and then helped her up onto the seat.

"Where's John this morning? I thought I'd have to fight him off in order to be your escort."

"He's visiting his family in Greenwood. We quarreled because I refused to agree to meet them and he left last night in a huff."

"You owe it to him to meet his family, Tutney," said Addison. "He's done everything but marry you, and I'm sure that's your decision!"

"My marriage or lack of it is my business, Brother. You insisted on your way, didn't you?"

She talked incessantly as they rode toward Belgrove School. She was still going on over Addison's agreeing to take on the three other Reisdale children.

"I told you marriage would tie you down before you established yourself in a practice, Brother! Now, Blanche has manipulated you into taking in her whole family. I can't believe you have let this happen!"

"Blanche has never manipulated anyone. She's too honest! Besides, hasn't it occurred to you I might be happy about the prospect. You know how I like children, Tutney."

"If you had looked after two boys who weren't your own and scrimped and scraped and done what you could to see they were properly educated, only to have one die and the other desert you, you'd understand why such a prospect is enough to sour the stomach!"

"I didn't desert you, Tutney. I'm still your Brother. Blanche is an asset, just as her siblings will be. I'm part of a real family for the first time in my life. Can't you be happy for me?" He had no idea how his words 'real family' wounded Tutney. Unfortunately, she was the one who had seen to it that everyone including Addison thought of her as invulnerable. As for his question about her being happy for him, Addison felt he already knew the answer. Tutney couldn't be happy for anyone she couldn't control.

'Poor John Parker,' he thought.

"Blanche has been a loyal daughter to Mr. Reisdale since Mrs. Reisdale died and she wants to continue, and I 'm going to help her."

'Blanche, Blanche, Blanche' thought Tutney. She handed Addison a letter to mail.

"What's this?" he asked.

"It's a letter to Dr. Sullivan, if you must know!" said Tutney pertly.

Tutney had written Dr. Sullivan frequently since moving to Falkirk and Addison had mailed several of these letters and was rather puzzled as to what the subject matter might be. As they reached the schoolhouse Addison pulled back on the reins.

"Whoa!" he commanded Mag and Mae. "I'll carry these things inside for you, Tutney. Is there anything you need?"

"Brother, you amuse me!" she said snidely. "You're too busy looking after Blanche and her brood to be able to help me ... besides, I learned not to depend on you a long time ago."

"Well, if there is anything ... "

"There's not!" Tutney said as she took her things from his arms and headed into the schoolhouse.

On his way back to the clinic Addison went into the post office. Apparently, Ida Sprayberry had hired a young woman to help with the mail. She was very attractive and expensively dressed and didn't look very much like a mail clerk. She looked at Addison and smiled, then again turned her attention toward the mail, sorting and placing letters in designated stacks.

"Good morning, Dr. Blair," said Ida warmly. "What can I do for you?"

"Good morning, Mrs. Sprayberry. Could you please mail this letter for Tutney? She'll never forgive me if it doesn't reach its destination."

"Why of course!" she replied. She noticed her companion looking at Addison and waiting to be introduced.

"Dr. Blair, this is Eliza Sprayberry, my sister-in-law."

"Pleased to meet you, Mrs. Sprayberry," said Addison politely. "Are you going to be a new neighbor?"

"Oh, no, I'm just visiting. My husband Edward, Ida's brother, just passed away this summer and I needed a change of scenery.

"Oh, I'm sorry," said Addison. "Well, I hope you enjoy your stay!"

"Thank you, Dr. Blair. I like this town."

"It's a very good place to live," he replied. "I've only been here a short time myself. I have a medical practice on St. Andrews Chapel Road. I'll be glad to help you if it is ever necessary, but I hope our environment will be healthy for you."

"I hope so, too," said Eliza.

"Good-bye, ladies."

"Good-bye, Dr. Blair," the women both said in unison.

Addison's practice was pretty busy and everyone in Falkirk now knew him quite well. Blanche proudly introduced herself as 'Mrs. Doctor Blair' wherever she went, and people were never without a kind word for her new husband. They became quite familiar with his rig as he made his way through Falkirk and the surrounding county on house calls or to run errands. Blanche always tried to be home at lunch so she could have his meal ready and he wouldn't have to close his practice for an hour, as many of his patients walked from their homes or jobs to be seen by him.

Addison was quickly learning his young wife was a social butterfly. She loved nothing better than having guests and every holiday afforded a chance to prepare elaborate meals for which she used all the linens she had inherited from her mother, as well as those she spent hours embroidering on the nights Addison was out treating very ill patients. To complete her kitchen she purchased a new set of cookware on installment from Sully's, determined to save enough grocery money so she wouldn't have to ask Addison for it. On its arrival, she was away at a friend's house and this awarded Addison an opportunity to get the best of her, which he loved to do, and to unnerve the delivery boy at the same time.

"Why, I by no means ordered any cookware!" declared Addison.

"What about the Mrs.?" the courier asked timidly.

"She never makes purchases without my knowledge," said Addison, perhaps a little perturbed she had done just that. When the courier took him seriously, Addison let him leave with the much-desired wares still in his buggy. That evening he told Blanche about the incident and she informed him of her order.

"I'll go to Sully's and straighten this out," she said. "And Addison, please don't interfere with my delivery next time. I've saved the money and I can take care of this myself."

When the delivery boy came the second time, Blanche was away again and Addison decided to take his prank a little further.

"I told you before," said Addison with a serious face, "I never ordered any cookware."

Weeks passed without delivery and Blanche was anxious for the cookware and went by Sully's Market to check on her order. She learned from Abe Sully that Addison had again refused its delivery. She was furious. She left for home and this time when she arrived, instead of entering the kitchen door at the back of the house, she barged right through the waiting room of the practice and into Addison's office.

"How dare you play jokes on me, Addison!" she said. "I was so humiliated. Mr. Sully has figured out that one of us is mad, and I know which one!"

"What are you talking about, Blanche?" asked Addison innocently.

"You know what you've done, Addison! You've returned my cookware again!" As she left in an uproar she dropped her groceries in the hall but refused his attempt to help her gather them.

"Don't you expect any supper from me tonight, Dr. Blair!"

Addison was too busy with patients that afternoon to give Blanche's anger much thought. He had no recollection of it as he locked up the practice, but it didn't take him long after walking through the kitchen door to recall what had happened earlier that day. Blanche was still pouting and made no acknowledgement of his presence.

"Darling," he said, "I'm sorry. Please don't be upset!"

"Why not?" snapped Blanche. "You know that's what you want! You like nothing better than to get me upset!"

"You know I love you, Blanche."

After a long silence he dared to ask, "What's for supper?"

"I've had supper, and I told you earlier not to expect any from me!"

"Well, I can do without supper," said Addison coyly, "but can I have a little kiss!"

It was the last straw. Blanche immediately began to sob and ran out of the house with Addison on her heels. When they reached the well he scooped her up into his arms, holding onto her while she writhed and wriggled her legs in a desperate attempt to escape.

"Now, Baby."

"Don't you baby me, Addison," she shouted, still crying.

"Well, if I'm that bad, Blanche, why don't you leave?" he asked teasing her further. Blanche stopped sobbing, wiped her nose and looked up at him teary-eyed.

"I would," she said, "but I don't have anywhere to go!"

Addison began to laugh hysterically and his laugh was so infectious Blanche gave in.

"So that's why you put up with me, you pretty little hypocrite!"

"Put me down," she said beginning to giggle, and the two of them walked arm-in-arm back into the house.

"I'll go to Sully's tomorrow," promised Addison, "and buy the cookware straight out. Now don't go ordering things you need without telling me. I'd have bought it for you!"

"I don't want to depend on you for everything, Addison," said Blanche earnestly.

"Darling," said Addison. "That's what I'm for!"

Blanche had hardly recovered from this incident when Addison riled her again. She had planned a wonderful luncheon for three of her friends, Evelyn Cobb, Grace Chapman and Ruby Kitchens who had been her school friends since first grade. She arranged a beautiful glass vase with blue and pink hydrangeas as a centerpiece and set the table with her very best flatware. She chose a blue linen tablecloth but soon discovered she had only four matching napkins, so she walked around the house to Addison's office to solicit his discretion about the missing napkin and he agreed to comply.

When two of the girls walked in at noon, Addison was hospitality personified.

"Hello, Grace ... Ruby," he said. "Come have a seat at the table."

A few minutes later, Evelyn Cobb arrived.

"Hi, Dr. Blair! We're so looking forward to one of Blanche's lunches."

"Well, I don't think you'll be disappointed. Blanche has everything just about ready."

Blanche presented a wonderful spread of southern fried chicken, macaroni and cheese, butterbeans, biscuits and blackberry jam.

"Please ask the blessing, Dr. Blair," said Blanche, who always addressed him formally around everyone but family.

They joined hands and bowed their heads.

"Lord, you have made this meal ready for us and we are ready for it!"

said Addison curtly. "Amen."

Blanche gave Addison a glare, smiled pensively at the girls and began to pass around the food.

"I'm attending a cooking school," said Grace. "Our church is sponsoring the school and has asked Marian Bhuket who is a chef in New York to teach the classes."

"How nice!" said Blanche.

Grace tried not to notice Addison repeatedly wiping his mouth on his sleeve, but it was very evident to Blanche who was growing increasingly agitated.

"How far along are you?" Blanche asked of Ruby who was pregnant with her first child.

"Six-and-a-half months," said Ruby.

"How nice!" said Blanche again attempting to ignore Addison as he deliberately made a spectacle of himself, wiping his mouth on his sleeve once more.

"I'm feeling really well now," Ruby continued. "The first two months were difficult because of nausea."

"I can identify with that," interjected Evelyn.

"You're fortunate you're over that, Ruby," said Addison, obviously using his sleeve again. "Some women are nauseated for the full term."

Blanche gave Addison another glare and the more agitated she became the more he liked it. Finally, he struck the final blow.

"Blanche," he asked pitifully, "do you have a flour sack in the kitchen I could use for a napkin?"

There was no use in Blanche getting upset. She couldn't stay mad at this man whose delight it was to frazzle her. She couldn't help but laugh, and the girls joined in.

Addison also teased her siblings and kept the house filled with laughter. Darby, Claire and Sammy delighted in his antics and each was developing his own unique sense of humor. The three of them seemed to change every day, especially Sammy and Claire who were in the throes of puberty. Sammy's voice was changing and Blanche and Darby together had already had a talk with Claire about "the monthlies" and introduced her to her first brazziere.

Mr. Reisdale would sometimes come and get the children for the weekend but he met a young woman from north Georgia and his visits with the children were getting less and less frequent, although he was faithful to send money each month. Meanwhile, Blanche remained diligent about helping the children with homework, and sewing to keep them in school clothes that were as much in style as possible. She depended on Addison to maintain Sammy's haircut and take the children to Sully's for new shoes when necessary.

Once in a while, Tutney would have the children over for the weekend. They loved to stay with her, listen to her stories and help with her garden but they hated drinking the creamy milk she got from Baby, her cow, and pushed on them at every meal.

John Parker, apparently, had finally given up on Tutney and moved out. All of Falkirk was abuzz about this last tidbit of Tutney's scandalous affair, but Addison never asked her for an explanation and she never gave one.

Rearing her sisters and brother was very rewarding for Blanche. They all did well in school, which was a tribute to her patience. It seemed they would just finish one year when the next would start and getting them registered again, coming up with clothes and shoes that fit and arranging transportation to the school was a demanding routine. Addison hired Mattie Banks to come to the house every day to help with the washing and cleaning, and had Otis take the children to school. Blanche and Addison became so involved with trying to make a home for the children they had very little time for themselves.

Addison, along with Shelton Cole and a few other compassionate Falkirk citizens established a school for the Negro children in an old two-story Victorian farmhouse. It was several miles from town out Stoneville Road. Blanche and Addison together attended the PTA at Belgrove School and usually chaperoned the children's special events, which were held at the Town Hall. Darby and Claire were always two of the best-dressed young ladies at every gathering. Sammy adored 'hanging out' with the guys and Otis once caught him smoking in the barn. That same afternoon Addison attempted his first 'man-to-man' talk about the perils of tobacco and alcohol and the meaning of the 'birds and bees,' but it seemed Sammy was already pretty well-informed

Blanche had begun a tradition. Every Christmas the family gathered for food and fellowship and Blanche called it 'The Blair Party'. Blanche did the decorating and cooking and Addison saw to it Otis and Mattie were there to clean and scour the kitchen before and after the event. The children provided the entertainment by coming up with an original skit.

Tutney had met Georgia Senator Tom Watson at a political gathering and he was so impressed with her intellect and spirit that at his suggestion she agreed to attend the Democratic convention in his place in the summer of 1912. She had saved enough money to pay for the train fare and meals and Blanche and Addison promised to see after the cow while she was gone. They saw her off at the train and Blanche couldn't help being pleased over Tutney's taking this trip. She knew that during her young life Tutney had been tied down with Addison and Walter and after that had dedicated herself to one primary school or another, taking little time for leisure.

The convention turned out to be an unusually long one and William Jennings Bryan who had been called "the silver-tongued orator" after he made his "Cross of Gold" speech at the Democratic National Convention in Chicago in 1896, played a large part in the current convention. It was believed he had an underlying desire to become the presidential nominee by default after the party was torn apart by the feuding of the supporters for Woodrow Wilson, governor of New Jersey, and Champ Clark, Speaker of the House. When Tutney returned after over three weeks she excitedly related her experience, which included meeting many dignitaries while she was there. She boasted that when William Jennings Bryan got up to address the convention and spoke of his first, second and then third runs for the presidency, she had risen to her feet and shouted, "Three strikes and out!" According to Tutney the whole convention took up the chant 'three strikes and out, three strikes and out, three strikes and out' for so long that poor Mr. Bryan had to leave the platform and sit down. Addison didn't doubt Tutney could be that bold and although he was never able to substantiate her story, he believed it probably occurred just as she said.

He was glad for Tutney but found politics fickle at best. He knew Senator Watson had once been a supporter of Bryan and had been touted as the best vice presidential choice on the populist ticket, but Watson had now become part of Bryan's greatest opposition. He no longer seemed to be an anti-Wall Street, pro-commoner Negro sympathizer. He was now thought by many to be a proponent of slavery. It lost him many of his moderate supporters, including Addison. Ultimately, Woodrow Wilson won the democratic nomination that year with Thomas R. Marshall, governor of Indiana, as his running mate. Many felt the populist party had made its last stand. In November, Woodrow Wilson won the presidency.

The next few years for Dr. Blair and his young wife went harmoniously by. The girls became young women and even Sammy had become quite responsible. Blanche held a graduation party for Darby inviting her family, Tutney and Darby's fellow students, along with her father and the woman he was courting. It was a great success and only two years later she found herself planning another, this time for Claire. She invited the whole town for dinner in the garden and an afternoon of croquet.

Darby proved to be quite impulsive and moved with a girlfriend and her family to Jacksonville, Florida, right after her graduation to open a fish market and restaurant near the beach. Blanche had yielded to Darby's strong will and determination to be her 'own person' and hadn't tried to dissuade her. A few months after moving there she married a young Jacksonville man. Blanche wasn't surprised. She just hoped things would go well with her sister and the brother-in-law she had never met.

Claire, on the other hand, was a delicate and pretty young woman and very academic. She had decided to follow in Blanche's footsteps and attend State Normal School to become a teacher. She was very shy and after graduating just sort of fell into courting Joseph Hammond, a Falkirk widower who was twice her age. His wife had died in childbirth with their fifth child. Blanche felt he was much too old for Claire and that she would not be able to handle the responsibility of five children, but Claire was hopelessly in love and taken by Joseph's attentions. Instead of seeking a teaching job, she took a position in Atlanta as a secretary at Fulton Mills and rented a room in a boarding house on Boulevard Drive. She wanted to be near Joseph, who owned a furniture store in Atlanta.

Blanche's father eventually remarried, sold the home place and moved to a small north Georgia town to make a new life for himself. Blanche was upset that he had not left his property to his children. When he ran for mayor of their town he was elected, and after that seldom kept in touch with Blanche.

After Darby and Claire were gone and Sammy was well on his way to 'manhood', life became less demanding for Blanche but instead of feeling relief she found it depressing. She was used to having too much to do and now had time on her hands. With Addison's knowledge and a lot of luck she had not gotten pregnant, but she was beginning to want to have her own child. She wasn't sure how Addison would feel about it, since they had never really had a life of their own.

Ara Olivia

CHAPTER NINETEEN

In late February of 1913, Blanche began to experience bouts of dizziness. She was having trouble keeping things on her stomach and even had a fainting spell. Addison's life was pretty full with his practice and the friends he'd made in Falkirk, and he had not given much thought to having a child. When Blanche informed him of her symptoms he examined her and was ecstatic to find she was pregnant, and that he would be the one to tell her. Blanche was thrilled and wasted no time buying soft cotton and lace and starting on baby gowns and hats. Her happiness was infectious and Mattie Banks knitted several pairs of booties and got Otis to make a small wooden cradle. Addison and Blanche hired Harley Anglin to add a room next to their bedroom and paint it baby blue. Before the sale on the Reisdale house was finalized, Blanche and Addison had retrieved the crib George Reisdale had made for her just before she was born.

Blanche adorned the windows in the nursery with white eyelet, which to Addison was reminiscent of Walter's room before he died. It was the first time Addison risked hurting Blanche's feelings.

"I don't like the curtains," he said matter-of-factly.

"Why not?" asked Blanche. "They're beautiful ... feel how soft!" Addison didn't budge.

"I don't like them, Blanche. Can you find something else, something heavier?"

"Why, of course, Addison, if you insist, but ... "

"Thank you, Blanche." She was quite puzzled by his insistence but gave the eyelet curtains to her friend, Ruby Kitchens, for her nursery and purchased baby blue cotton muslin as a replacement.

Tutney was shocked at the news of Blanche's pregnancy but this didn't keep her from insisting on naming her future niece or nephew.

"'Elijah Clark' Blair if it's a boy!" she mandated. He's one of our ancestors and a hero of the Revolution."

"It's going to be a girl, Tutney!" Addison assured her.

"I suppose God has nothing to do with it, then?" she asked him.

"I didn't know you thought God had anything to do with anything." Addison replied.

Tutney ignored him.

"Well, if it's a girl you should name her 'Katherine Elizabeth'. It's a royal name."

"The Blairs are not kings," Addison offered. "They're descended from Scottish granite masons. Besides, Blanche will name our child, not me."

By June, Blanche had already gained twenty pounds. She had begun to have some swelling in her ankles, but she hadn't slowed down. St. Andrews Chapel Methodist Church had built a new addition and selected Blanche chairman of the Women's Guild. She was responsible for cleaning and decorating the new sanctuary. She solicited the help of Evelyn Cobb and schoolmate Stella Jean Scarborough, to get everything ready for the very first worship service in the new building.

"I wonder who'll be the first funeral in our new church," Blanche mused.

"Probably, Mr. Flake," replied Stella Jean. "He's going to be ninety-seven his next birthday and he's nothing but skin and bone!"

"Most ninety-seven-year-olds are skin and bone," interjected Evelyn.

"I think Stella's right," said Blanche. "Mr. Flake can hardly walk, even with his cane; and his daughter Lorene told me she has to do everything for him, including giving him his baths."

"Really, death is something we needn't speculate about," added Evelyn, who was known for her tendency toward drama. "'To everything is appointed a time; a time to live and a time to die.'"

"Well everything seems to be in order, girls," said Blanche exhausted. "Doesn't it look beautiful?"

"It does," said Evelyn.

"Why don't the two of you come have lunch with Dr. Blair and me?"

The two of them rode home with Blanche in Dr. Blair's buggy. They were surprised when Addison actually had lunch ready. He had warmed leftovers from the night before, prepared slices of buttered toast and opened up a fresh jar of strawberry preserves. There was plenty for everyone. Blanche made a pitcher of tea and they sat down to eat. The meal was good and filling. Addison returned to his practice and left the women to giggling and gossip.

That night he closed the practice and just as he reached the kitchen door, Mattie Banks came up behind him.

"Mattie, are you sick?" Addison asked.

"No, Dr. Blair. I jes' came to tell you be sho' and call me when Blanche is ready to delivah," she said sincerely. "Nobody can help you take cah o' her bettuh 'n me!"

"I promise, Mattie," said Addison, feeling he and Blanche truly would want no one else's help but hers.

"We gon' bring you a fine baby!"

"I'm sure you will, Mattie. I'll be sure someone comes for you as soon as Blanche goes into labor! I promise. Now you get on home and get Otis his supper. He'll be looking for you!"

"Oh, he knows wheah I is!"

"See you later!" said Addison as he turned and walked up the back steps into the kitchen.

"Who was that?" asked Blanche, as she put two bowls of chicken soup on the table.

"It was Mattie," said Addison.

"Why didn't she come in?"

"She just wanted to talk to me ... to be sure I took care of you!"

"Me?!" said Blanche. "She wants to take care of you! She's been telling everybody in town you're a 'white angel.'"

"I know," said Addison.

"I'll offer thanks," said Blanche. She wasn't often given to teasing when it came to saying grace, but this time she bowed her head and almost giggled at what she was about to say.

"Dear Heavenly Father, thank you for this food and your many blessings. Please take care of the girls, Sammy, and this baby ... and, Father ... especially make us worthy of our 'white angel'!" Addison grinned like a Cheshire cat.

The next few weeks at the clinic were quite demanding. Evelyn Cobb's son, Ethan, contracted a severe case of measles and became seriously ill. Addison admitted him to the St. Mary's Hospital in Athens and traveled there once a week to check on him. Fortunately, he responded to treatment and was able to come home after a month. There was an epidemic of flu in Falkirk and Addison was barraged with patients running fevers and riddled with cough and congestion. He had to solicit a nurse from Athens, Marie Ford, whom Michael Balfour had recommended to help him. Tutney agreed to let Marie stay in her spare bedroom. Blanche included her at lunch and Addison paid for her suppers at Sully's every evening. Eventually, the patient load became lighter but Marie had been such a help to Addison he offered her a permanent job. She moved in with Tutney and worked each day from nine a.m. until five p.m. in Addison's practice.

By early fall Blanche was becoming more and more restless and uncomfortable. She carried the pregnancy high in the pelvis and it pressed on her diaphragm so she had trouble breathing. She wasn't comfortable lying flat and resorted to sitting up in the parlor to sleep.

The first week in November, there was a terrible storm. The rivers and creeks around Falkirk were almost at flood level. The rain-soaked roots of several large trees had given way and the trees had fallen across some of the vital roadways in the county and had to be removed. Mayor Cole borrowed wagons from several of the townspeople and hired colored men to transport the colored children to and from their new school out Stoneville Road. He was receiving a lot of criticism, especially from Slye Campbell and his crowd, for 'givin' the niggers special treatment.'

One afternoon in the middle of that week Addison was examining his last patient, an elderly woman who had come in after several days of influenza, when Marie came rushing into the room.

"Dr. Blair," Marie said urgently, "It's Blanche. She's in the parlor and is pretty sure she is in labor." Addison hurriedly wrote his patient a prescription and sent her home. He grabbed his medical bag and rushed to the parlor.

"Blanche," he said excitedly, "You think it's time?"

"You're the doctor," she said worriedly. "I'm just the one whose worn out from nine months of infirmity."

"A baby's not an infirmity, Blanche, and delivering one is the most natural thing in the world."

"Don't patronize me, Addison. Right now I'm feeling anything but 'natural'!"

"Sorry, Darling," said Addison. Just lean on me and let's get you to the examining table.

Blanche was having very strong contractions. Addison asked Marie to sterilize the necessary instruments and walked Blanche to his examining room. He helped her up onto the bed. He decided not to rupture her membranes for fear of making her first labor too fast and hard.

"Go to Tutney's," he said to Marie. "Ride with her to get Mattie."

"But Dr. Blair, the roads are awful."

"I promised Mattie," said Addison. "You've got to get her."

Blanche could hear what they were saying, but she was fighting to endure the contractions and not concerned about what was going on around her. Marie threw on her raincoat and walked up to Tutney's. When Tutney got the news, she and Marie hurried back to Addison's clinic. Tutney hitched up his horses and buggy and rode down Stoneville Road to pick up Mattie. Both Mattie and Otis climbed into the rain-filled buggy with hat and umbrella and the three of them made their way back up the muddy road to town.

When they arrived Mattie and Tutney went promptly into the clinic, and Otis put Addison's rig back in the barn.

Blanche was about to deliver. She felt panicky and began to hyperventilate.

"Suddenly, I realize I no longer have any taste for childbirth!" said Tutney as she retired to the parlor to wait.

Marie had begun to sterilize the instruments when Addison looked up and saw Mattie.

"Wash your hands and get in here, Mattie ... calm her down and get her ready to push!" Mattie quickly complied. She slid in beside Blanche and stood by the bed. She bathed Blanche's forehead, took her hand and began to encourage her.

"I's not surprised 'dis baby coming t'nite, Miss Blanche. You know, de rain always bring on babies. Come on now, you got pushin' to do. Jes' take it easy, you can do it! When you feels a pain comin' jes' breathe slow and push ha-a-d!"

After a few minutes, Mattie declared, "heah come anotha one, Miss Blanche. Now, push ... push!" Blanche clinched her fists and bore down as hard as she could. She felt as if her insides were going to come out, but she was determined to get it done. Suddenly, she let out a terrible shriek. It was the first sound she'd made. The baby's head delivered.

"You done real good, Miss Blanche," said Mattie.

Dr. Blair quickly delivered the infant and cut the cord, asking Marie to get it tied and secured. He held the baby up by her feet.

"Nine pounds, Mattie." He slapped the baby's back and the room became filled with the soft, demanding cries of a baby girl. Addison couldn't hide his joy. Tears began to streak down his face as he handed the baby to Mattie, and turned his attention back to Blanche, who despite his preventive incision, required a few stitches. When this was done and he was sure she was stable he discarded his lab coat and washed his hands. He walked over to Mattie and his new baby girl. He took her in his big hands, kissed her cheek and put her into Blanche's arms.

"Just look at your daughter, Darling," he said.

"*Our* daughter, Addison," said Blanche, now calm and out of pain.

"She's beautiful!" said Addison. "What's her name to be?"

"She's Ara Olivia," said Blanche and began to cry softly. "Do you think mother can see her?"

"Of course, " assured Addison. "Of course, she can!"

Mattie was tearful, too, as she finished cleaning up. She then slipped quietly out of the room and into the kitchen and went to find Otis to take her home. She had done her job. She had been there for Dr. Blair. Tutney managed to get a quick peek at the new arrival and congratulated the new parents before climbing into Addison's buggy so Otis could drop her off at home.

Addison didn't want Blanche to be up on her feet so that night he got up with the baby several times. He changed her, wrapped her in a blanket and brought her to Blanche who nursed her until she fell asleep. Then, he burped her and put her back in the cradle.

Blanche's Aunt Madeline had an announcement of the new arrival put in the Falkirk Star.

'Dr. and Mrs. Jeffrey Addison Blair, the former Mary Blanche Reisdale of Falkirk, announce the birth of their first child, a daughter, Ara Olivia Blair, born November 14, 1913, weight nine pounds, two ounces. The paternal grandparents are the late Lycurgeus McElsworth Blair and the late Sally Olivia Blair of Marbleton. The maternal grandparents are George Washington Reisdale and the late Ara Olivia Reisdale of Falkirk. Paternal Aunt, Tutney Key Blair of Marbleton.'

Blanche had suggested mentioning Tutney and Madeleine had complied.

For the next few weeks Blanche and Addison got very little sleep. Mattie got Otis to bring her to Dr. Blair's house every morning and she looked after Blanche during the day. She cooked, cleaned and helped care for the baby. Addison insisted Mattie not let Blanche put a foot on the floor for three weeks. Mattie proudly told all her kin about her important assignment.

Ara Olivia was a beautiful baby. Tutney adored her, as she was the closest thing to Addison, and she opened up a savings account for her at the South Albert County Bank. She bought a sterling bracelet from Beacon Jewelers and had it inscribed 'Ara Olivia Blair, November 14, 1913.' Her visits to see Addison and Blanche became more frequent.

Addison made sure that at one month Ara Olivia had a red velvet coat and hat trimmed with white rabbit fur and a white fur muff like the one Blanche had worn the night he told her he wanted to court her. She wore the tiny muff tied to her little wrist with a red satin ribbon. Ara Olivia was presented at the traditional 'Blair Party' and passed from lap to lap after the Christmas meal. Blanche was an adoring mother and Addison admired her more than ever. She had a fragile strength about her and was instinctively good with the baby who flourished, steadily gaining weight and becoming more vocal. Addison could hardly take care of his practice for running back to the kitchen to coo and kiss his new little girl.

"You're such an 'itty-bitty', " he said to her and after that he called her 'Bitty.'

Blanche was determined Ara Olivia would love and respect her father.

"See your father, Ara Olivia," she would say. "Isn't he something? You're a special girl you know. Your daddy is a wonderful doctor!"

"Stop making me out to be a hero," Addison would remark.

In early May, when Ara Olivia was six months old Addison and Blanche arranged with her uncle Clayton for their infant daughter's baptism. On that particular Sunday it was very hot and had already reached eighty-nine degrees by ten o'clock. Blanche felt cruel dolling Ara Olivia up in a white organza dress. Over her dress, the baby wore the pink sweater, matching booties and hat Mattie had made for her.

Just as the three of them reached the barn to get into the buggy a carriage came down the road stirring up a dust cloud, which floated and settled over them. Blanche took Ara Olivia's receiving blanket and shielded her with it as she climbed up onto the seat. The sun beat down on them on the way and Blanche was relieved when they finally reached the church and she managed to get the baby inside. The pews fluttered with paper fans, looking like rows of dominoes. Blanche requested that Addison carry Ara Olivia to the front of the church because she knew how much he loved showing her off.

Pastor Reisdale delivered his sermon, which Blanche felt would never end.

'They do this backwards,' she thought to herself. 'The baby's good humor on arrival is wasted and by the time the pastor's ready the baby is hungry, tired, soiled and anything but sociable.'

Finally, Pastor Reisdale requested that Blanche, Addison and little Ara Olivia come to the front of the church.

"It is a sacred occasion," he began, "when one of our most beloved families brings their firstborn before the Lord to receive His blessings and to be dedicated to His service." He reached out for Ara Olivia and took her into his arms.

Ara Olivia twisted, turned, and stretched to reach for Addison. Addison shushed her and patted her on the head, which only intensified her desire to be back in his arms.

"Da-Da," she demanded loudly. "Da-Da!" She began to wriggle to get out of Pastor Reisdale's grasp. He finally gave up and returned her to her father.

"The way you have made her repeat it," whispered Blanche, "Anyone would think you were the only 'Da-Da' in the world."

"I am the only one who has a Bitty," he whispered smiling.

"In Dr. Blair's arms is Miss Ara Olivia Blair," Pastor Reisdale said to the congregation. "Everyone in favor of welcoming her to our rolls, promising as her church family to encourage and strengthen her as she grows in her commitment to the service of our Lord, let it be known by your uplifted right hand."

The congregation unanimously held up their hands in support.

Dipping his fingers in the sacramental water, the pastor declared, "I hereby christen thee Ara Olivia Blair and bestow upon thee the grace and protection of Our Lord, Jesus Christ in the name of the Father, and the Son, and the Holy Spirit. Amen."

Bitty winced at the cool drops on her forehead, and when Addison lifted her up and presented her to the congregation, she smiled as if she knew exactly what was happening. Addison had never felt such a proud moment and determined Bitty would have every Christian advantage he could provide. In his idealism, he mistakenly believed he would do everything right. When Blanche's Uncle Clayton finished the ceremony, her father and all three of her siblings came to the front to congratulate them. It was almost like old times for Blanche, although her father seemed somewhat hesitant to acknowledge his granddaughter before his new wife.

"Does she look like mother?" Blanche asked.

"Perhaps, a little," he said reticently.

In a rare moment alone with him she spoke to him about Claire. "Please talk to her Papa, and tell her she's too young to marry a man of forty with five children."

"You know I have no influence over Claire," he answered. "She's yours more than mine now." The father she had so idolized was turning out to be one of her greatest disappointments.

As they left the church Blanche invited all the family along with Marie, Mayor Cole and his wife, the Sully's, the Malones, the Cobbs and the Scarbroughs for Sunday dinner. After a few rounds of croquet and a tremendous feast with everyone full of homemade ice cream they sat out in the yard under the trees and the women discussed babies, while the men discussed the federal government and the weather until the afternoon gave way to twilight.

Darby and Claire both stayed the week to visit with Blanche and Ara Olivia. While there, Claire announced her intentions to marry Joseph Hammond in August and promised to send invitations to the wedding. Blanche tried to be happy but inwardly had a terrible premonition about Claire's future marriage.

The following week was over too soon and everyone said their goodbyes. Claire was going home with Darby to Jacksonville for a brief visit. Addison got Otis to drive them both to the train station in Athens.

At the end of May, Sammy graduated from high school, and the family was together again. This time George Reisdale actually seemed proud of his son. Sammy was very handsome and looked very much like his elderly father--the same cleft chin and green eyes. Sammy's girlfriend, Trudy, was becoming more and more of a fixture at family events and the two seemed destined to marry. Blanche approved. She thought Trudy a very sweet, though somewhat giddy, young woman. Addison seemed to think Sammy needed a more intellectual match but kept his opinion to himself. He didn't want to upset Blanche, who loved Sammy as if he were her own.

In August as promised, Blanche and Addison received an invitation to Claire's wedding and she and Addison made arrangements to attend. It was an elaborate affair indeed. Joseph's two sisters, the bridesmaids, and Darby, the maid of honor, wore pale pink. The groom's attendants were in gray tuxedos. Held at the First Baptist Church in Atlanta on Peachtree near where Joseph now lived on Clifton Road, the reception included a full-string orchestra and soloist. Blanche had helped Claire make a beige linen suit and gave her shoes and a beige hat and veil as a wedding gift. Blanche wished her the best and prayed God would bless the marriage even though her opinion of Joseph hadn't changed.

Addison made sure everyone noticed Bitty in the soft pink dress Blanche had made, and when it was time to depart everyone gave her kisses. She now could say 'Da-Da', 'Ma-Ma', 'Bye-bye' and endlessly babbled all kinds of blurbs that sounded like words, repeating her strange vocabulary over and over. She loved to wave and would persist until people reciprocated. Blanche wondered how Addison had ever lived without her. She was in his arms so much of the time she seemed permanently attached.

The last week in August, Addison and Blanche took the baby for a visit with Grace and Barry Reynolds, who also had a new baby daughter. Barry was the boy Grace had met on the hayride in Carrollton. She'd married him just as she had vowed that afternoon in their dorm room years before. Grace had become an accomplished chef since her cooking school days and treated them to roast lamb with mint jelly, parsnips, squash soup and other things rarely served in the South. After supper the proud parents watched their infant daughters and compared first food, first turn-overs and first words. Grace's daughter would point at Ara Olivia and say "Ba-bee!" and Ara Olivia would stare quizzically back as if to say, 'and what do you think you are?'

On the way home, Blanche nursed Ara Olivia who promptly went to sleep in her arms.

In mid-August when she was only nine months old Ara Olivia took her first step. Addison had just locked up the clinic and come through the kitchen door when Ara Olivia suddenly let go of a chair and raced across the floor to him.

"Da-da, Da-da!" she screamed with glee.

"Bitty," cried Addison reaching out and gathering her up in his arms. "You're wonderful! Did you see that, Blanche?"

"Yes, she's been waddling around the kitchen all day today ... and where are you going?"

"To show her the moon," he said. He carried her out into the warm night. The summer days were hot and unbearable, but the nights were perfect.

"Look up there, Bitty!" said Addison. "Do you see that moon? That's Daddy's moon. He asked God to make it just for you!"

"Moo-o-on," said Ara Olivia, pointing her tiny finger toward the sky.

"That's right, Bitty."

"Moon," repeated Ara Olivia.

"Mother, come out here!" Addison shouted to Blanche.

"Moon!" repeated Ara Olivia pointing again at the large yellow orb then looking at Blanche as she awaited her approval.

"See what a bright girl, we have?" asked Addison.

"She certainly is!" said Blanche. "She's just like her father!"

Ara Olivia reached up and grabbed Addison's ears and put her open mouth to his to give him a very wet kiss, as if in agreement.

CHAPTER TWENTY

December came and Ara Olivia experienced her second Christmas. This time Addison bought her green velvet with a white sweater and leggings and commissioned a family photograph. Ara Olivia complied with a smile, as if she knew how many times her daddy would show this off to his patients and friends. She tore open all of her presents with glee, giving one individual gift her attention just long enough to remove the wrapping and ribbon and then reaching for another. After a day of eating, visiting with family and being held continually, a very sleepy Ara Olivia became tired and cranky and Blanche discovered she was cutting her first tooth.

"The only thing she's been late doing," said Blanche.

"But she'll have better teeth! Very clever, Bitty!" said Addison

"She's not very clever right now!" said Blanche. "She's ill as a hornet! I think you're Bitty needs to get to bed."

Blanche quickly bathed Ara Olivia and washed her hair. She brought her back into the parlor soft, clean and smelling sweet to say goodnight to her father.

"Good-night, Bitty," said Addison. "Daddy loves you!" Blanche took her to the crib.

"Good night, precious!" she said as she tucked her in. She turned out the light and went to the kitchen, made coffee and joined Addison in the parlor presenting him with a cup.

"What a wonderful Christmas," mused Addison. "Bitty makes everything more special!"

"You don't love her, do you?" teased Blanche.

"I certainly do!" he replied giving Blanche a kiss. "Just as I do her mother."

The two of them retired to the bedroom. About four hours later they were awakened by Ara Olivia's crying.

"I'll check on her," said Addison rubbing his eyes. He got up, grabbed his robe and slipped into his bedroom shoes. He washed his face and hands and headed for the nursery. After a few minutes he shouted to Blanche.

"Blanche! Bring a cool washcloth. She's running a little fever." Blanche quickly appeared looking worried and gave Addison the wet cloth.

"She's burning up!" she said touching her forehead. "Addison, what can I do?"

"No, she's not that hot" he said. "Don't worry, darling. Children run a fever at the drop of a hat. It's probably just a cold."

Addison bathed her face and neck and she stopped crying. He handed her to Blanche who sat down in the chair and began to rock and sing her a lullaby. When Ara Olivia finally went to sleep Blanche rose from the chair and tiptoed to the crib, laid her down on her stomach and covered her with a light blanket. She sat beside the crib while Ara Olivia slept. Addison sat beside her in a straight chair he had brought from the kitchen. A couple of hours passed and the baby awoke crying again and this time was running an extreme fever. Addison noticed her neck had begun to swell.

"Blanche, we need to get Uncle Cambridge to come check on Ara Olivia. Go get Tutney and ask her to take you to get Otis. I don't want you to ride to the Banks' house alone."

"Is she going to be all right?" Blanche asked anxiously.

"I hope so, Blanche," he said with concern. "I think so ... now go on and be careful!"

In a few minutes Blanche and Tutney returned. Marie also came, having agreed to ride with Tutney to get Otis so Blanche could stay with Addison and Ara Olivia. After about an hour Tutney and Marie arrived back at the house. They stayed there while Otis left immediately for Harrison to pick up Cambridge Blair. Addison stood by the crib and Blanche sat in the rocker anxiously watching. He tried to convince her to go back to bed but she knew he was worried and needed her presence as much as she needed his.

They both kept watch through the night with Tutney and Marie in the kitchen keeping hot coffee made. Otis returned in the early morning hours with Cambridge Blair following in his own carriage. When he walked in, it seemed to Addison and Blanche as if eternity had passed.

"Uncle Cambridge!" said Addison, very relieved.

"Let me have a look at her, Addison," he said. He opened her mouth.

"Her throat is coated," interjected Addison.

"I see it is," said Cambridge. "Her neck and jaws are quite swollen. You know what it is, don't you Addison?"

"I'm afraid it may be diphtheria," said Addison warily.

"It is diphtheria ... and we need to get her to Athens Regional right away."

"What is it?" said Blanche. "Tell me. What's wrong with our daughter?"

"It's diphtheria, Blanche," said Cambridge. "I'm sure you know that's serious. Now, help us get her ready to go, quickly!"

Blanche began crying so hard she could hardly see as she frantically changed her little daughter and put on her gown and leggings. She quickly pushed Ara Olivia's little arms into her sweater and pulled her warm knit hat over her head. Ara Olivia was too weak to protest. Uncle Cambridge got Otis to water all the horses and get both rigs ready to start out again. Blanche wrapped Ara Olivia in warm blankets and the three of them headed for Athens in Cambridge's carriage, with Otis and Tutney following in Addison's buggy. After three hours they all arrived at Athens Regional. A nurse took Ara Olivia into her arms, pulling off her clothes as Cambridge led them through the hall to the nursery.

"Addison, if you want me to treat her you'll have to trust me!" said Cambridge. "In the case of a serious illness it's never a good idea for a physician to treat his own family."

Addison hesitated. To trust Bitty to the care of any physician, even his Uncle Cambridge who he knew was the best, was a very hard thing for him to do.

"Do what you have to do," he said finally, watching anxiously as Cambridge carried Ara Olivia to the operating room.

Blanche grabbed Addison's hand.

"Please pray for our baby, Addison. I can't do it."

"Father, how we thank you for our little daughter Bitty, and for the beauty and the joy of her. We've never been so happy. We want to keep her. Please, God, let us keep her."

Cambridge placed tubes into Ara Olivia's throat. This was a new therapy to prevent patients from suffocating from the membrane growing over and obstructing their airways. He also administered antitoxin to neutralize poisons released by the bacteria. Soon, Ara Olivia was returned to the nursery. It seemed she was going to be all right. Her fever subsided completely and she seemed to be having less trouble breathing.

At nine o'clock that evening Uncle Cambridge examined her again. He called Addison and Blanche into the room. He shook his head.

"She's dying."

"Uncle Cambridge?" entreated Blanche.

"I'm sorry, Blanche. There's nothing we can do."

Blanche standing beside the crib looked down at her child. It broke her heart to see her so swollen she was unrecognizable. Blanche stroked her baby's face, tears burning her own cheeks.

"Bitty ... don't give up!" said Addison.

He picked her up and held her to his chest. As he softly rubbed her eyes, she opened them.

"Da-Da," she said wearily. She didn't cry. She rested her swollen face against his neck and reached up and grabbed his ears.

"Night-night, Da-Da," she said, and closed her eyes.

Suddenly, her little arms dropped lifeless to her sides. Addison's big hands squeezed her more tightly.

"Night-night, Bitty," he said in a broken voice.

"No-o-o-o!" screamed Blanche. "Oh, God, No-o-o-o!" Addison reached out to pull her closer and the two of them stood there motionless, desperately clinging to each other and to their dead child. The room was dark except for a dim light from the hallway. Tutney stood discreetly in the corner watching, speechless for the first time in her life.

The following days went by in a blur. It was impossible for Blanche or Addison to isolate the feelings they were having, which were a mixture of guilt, devastation, denial and anger at God for such a testing of their faiths. Memories flooded their stunned minds and broken hearts. In a short thirteen months Ara Olivia had transformed them and given them a glimpse into God's unconditional love, but how He could take this child loved by so many was difficult to comprehend. Addison asked over and over again, 'Why', and each time he had a revelation, however small, of God's own sacrifice.

Everyone was supportive. The next day Blanche's friends lavished her with love and understanding as best they could. The community produced a bountiful supply of special dishes to express their empathy for Falkirk's beloved physician.

Let not your heart be troubled. You believe in God, believe also in me. In my Father's house are many mansions. If it were not so I would have told you. I go to prepare a place for you, and if I go and prepare a place I will come again to receive you unto myself that where I am there you may be also. (John 14:1-3)

CHAPTER TWENTY-ONE

The evening of the wake Blanche tried to stay busy with preparation for the occasion, motivated by a determination not to think at all to avoid feeling her unbearable loss. Preparing the nursery for receiving her daughter's little body brought floods of tears, as she hypnotically folded little dresses and gowns and dusted off a rocking horse made for Ara Olivia by Otis as a Christmas gift. She decided Ara Olivia would be buried in the green Christmas velvet Addison had bought for her. Blanche sat quietly in the nursery most of the day, while Addison stayed in the parlor reading. There was very little conversation between them. The sadness that filled their hearts went without saying. Mattie who had come to help out heated lunch and called them to the table, but they sat quietly and picked over their food.

George Reisdale came with his new wife and her son, Aaron. They arrived an hour before guests were expected.

"Oh, Papa," said Blanche falling into her faither's arms, weeping.

"Mary Blanche," he said tenderly. "I wish there were something I could do." Blanche welcomed his embrace.

Tutney came shortly after, grieving, though it didn't show. She had become more attached than she would have believed to her brother's first child.

"Brother," she said putting her hand to Addison's cheek.

Claire and Darby arrived and embraced their sister, weeping with her for several minutes. Sammy came with Trudy, his new bride. The two of them had eloped the week before Christmas. Sammy tried to make small talk with Addison, unaware of how to respond and filled with memories of the loss of his mother. Friends were kind, but there was no comfort to be found. Even prayers seemed empty and falling on deaf ears.

The following day just as the funeral started Blanche spotted old Mr. Flake hobbling into the church with his cane to pay his respects. His daughter held him by his other arm and helped him to a pew. Blanche recalled her remarks about the first funeral in the new church.

"I never dreamed it would be my baby," she whispered to herself.

Somehow they got through it, hearing voices but not words, seeing people but not faces. The numbness seemed to be the one thing that would help them to survive the life they suddenly faced without Ara Olivia. Pastor Reisdale reminded them they would see her again in Heaven and, although these words had helped with former griefs, this time they seemed lacking.

Later, standing in the cemetery Blanche agonized as they lowered the small coffin into the grave. She became weak and faint and Addison pulled her to him to steady her. After a brief prayer, everyone walked by to express sympathy and one by one they all left. Sammy took Blanche's arm and walked her toward his buggy.

Suddenly, Addison realized he was all alone. He was tortured by conflict.

'If I had treated her myself, I might have saved her,' he couldn't help thinking, but he knew he was being unfair to his Uncle Cambridge who had done his very best and who had much more experience in treating diphtheria. When he remembered Bitty's goodnight he began to weep inconsolably.

'So this is the sting of death,' he thought. Somewhere within his heart he heard God answer.

'There is a day of resurrection, Addison – an appointed day, but it is not today.' Addison pulled his handkerchief from his pocket and dried his face. He walked back to the church to find Blanche but she had already left with Sammy for home.

Blanche went into a deep depression and for the next two months took to the bed. Addison wanted to help but was so deep in his own grief as to be unaware of her terrible state, thinking somehow it would just go away. He did set up a roll-away bed in the kitchen and ask Mattie to come and stay. She became a permanent resident for a time. She fixed

Blanche's meals and had supper for Addison at the end of the day. She did the washing and even tidied Addison's waiting room once a week. Addison found it incredible the way she worked tirelessly to lighten their burden. In the days that followed, Addison never seemed to make it back to the kitchen before seven in the evening. Blanche was so out of it she didn't notice. Mattie guessed he was pouring himself into his work to keep from facing the death of his child.

One day in late January Mattie told Addison she had to leave early on Friday and be off for the weekend, as she had promised to sit with little Blair while the Sims traveled to visit relatives in south Georgia. Mattie got all the laundry done and prepared food ahead so Addison could warm a plate for Blanche and himself. She packed up her muslin bag and left, promising to be back early Monday morning. Otis came in his old hay wagon to pick her up and the two of them started for home. Since it was quicker they decided to travel out St. Andrews Chapel Road a few miles to River Road, and then, cross over to the main route. On the way they passed by St. Andrews Chapel Church. Mattie looked toward the cemetery and saw the dark figure of a man bent over one of the graves. He appeared to be reading.

"Lawdy mercy, Otis, look yondah! It Docta Blair." Mattie gasped. So dat why he so late gettin' home to Miss Blanche evuh night. He comin' out to dis cemetery."

"Yessum," said Otis. "Pastor Reisdale say he out heah most ever' evenin' broodin' over that chile. I tol' him he need to tell Miss Blanche, but he say he ain't gone put narry burden on huh, upset as she is. He say it Docta Blair's way of grievin' and to let 'm' lone."

"Bless his heart," said Mattie. "I sho' wish I could hep, but I cain't. No one can hep him now but sweet Jesus. What you reckon he readin'?"

"Lawd, Mattie, how I know?"

Tutney was on the way home from the schoolhouse one evening and caught sight of Addison in the cemetery. She stopped and got down from the buggy then walked through the soggy grounds to Ara Olivia's grave where Addison sat on the rock wall around the family plot with a book in his hand.

"What on earth are you doing?" she said. Addison was startled.

"And what are you reading?" Tutney took the book from his hand. It was Edgar Allen Poe's famous poem, "The Raven", and Addison had underlined the anguished words, 'Quoth the raven, "nevermore"'.

Addison looked up at her and in that moment broke down. He turned his face away to hide the deluge of tears but began to sob uncontrollably.

"I can't accept this, Tutney. I miss Bitty. I think everyone is tired of my grief and I really don't know where to go from here."

Tutney looked in amazement at this hulk of a man who was her brother sitting there weeping. Somewhere deep inside she understood but something kept her from connecting with this kind of grief.

"I don't understand you, Brother," she said. "Where's your 'Christianity' now? You're the one who believes in the glorious hereafter when we mere mortals will 'put on immortality' and be reunited once again to live in eternal bliss, crying, 'Grave, where is thy victory?'

Addison saw on his sister's face an expression he'd never seen before. A pall, empty, resignation ... an unbelievable, obvious contempt where there should have been sorrow, and it frightened him. Tutney rambled on.

"It's not death you can't accept, Addison. It's life! This is life! Flowers shrivel, dreams vanish, the harvest spoils, things die---people die. But does time stop?" She continued. "No, time ticks on, and young girls grow old and are left alone." For a long time Addison said nothing. Then, he stood and looked his sister in the eye.

"You're not talking about Bitty," he said, "and you're not talking about my grief. You're talking about yourself. Why is it everything ends up being about you, Tutney? Everything you say is full of the bitterness and unforgiveness you harbor for every little slight you've suffered. But I'm just never able to give up on you. I know you're incapable of sharing my grief and yet I've just asked you again. I needed to talk about Walter's death but you didn't know how to comfort me then. You knew only how to turn your feelings off and withdraw to that place you go where no one else can come. 'This is life!?' No, Tutney, I don't accept that. I'm hurt and I'm angry, ... but I know God is good and things 'work together for good to those who love the Lord and are called according to His purpose.' Life is togetherness, celebration and in sad times, sharing. God is the sustainer of life. God is love." Addison picked up his hat and coat off the rock wall.

"Seems, I'm answering my own questions," he said, somewhat

surprised. "Isn't that something!"

"Can't you see, Brother? God did this to you! God took Walter, and now he has taken Ara Olivia!"

"Ara Olivia was sick and God took her home, Tutney. I know my faith is struggling ... it will survive ... but, Tutney, I truly fear something in you has died, something very precious ... and I hope you'll find it again!"

He started to walk away, then turned back.

"Please don't mention to Blanche I was here."

CHAPTER TWENTY-TWO

When Mattie found Blanche in the kitchen preparing breakfast she was thrilled. For weeks Blanche had expressed no interest in anything. There were no more tears. She mostly stared at everything and at nothing. Mattie tried in her simple way to encourage her.

"It sho is good to see you up dis mo'nin." Blanche didn't answer.

"What you wants for lunch, Miss Blanche? I'll go up to Sully's and git anythin' you wants."

"I'm all right, Mattie," managed Blanche. "Just fix whatever you think Addison would like."

"You know, Miss Blanche, you an' Dr. Blair needs to talk. Grief a terrible thing, sometimes talkin' make it easier ... and Dr. Blair need you." Blanche gave Mattie a puzzled look. Addison hardly spoke to her anymore. She knew he was hurting like she was but she hadn't stopped to think how affected he had been by the loss of Ara Olivia. He rose early each day and starting seeing patients. He showed no evidence of devastation.

"Men's diffunt," said Mattie, picking up on Blanche's thoughts. She didn't dare say more but went toward the bedroom to make the bed and to pick up soiled clothes and start the weekly wash.

Blanche took Mattie's advice and determined to reject self-pity. She tried to focus more on Addison's needs and life slowly became more tolerable. After a few more weeks Mattie was able to return home.

Addison still ended every evening at Ara Olivia's grave.

Blanche figured it out and finally asked him point blank, "Why are you getting home late every evening, Addison? You're not spending time at the cemetery are you? You know there's nothing there." Addison gave Blanche a blank look and she said no more.

When the long winter was finally over and the daffodils began to spring up over the hills of Falkirk, Addison started giving thought to building a clinic and hospital. He hoped it would give both he and Blanche something to look forward to, he toward the new facilities and she toward using the additional area available in the house as the formal living and dining rooms she'd always wanted. He planned to put the hospital at the back of his property and create an entrance off Athens Road. He would run the driveway between Slye Campbell's property and his own. He had asked Shelton about an architect and he had recommended Aubrey Reardon, who he said had an excellent reputation. He told him Aubrey had designed the new Falkirk Library and that Harley Anglin had worked with him and held him in high esteem. Addison contacted Mr. Reardon and invited him to the house to discuss exactly what he had in mind for the hospital. Mr. Reardon said he'd come by on Wednesday evening, and Addison asked Blanche to prepare a special meal. At six o'clock there was a knock at the clinic entrance. Addison went to the front of the house, introduced himself to Mr. Reardon and brought him around to the kitchen door.

"This is Aubrey Reardon," said Addison. "Aubrey, my wife Blanche."

"So glad to meet you," said Mr. Reardon. "It certainly is nice of you to feed me."

He seemed very congenial to Blanche. She showed him to the table and took his hat and coat to the bedroom.

"Everything's ready," she said on her return. Mr. Reardon enjoyed the meal immensely making a pig of himself, which delighted Blanche. The last thing she wanted was for someone to pick over a meal she'd prepared. When they were finished Blanche quickly cleared the table.

Addison and Mr. Reardon sat down with paper and pen to collaborate on a design for the new hospital. Together they came up with a tentative plan. There would be a four-hundred square foot registration area, waiting room and bathroom at the center front of the building and two long wings extending at an angle from the opposite ends of that area.

The hospital wing on the left would consist of six patient rooms, three on each side of the hallway with two bathrooms at the end. The lab and nursing station would be at the front directly behind the registration area. The clinic wing on the left would include a waiting room, office, examining room and bathroom for Addison on one side of the hall, and another examining room and two supply rooms on the other side. There would be a large parking area for carriages and a hedge row would be planted to provide more privacy for Addison's and Blanche's residence.

"It's going to be a great project, Dr. Blair," said Aubrey. "I'm looking forward to working with you."

It took Aubrey Reardon four weeks to finalize the plans and present the blueprints to Harley Anglin whom Addison had chosen to contract the job. Harley estimated the cost of building and Addison took his figures to the South Albert County Bank to obtain a construction loan. Harley got the permits from the city and county, and soon brought in a grading crew to prepare the grounds and foundation for the building.

Blanche didn't start planning the renovation on the house. She wanted to wait until the hospital was completed so she wouldn't be disappointed if Addison had to practice in their home longer than expected. She was really lonesome with Addison so engrossed in the building of the hospital so she tried getting involved again in the Women's Guild at the church to occupy her time. She also spent some time with Tutney. Tutney would fix coffee and the two of them would grade papers.

One evening Tutney showed Blanche a brochure of memorial stones for Ara Olivia. She pointed out one with a lamb sitting on the top of the stone and the words "Little Angel" engraved just beneath. Blanche detested it.

"Ara Olivia wasn't an 'angel,'" she said. "She was our child!"

"Well, pick one you like, but it's time you and Addison get a headstone for Bitty. It's a disgrace for a physician's daughter to be without a memorial for this long!"

"Addison will have to help me, Tutney. I just can't think about it right now." It was difficult for Blanche to cope with people at times. They just didn't seem to understand that for her, grief over Ara Olivia had only deepened, though she tried not to burden others. She decided visits with Tutney were definitely not the answer.

She tried to sound interested when Addison talked about the hospital but her thoughts were always of children. She desperately wanted to get pregnant again but Addison felt it was too soon. He said her body needed more time to recover. She feared losing Ara Olivia had thwarted his thoughts of future fatherhood forever.

Fortunately, Blanche received a reprieve from her loneliness. Grace Reynolds sent her a letter about an upcoming State Normal School Reunion for the class of 1907. It was to take place in June. Grace was very excited about the festivities planned for that week and wanted to persuade Blanche and Addison to join her and her husband Barry at the Athens Inn for the weekend so they could attend the reunion together. Blanche decided to approach Addison about it. That night she prepared pot roast, one of his favorites. She lit a candle in the center of the table.

"What are you up to?" Addison asked smiling.

"Nothing," said Blanche. "I just wanted supper to be special. I know how hard you're working on the hospital."

"It's more than that, Blanche. I know you. You have something to ask me."

It was aggravating that he could always read her so well, but it made it easier for her to bring up the subject.

"Grace Reynolds wrote me about the State Normal School reunion," she said.

"And?"

"And I want desperately to go!"

"Well, we can't have you desperate, Darling!" Addison teased. "We'll go!"

"You're not going to give me an argument? Say you're too busy?"

"Blanche, I am busy with the hospital ... but you know you come first. Why are you still so hesitant to ask me for anything?"

"Because you're a physician and I know your work is important." Addison walked over to Blanche's chair and looked into her eyes.

"Everyone's work is important but the most important thing to me will always be you!" He kissed her more tenderly than he had in a long time. "Make the arrangements."

Blanche promptly wrote back to Grace. She enclosed a check and asked her to reserve a room at the Inn for her and Addison. She got Evelyn Cobb to help her pick out fabric for a ball gown. Because Addison liked her in green she chose green satin brocade and started on it right away. She couldn't believe how she looked forward to seeing Grace and her other schoolmates again. Addison asked Harley to step up the pace on the hospital as much as he could. He wanted him to be able to get the addition to the house finished so Blanche could get it furnished and decorated before the Christmas holidays. Everything was progressing well.

Addison suggested finishing the building in stucco but Harley advised against it saying that getting it right was difficult and not getting it right would be a disaster, so clapboard siding was used and painted white. Green shutters were placed on both sides of every window and Harley built a breezeway out in front of the registration area so buggies could pull under it and people arriving and departing would be protected from inclement weather. Addison had spoken with Shelton about the number of beds needed for the town and the new hospital was going to be large enough. In fact, he was hoping he wasn't overbuilding. When the construction was finally completed Harley did the landscaping on his own. He said it was his contribution to Falkirk, but it really was his gift to Addison. Shelton Cole purchased and donated a large elegant chandelier for the lobby and registration area.

Addison got Blanche to put an article in the paper inviting the public to the dedication of "Ara Olivia Hospital" on Saturday, the eighth of May, 1915. It turned out to be a special day for everyone in Falkirk and almost everyone came. Blanche prepared dozens of hors d'oeuvres and Evelyn Cobb made several gallons of raspberry punch. Aunt Madeleine provided the punch bowl, cups, serving platters and napkins and Tutney agreed to be hostess. She was in her element showing all the visiting physicians and dignitaries through the lab and patient rooms. Marie had gotten Addison to employ another nurse, Edna Duncan, who was one of her peers from Athens. The hospital already had its first patient, Andrew Ross' mother, who had contracted pneumonia while on a visit to see her son.

Claire and Joseph came from Atlanta with Sammy and Trudy but Darby sent her regrets. Blanche wondered if Darby's husband just didn't want to be included in family events. Addison's Uncle Cambridge and Aunt Abigail came from Harrison, and Mr. and Mrs. George Reisdale came to offer their congratulations. Blanche was so excited for Addison. Finally, he would have the kind of facilities he deserved and be able to do something for Falkirk he had dreamed of since he first moved there. The celebration lasted until about eight-thirty. After people began leaving Blanche and Madeleine worked hard to get everything cleaned up. Addison had Otis take Evelyn and Tutney home, and Uncle Clayton and Madeleine left for home in their carriage. Blanche and Addison waved their good-byes and, exhausted, walked back into the house.

"Now you can start on the living and dining rooms, Blanche. Whatever you want! Nothing's too good for you!"

"You're very proud of this hospital, aren't you, Dear? Don't let it go to your head, Dr. Blair!" It had been awhile since she had called him that.

"'Ara Olivia Hospital', if only ... "

"Let's go to bed. It's been a long day," said Blanche. She knew she had cut him off but she couldn't yet bear speaking about Ara Olivia, especially on happy occasions.

The following week Blanche began plans to remodel their home. Addison told Harley Anglin to hold nothing back. Blanche had Harley design and build a front porch across the entire length of the house with Georgian-like columns, and she selected a beautiful, massive double-door with stained glass windows for the front entrance. She chose two huge European lanterns to be hung on each side of the doors, and requested that Harley build a bay window in the parlor that would look out onto the porch. She extended the kitchen and had Harley add a spacious eating area where she placed her mother's round oak claw-foot table. There was a wall of large windows that looked out onto the back acreage and the hospital. The top panes were of stained glass. She ordered a large dogwood tree and had Harley plant it outside in plain view, and from this she hung a bird feeder.

Blanche arranged for her and Addison to have portraits made and hung them on each side of the fireplace in the parlor. She purchased a Duncan-Phyfe sofa and two wing-backed chairs, along with a French provincial tea table. She designed beautiful draperies of pink and green floral damask, which fell from ceiling to floor in the parlor. When everything was done, she hung tremendous green ferns on the porch, one between each of the four columns.

Blanche was so pleased she decided to plan a house-warming. She invited their families and closest friends and everyone from the church. She asked Grace if she and Barry would come early to help. Blanche prepared all the finger foods and a citrus punch and once again depended on faithful Madeleine for serving dishes and glasses. Mattie helped Blanche clean and decorate with leaves and blossoms she gathered from the magnolias and camellias on Shelton Cole's estate. She embroidered a tablecloth with a border of magnolia blossoms and green leaves and crocheted delicate doilies and tied them around paper-wrapped pieces of divinity for party favors.

When Grace arrived Blanche led her to the kitchen to help with the last minute preparations.

"You look wonderful, Blanche," she said, "and the house is beautiful. I know you're pleased!"

"Thank you, Grace."

"Are you doing all right? I've never talked to you about Ara Olivia. I heard Dr. Blair spends every evening at her grave."

"Who told you that?" asked Blanche.

"Oh, one of the ladies who is planning the reunion. She went to school with Tutney at State Normal."

"Oh." Blanche was afraid people would find his behavior morbid and even she found it strange. There was no comfort there for her but she had always been a realist and not one to dwell on the past.

"Bless his heart," said Grace. "He loved her so much. I'm not surprised he finds it so hard."

"We're looking forward to the reunion!" exclaimed Blanche, willfully taking the conversation in a different direction.

"Won't it be great?" agreed Grace. Barry and I have made all the arrangements and I've bought a beautiful lavender satin gown and gloves. What will you wear?"

"I'm making my gown," said Blanche. "I'm still working on the design."

"I wish I could keep up with you, Blanche."

"Don't be silly," Blanche protested. "I've never seen you fail at anything once you made up your mind. Now, help me get this food on the tables so I can go slip on my dress and gussie up a little."

The party was a sensation. The house was filled with laughter and gaiety for the first time since Ara Olivia had died. Grace saw to it that everyone was welcomed. Addison was overwhelmed with all the fanfare and stepped outside for a breath of fresh air. He watched Blanche through the lighted bay window as she mingled with their friends and acquaintances and served the foods she'd prepared. He continued to be amazed by her resourcefulness. Their home was now one of the most attractive in Falkirk and his life seemed charmed. He was dedicated to his profession and enjoyed the fellowship of the Falkirk gentry. He still lived with the emptiness left by Bitty's death but seeing Blanche begin to flourish again made him determined to give her a happy future.

CHAPTER TWENTY-THREE

Addison got Marie to reschedule his appointments for the first week in June. Cambridge and Abigail were coming to stay at his home and Cambridge agreed to administer care to the patients that week, as well.

The date finally came. As soon as Addison and Blanche arrived in Athens on Friday night they went to meet Grace and Barry at the Athens Inn. When everyone was dressed, the four of them walked to the ballroom together. Blanche had embroidered the border of her green skirt and the cuffs of her sleeves with gold scrolling, and wore a gold headdress with emerald necklace and earrings that had belonged to her mother. Addison rented a tuxedo in Athens and the two of them made a grand entrance to the Southern Magnolia Ball Room. The reunion committee had hired a string band from Savannah and a young baritone crooned all night long to 'Moonlight Bay', 'Apple Blossom Time' and 'After the Ball'. Blanche and Grace were having the time of their lives and Addison and Barry were gracious escorts. Blanche caught a glimpse of Jim Watkins with a young blonde woman in a velvet gown. His parents were hosting the ball. He stopped in the middle of a dance when he saw Blanche, nodded and threw up his hand. She felt conspicuous.

"Just think," she said to Grace, "If I'd married Jim I'd be a rich society dame."

"You mean a rich divorcee, don't you? That's his third wife."

"No!"

"Oh, yes! The first Mrs. Watkins was a Boston debutante, the second a teacher from Arkansas, and I understand this one is a waitress from

Philadelphia. He seems to be spanning the nation and working his way to the bottom. So far this marriage has lasted a record six months."

"Six months?" asked Blanche. "I did make the right decision, didn't I?"

"Do you have to ask? Everyone loves Dr. Blair, Blanche. If anything ever happens to you, we're all in line."

"He's a good man, Grace, but not without his imperfections."

"Well, he is a man, isn't he?" replied Grace, smiling.

There was a buffet of shrimp, cheese straws, fruit and cucumber sandwiches. They each ate their fill but after all the dancing the men still felt hungry, so the four of them rented a carriage and rode to a cafe in Athens where they had hearty roast beef sandwiches and mashed potatoes.

When they got back to the Inn, Grace and Barry retired but Addison and Blanche walked over the grounds. Two large weeping willows bent over a large pond and in the moonlight there was the pink glow of creeping phlox along its banks. Blanche and Addison sat in a swing listening to the rippling water at the edge of the pond and the songs of two whippoorwills greeting each other across the dark sky. It was good to be together away from the practice, away from their entourage of friends and family. Blanche's face glowed softly in the low light. Addison was staring at her as he sometimes did, and this time she didn't feel coy. She wanted him more than ever. That night their lovemaking was special, touched by the magic of the evening and the thrill of being away from the routine of home. For the first time in a long while, their thoughts were only for each other.

CHAPTER TWENTY-FOUR

It was hard for Blanche to adjust to getting back to Falkirk to face the reality of all that had happened to them the past year. The reunion had been a break for Blanche from the constant thought of Ara Olivia and the emptiness she felt. Addison found solace in his new routine at the hospital, which after only six weeks was already at full capacity. His clinic practice was steady as always.

Dudley Banks came by late one afternoon to tell Addison Mattie was sick. She had been losing weight without explanation, coughing incessantly at night and was getting very weak but was still trying to manage the house and cooking. Otis was worried. Mattie hadn't complained but it was obvious something wasn't right. Addison asked Blanche to ride with him out Stoneville Road to the Banks' house that night. Unexplained weight loss was never a good sign and he didn't want to be alone if there were a chance Mattie was bad. When they arrived he could hear Mattie coughing in the kitchen. She didn't know he was coming.

"Lawdy, Docta Blair, what you mean sneakin' up on ol' Mattie like dis. I's a mess!"

"You look fine to me, Mattie, but the cough doesn't sound good. How long have you had it?"

"Not too long, maybe a week."

"Now you needs to be true wid Dr. Blair, Mattie," said Otis. "She had dis heah cough for more'n a munt' now."

"Is that right, Mattie?"

"Well, I reckon so, Docta Blair."

"Let me listen to your chest, Mattie."

"Otis, get Miss Blanche a chair and some iced tea. She gon' think we don' know how to treat comp-ny!" said Mattie.

"Don't worry about me, Mattie. I'll be fine. We need to take care of you this time."

"You have a lot of congestion, Mattie. Are you coughing anything up?" asked Addison.

"I staa'ted Saad'y coughin' up a l'il blood."

"Save it in a mason jar next time, Mattie, and have Otis bring it by the hospital. We need to know what's going on."

"I will, Docta Blair," promised Mattie.

"Mattie, I'm going to show Otis how to make a mustard pack. You need to be wearing one on your chest around-the-clock. Every twelve hours he needs to take off the old one and put on a new one and have it good and hot when he puts it on." Addison had Otis retrieve ingredients from Mattie's cupboard and while Blanche talked with Mattie, he showed Otis how to put together a good mustard pack.

A little later Addison and Blanche bade the Banks good-bye and headed back home. On the way, Blanche felt sick. She made Addison stop the buggy and let her out. She vomited at the side of the road and Addison pulled a towel from his medical bag, and Blanche wiped her face and blew her nose. She couldn't understand why this came on so quickly but she assured Addison she'd be all right till they reached home.

The house still smelled of fresh paint from the remodeling, which made it hard for Addison to sleep, but Blanche was asleep as soon as she crawled into bed. Addison felt guilty for asking her to ride with him. She had always had to have her rest to keep going. He finally gave up on sleeping himself and went to the kitchen to read.

The next morning Otis brought by the specimen requested by Addison who was worried Mattie might have tuberculosis but wanted to wait until the cultures were back. If he were right, she needed to be hospitalized in an isolation ward but none was available for the colored. At the least, she and Otis would have to be quarantined.

Blanche got up and fixed a good breakfast before Addison left. He had changed his clinic hours. The clinic wing didn't open until ten in the morning, and closed at six in the evening. This gave Addison two hours in the hospital every morning. Marie and Edna managed to attend to both the hospital and clinic patients, and handle the books. The two of them alternated between the clinic and the hospital every day, and every-other-night one of the two had hospital duty. Velma Sims was hired as a cleaning woman for the hospital at night. If everything was quiet and there were no serious cases, the nurse on duty would rest on the couch in Addison's office or in a hospital bed if one was available. Velma would check on the patients as she went from room to room cleaning, and notify the nurse if a patient had an urgent need. If there were an emergency the nurse would send Velma to summon Addison. Thus far, the arrangement had worked quite well.

As Addison was getting ready to leave for the hospital one morning he heard Blanche in the bathroom vomiting again.

"Blanche," shouted Addison from the kitchen. "Come to the clinic just before lunch today and let me have a look at you."

"Why, Addison?" she shouted from the bathroom.

"Is your period late?" he asked.

"A few days I guess," she shouted. "But that's not unusual for me."

"You come by just the same. You may be pregnant!"

Blanche ran to the kitchen. She was disappointed not to see excitement on Addison's face, but she couldn't hide her own feelings.

"You really think so?!" she asked exuberantly.

"We'll see," said Addison.

Marie was mopping the floor of the lobby when Blanche arrived. Addison was fortunate Marie was the kind of person who didn't feel above doing anything that contributed to the efficiency of the hospital.

"Hello, Marie," said Blanche.

"Hi!" said Marie. "My, you look pretty!"

"Why, thank you!" Blanche had dressed in her favorite dress. For her this was going to be a special occasion and she wanted Addison to know from the start she looked forward to another child.

"Is Addison in his office?" Blanche asked.

"He was when I went by a few minutes ago, Blanche." She started to put down her mop.

"Oh, no, don't stop! I'll go and find him."

She found Addison engrossed in another article about tetanus and intermittently sipping hot coffee. Blanche thought he consumed far too much coffee for his own good but he dismissed her concern about his health.

"Hello, Darling!" said Addison rising to his feet to give Blanche a kiss. He examined her in the next room. It took him only 5 minutes to come to a conclusion.

"You're about six weeks' pregnant, Blanche," he said matter-of-factly.

"Are you sure?" she asked pensively, afraid to believe it.

"Seems our trip to Athens was more eventful than we thought?"

"Oh, Addison ... you are happy, aren't you?"

"Of course, I'm happy ... but you and I both know there will never be another Bitty."

"This child isn't supposed to be another Ara Olivia, Addison," said Blanche. "She'll have her own personality, her own dreams, and her own sweetness!"

"I'm sorry, Blanche. I didn't mean to take away from your excitement."

"Our excitement, Addison!"

"Our excitement," he confirmed giving her a kiss. "Now get yourself back together and I'll take you to Sully's for lunch." As the two of them left, Marie reminded Dr. Blair his next patient would arrive at one-thirty, and he assured her he'd be back, promising to bring back sandwiches for her and Edna.

Addison followed Blanche out to the buggy. He noticed she already had a glow about her, the way she had when she was pregnant with Ara Olivia. He determined not to let her know he feared he could never love another child like he loved Bitty, or that he was thinking he couldn't survive another devastating loss.

Naomi Sully brought Blanche and Addison beef stew and talked them into trying pecan pie to finish off their meal.

"It's delicious," said Addison.

"Thank you, Dr. Bl--," Naomi stopped short and stood staring out the front window.

"Here comes Dudley Banks," she said. "He looks mighty distressed!"

Dudley threw open the door, out of breath and barely able to speak.

"Dr. Blair," he gasped. "It's Mama. She gone and passed out. Daddy put her on de bed and wuz fannin' her face but when he see she not gon' wake up he send me fo' you. Miss Marie say you wuz at Sully's, so heah I is."

"I'll get Abe to take Blanche home," offered Naomi.

"Thanks, Naomi! Let's go!" Addison climbed up into Dudley's hay wagon. By the time they arrived at the Banks home, Mattie was sitting up on the front porch. Otis was still fanning Mattie's face and she was drinking a glass of water.

"Have you been behaving, Mattie?" asked Addison, "because if you brought this on by doing too much I'm going to take a stick to you!"

"Mercy, Dr. Blair," I ain't been good for nuthin'. Otis been doin' all the cookin' and cleanin'. He even help me to bed nights and he sho do keep dat mustard pack on me."

"Well, good! At least you're trying to be good."

"Tryin'? I couldn' do no diffunt, ain't got the stren'th!"

Addison listened to Mattie's chest. The congestion was worse. He looked her right in the eyes.

"Mattie, you're a no nonsense woman and I'm going to be straight with you. I think you have tuberculosis. I still don't have the culture back, but your congestion is worse today. You're going to have to stay in bed awhile. You can't let anyone come into your room but Otis and Dudley. I'll get masks for them to wear when they're with you. We don't want them to contract the disease. Can you promise me you'll stay in the bed until I tell you everything is okay?"

"I do my bes'," said Mattie compliantly.

"I hope so. I need you too much to let anything happen to you!" he patted her on the shoulder.

"Well, I'd better get back to the hospital. I guess Marie's figured out by now where I am, if Blanche didn't let her know."

"I'm sho Miss Blanche tol' her," said Mattie. "She ain't 'bout to leave nobody hangin'. You bettuh be takin' cah o' dat sweet lady, and lettin' this old, ugly colored woman be."

"I can take care of you both, Mattie," laughed Addison.

Mattie's culture was positive as Addison had suspected, but she complied with bed rest and Otis was a faithful nurse so over the next few months she steadily improved. By mid-November Addison gave her the okay to get out of bed. No sooner had she gotten well than Addison got sick. He had been treating a boy from Jackson for diphtheria, using all the techniques he'd learned from watching Cambridge treat Ara Olivia. The child recovered and even though Addison felt ill, he continued to work, trying not to get too close to his patients. Blanche pleaded with him to cancel appointments for a week and try to rest and recuperate. One evening he came in late saying he didn't want supper and was going right to bed. Blanche put away the meal she'd prepared and went to the bedroom to check on him and found him burning with fever.

"Addison, you're not going to the hospital in the morning," she said adamantly. "I'm going to see Marie first thing to let her know you won't be coming. You've let this go on far too long, and I refuse to let you do another thing until this fever and cough is gone. She and Edna can take care of the patients. It's not like you're miles away. They can come get you if there's an emergency."

"Now, don't go making a mountain out of this, Blanche. Sickness is always worse at night. I'll be better in the morning."

"Well, better or not, you're not going in and that's final! Besides, it's dangerous to your patients for you to be around them when you're ill."

Addison felt too ill to argue, especially when he knew she was right. He asked Blanche to bring him some cold water, which he gulped down.

"You won't be upset with me if I just try to sleep, now, will you Blanche!"

"I'll be upset if you don't!" He was obviously having chills and she pulled the blanket up and tucked it around and behind his neck.

"Good night, Addison."

Blanche went back to the kitchen and made a pot of coffee. She decided she'd work on pillowcases. Engrossed in the needlework she became unaware of the time. She started to nod, so she put her sewing away and went to get ready for bed. When she checked on Addison she noticed he was extremely pale.

"Addison!" she nudged. He didn't respond.

"Wake up, Addison." She felt his face. His skin was cold and clammy and she was sure he'd fainted.

"Oh, God, Addison!" She ran to find her shoes, pulled them on and ran out of the house toward the hospital.

'Please don't let anything happen to Addison,' she prayed as she hurried across the yard. It seemed to take forever. Marie was going over patient charts when Blanche rushed into the lobby.

"Something's happened to Dr. Blair!" Marie said instinctively when Blanche appeared.

"He's passed out in bed, Marie. He was burning up with fever but now he's cold and his night clothes are soaking wet. Please help me!"

"I'll go tell Edna to take care of things here and I'll go back with you," said Marie. She ran down the hall to find Edna and in a flash returned, and she and Blanche ran back to the house and found Addison still out cold.

"I'll stay here with Dr. Blair," said Marie. "You go get Joe Malone. Tell him to get Otis to go get Dr. Cambridge in Harrison and bring him back to see Dr. Blair."

Blanche hurried up to the Malone's and found Joe in the carriage house.

"Joe!" she shouted. "Dr. Blair is ill! Can you take your buggy to Otis' house and get him to go for Uncle Cambridge? I think we're going to need him."

"What happened?" asked Joe.

"Addison's had a cough but he insisted on working till all hours, and now I'm afraid he may have pneumonia." Joe quickly harnessed the horses and hooked up his rig.

"Get in," said Joe. "I'll run you back by to get Dr. Blair and we'll get him to the hospital first, then I'll go get Otis." When they reached the house Marie and Blanche wrapped Addison in a blanket as best they could, and the three of them carried him to the buggy. Joe drove the buggy across the yard and up under the breezeway, and Edna came out and helped to get Addison inside.

"Edna, is there a clean bed for Dr. Blair?" asked Marie.

"Bed three is available on the South Hall," Edna replied. When they reached the room Edna pulled back the covers. Together they laid Addison on the hospital bed and Blanche put a pillow under his head.

"I'm on my way to get Otis, Mrs. Blair," said Joe. "I'll be praying hard!"

"Thank you, Joe. Leave your rig at the house and take our buggy. Otis can bring you back home. He'll need two horses to make the trip to Harrison.

Joe hurried to the house and put his buggy in the barn. He ran to

Addison's house, hitched up Addison's rig and started down the Stoneville Road.

Edna went for some ammonia. She held it to Addison's nostrils and almost immediately he awoke.

"Dr. Blair," said Edna, "Are you all right?"

"Not as well as I thought," said Addison starting to cough.

"Tell me what I need to do for you!"

"Get ... " Addison didn't finish his sentence. Marie took charge.

"Go get some whiskey," she said to Edna. "We have some in the supply room in the first cabinet on the right as you go through the door. That'll get his circulation going again." In just a few minutes Edna returned with the whiskey. Marie held up Addison's head and gave him a shot and he managed to swallow it down. He roused a bit and opened his eyes. He recognized the fear on Blanche's face.

"Get Otis to get Cambridge, Darling," he said weakly. "He'll know what to do."

"Joe's already on the way to get Otis in our buggy and take him to Harrison," Blanche told him but he didn't hear her. He had already lost consciousness again.

When Joe got to the Banks' everyone was in bed and the house was dark. A dog began to bark. Joe knocked frantically at the door.

"Who is dat?" came a man's voice from the kitchen.

"It's Joe Malone, Otis. We need you. Dr. Blair is sick." Otis lifted the latch and opened the door.

"Wheah is he?" asked Otis.

"At the hospital," said Joe, "but he's in and out. We need to go get Cambridge Blair in Harrison!"

"Sho' do," said Otis. Le' me get dressed." It took him only five minutes to get into his overalls. He told Mattie Dr. Blair was ill and she insisted on coming with them. Otis drove to drop Joe off at home, and he and Mattie started toward Harrison.

"Joe, you be sho and tell Miss Tutney 'bout Dr. Blair," shouted Mattie as they left.

"Don't worry, I'll go now." Joe climbed up in his rig and headed to Tutney's apartment to awaken her. After three hard knocks, she came to the door.

"What in the world?" she asked Joe.

"Dr. Blair's sick, Miss Blair. You need to get up into the buggy and ride with me to the hospital."

When Tutney got there she found an office chair and took it into Addison's room. She sat down beside Blanche. Marie had gotten Addison somewhat stabilized. The shot of whiskey had seemed to subdue his cough, and Marie had made a mustard plaster for his chest.

"How is Brother?" Tutney asked.

"He's delirious," said Blanche. "He opened his eyes once or twice but hasn't shown any signs of consciousness since."

"What brought this on?" asked Tutney. "Shouldn't you be doing something!"

Blanche wasn't surprised Tutney seemed to be blaming her.

"Otis has gone to get Uncle Cambridge, Tutney." The two of them sat quietly in the room for the next several hours. Finally, Cambridge appeared.

"How long has he been like this?" he asked.

"He didn't eat anything and must have passed out sometime after I finished my supper," answered Blanche. "He did wake a couple of times, but only for a moment."

"He's worked himself too hard!" said Tutney.

"He certainly has." added Blanche. "He insists on attending to his patients personally, even when the nurses would do just as well. Marie's been telling him for a week his cough was getting worse and was going to get the best of him." Cambridge bent down to listen to Addison's chest.

"Um," he said nodding his head. "He's got a fight on his hands this time. He's filled with congestion. It's going to be touch and go for awhile. I'll plan on staying till he's out of the woods."

"What can I do?" said Blanche.

"You can go home and get some rest. It won't help for you to get under the weather. You've got to think of the baby. Marie and I will take care of Addison."

He turned to Marie who had just come to the door.

"I sure could use a comfortable chair."

Marie went to get Addison's chair from his office and put it beside the bed and Cambridge took a seat.

"I'm going, Uncle Cambridge," said Blanche. "But promise you'll send for me if anything changes."

"I promise, Blanche."

Tutney walked to the lobby with Blanche. She decided to wait there until Addison was better. When they reached the lobby they found Mattie and Otis sitting over in the corner.

"How Dr. Blair be?" Mattie asked.

"Oh, Mattie, he's not doing very well right now. I'm so thankful Uncle Cambridge is here. He's going to stay with him tonight and he's ordered me home ... says I have to think of the baby."

"He right, Miss Blanche. Don' you worry. We gon' stay right heah and pray fo' 'im, and de Lawd gone take cah o' him."

"I hope so, Mattie. I hope so."

Tutney deliberately took a seat on the opposite side of the room and pulled out a book to read. Though she appreciated Mattie as a hard worker and decent human being, she still thought it was improper for whites and blacks to mingle on any kind of social basis.

As Blanche walked back home she thought about the night Cambridge came to see Ara Olivia. She had no idea how sick her baby was that night. Now, she feared Addison was in serious trouble.

"God," she whispered. "Addison's a good man. He just has to get well. He has to be here for our baby. Please God."

She didn't get much sleep. She tossed and turned and occasionally dozed, but her dreaming was as bad as the reality, full of the faces of people who had died. Finally, she got up and went to the kitchen to make fresh coffee. When she looked at her watch it was five a.m. The coffee revived her and she decided to dress and return to the hospital. When she arrived Mattie was still there.

"Good mo'nin', Miss Blanche."

"Good morning, Mattie. Where is Tutney?"

"She jes' lef'. Dr. Cambridge tol' Miss Tutney wasn't nuthin' she cud do, so she say she haf to git to school?"

"Did Otis go back home?"

"No, he gon' to tell our folks to pray fo' Doctah Blair, Miss Blanche."

"Bless you both, Mattie."

When she went into Addison's room she found Cambridge in Addison's lab coat standing over the bed, looking quite different from the distinguished gentleman she knew. She immediately recognized the terrible swelling in Addison's neck and face.

"Oh no, Uncle Cambridge, it's ... "

"Yes, Blanche. It's diphtheria. He hasn't been conscious all night." Blanche began to cry.

"Now, now, don't despair ... just pray. He's a strong man and he has a good chance. I've just asked Marie to come sit with him. When she gets here I'm going to go lie down for awhile."

"You go ahead and get some rest, Uncle Cambridge. I'll sit with him."

Blanche took a seat in Addison's office chair and Cambridge walked down the hall toward the lobby. Occasionally, Addison would choke and seemed to have trouble breathing. He tossed and mumbled but didn't open his eyes. Marie soon came back into the room.

"Did you get some sleep, Mrs. Blair?" Marie asked.

"A little," said Blanche. I kept waking up and wondering how Addison was. Uncle Cambridge has just told me it's diphtheria."

"I'm sorry, Mrs. Blair, but Addison's uncle seems to know what he's doing. I don't think Dr. Blair could be in better hands. We're keeping very close watch on him." She bent to feel Addison's forehead.

"Can you continue cooling him down with this damp cloth? His fever's still extremely high. I need to help Edna take care of the patients this morning."

"Of course," said Blanche.

She moved to the other side of the bed and for hours bathed Addison's face and neck. She could hear commotion coming from the lobby, the water running and toilets flushing in the hall. She could smell medication and hear soft whispers and wondered about the other patients and their families. It was strange to see Addison in a hospital bed, totally dependent on the nurses.

For a week Addison lay gravely ill, delirious with fever. Cambridge settled in to stay and not only attended to him, but also, took care of the patients. Blanche stayed by Addison's bedside. By Sunday evening she was exhausted but kept watch. Marie came to the room frequently to check on them both. She told Blanche to try to rest and she would come in often to be sure Addison was stable. Despite her good intentions, Blanche fell asleep in the chair. A little while later she awoke to the comforting sound of a gospel hymn. It was Falkirk's colored community.

'Dr. Blair's black patients and their families have come to the hospital,' she said to herself. Cambridge came out of the office to disperse them, but Marie stopped him.

"Dr. Blair," she said, "You know he would want them to stay."

Pastor Jasper Ewing of the Beulah Baptist Church began to pray, raising his hands in supplication. "Fatha, heah our prayer this evenin'. Touch our good doctah with yo' healin' hands. Be wid our 'white angel' and make him well in our precious Jesus' name."

"Amen," the others echoed. They prayed until the early morning light. Blanche was touched by their loyalty and tears filled her eyes. Suddenly, a peace came over her. She fell asleep again to the singing of old negro spirituals. At eleven the next morning Addison awoke. God had heard their prayers. Uncle Cambridge was soon able to go back to Harrison.

CHAPTER TWENTY-FIVE

Blanche had done exceedingly well with her second pregnancy despite the stress of Addison's illness and was once again busier than ever. She seemed to find extra reserves of energy when she was expecting a child. The nursery was decorated and ready. She had only two months before delivery and was going to be happy with either a son or daughter but secretly hoped it would be another girl. She had Harley paint the new room a soft green and the crib and cradle white. She made ruffled organza curtains and talked Addison into ordering a plush boudoir rocker. She bought wind chimes and got Addison to hang them in the hall so they would resound with the soft breeze that blew through the house whenever someone opened the front door. Mattie started coming every Friday to clean and do Blanche's washing and ironing.

Tutney tried to name Addison's second child, suggesting if it were a boy he should be named after Dr. Ivan Sullivan, but this time Addison had already chosen a name. Although Bitty could never be replaced, he was sure this baby would be another girl. He was going to call her Dorothy Lenore—'Dorothy' because she would be the "gift of God" and 'Lenore' from Poe's poem; however, unlike Poe who gave in to despair over the death of his child bride, Addison believed God was going to let him experience the special love of a daughter once more.

Most of the time the hospital stayed full. Addison decided to make arrangements with Andrew Ross to inventory the medicines for the hospital at the drug store. Andrew hired Dudley Banks as a courier and every afternoon Dudley picked up Addison's patient prescriptions.

231

Andrew would fill them for the patients individually and send them back with Dudley to the hospital the next morning. It kept Addison from having to inventory medicines and keep track of invoices at the hospital.

There were still no hospital facilities for the Negroes so Addison continued making house calls to his colored patients. He delivered dozens of babies including Dudley's two boys and did many tonsillectomies in the Negro community. Most of his services were free or for eggs, chickens, milk, baskets, quilts or whatever items the colored could offer. It was heartbreaking for Addison that when colored patients were terminally ill they received little or no nursing, other than what their families could provide. In the case of death of a family member, Addison would put them in touch with the medical college who accepted cadavers for academic research from families who were too poor to provide interment for their loved ones. Addison hoped one day this would all change.

Falkirk was in the throes of winter. There had been a lot of extremely cold mornings when Addison felt the wind cutting through him as he walked over to the hospital. On the morning of February 10, 1916, Blanche went into labor. This time she was amazingly calm and things progressed quickly. At three in the afternoon she gave birth to an 8-pound 14-ounce baby girl, Dorothy Lenore Blair, with Mattie again by her side. That evening Addison made his last visit to Ara Olivia's grave.

'Well what do you think of your new sister, Bitty?' he asked. 'She's as beautiful as you, and she's going to be so much like you. He stood there for an hour, reminiscing, as he had done so often, about the day Ara Olivia had been born and the joy he had introducing her to Falkirk – even about the terrible sadness he felt when her brief life ended.

'Time to say good-bye, Bitty,' he sighed. 'Daddy will always love you.' He turned to walk away from his first child for the very last time-- and didn't look back.

Addison immediately began to teach his new daughter about 'Daddy's moon' and to show her off to everyone. Baby Dorothy was just as delighted with her father as Ara Olivia had been. Blanche had every reason to be jealous but it wasn't her nature. She was thrilled to see the two of them so close and to see a light in Addison's eyes again.

By late February hyacinths and jonquils began to peep through the grass in front yards all over Falkirk. Addison was anxious for warmer weather and for Dorothy to get old enough to take a buggy ride. By the end of April he was insisting Blanche and the baby ride with him on his visits to see the colored in the evenings. One night when they got home late, Blanche rocked Dorothy to sleep, singing to her an old love song.

Smile a while and kiss me sad adieu.
When the clouds roll by, I'll come to you.
Then the skies will be more blue
Down in lovers' lane, my dearie.

Addison heard her song coming from the nursery as he was reading in the parlor and closed his eyes.

"Thank you, Father," he whispered.

CHAPTER TWENTY-SIX

One morning when Dorothy was about twenty months old Blanche decided to make a pound cake. She spooned the batter of her six-egg cake into the pan and handed the empty bowl down to little Dorothy, who sat on the floor and began to lick the bowl and spoon.

After a few minutes little Dorothy began to plead.

"All gone, Mama." She held up the bowl.

"Yes, Dorothy, it's all gone," said Blanche. "Mama's put all the batter in the pan and it's baking now. In just a little while you can have a piece of Mama's cake."

"More," insisted Dorothy.

"Now, baby, there is no more. Let's go out and swing while the cake is baking. Mama will teach you a new song."

Dorothy was very much like Blanche, but her hair was black and curly, and she was large-framed and tall like her father. She had blue eyes and a dimple in each cheek and loved to sing. Blanche had already taught her several songs and it was becoming obvious she liked to perform. The more encouragement she received the more animated she became. As soon as she was old enough Addison told her about her sister, Ara Olivia, and how he had chosen Dorothy's name, which people very quickly had shortened to 'Dot'.

Little Dot loved sitting by her father's side when he was studying and occasionally he would speak in medical terms, which to his surprise she would try to repeat. She grew so fast Blanche was constantly sewing to keep her in clothes. Then, the inevitable happened. Blanche was pregnant again. This time she announced to Addison he was going to be a father again. In the late afternoon of August 11, 1918, Addison delivered Slye Campbell's first child, a boy, Roderick Stonewall Campbell. He had no more than left the hospital when he met Blanche making her way across the yard between labor pains. He took her arm and headed back into the hospital and two hours later his son, Jeffrey Addison Blair, Jr., was born.

Little Jeffrey loved his mother desperately and when he nursed he managed to get his tiny fingers into her long hair. When Blanche decided to get a bob because it was in fashion at the time, baby Jeffrey was devastated, but it wasn't long before he was grabbing her short curly locks with sheer delight. His eyes were green like Blanche's but the wide embodiment of innocence like those of his father. His hair was full, thick and chestnut in color and Dot, who at two-and-a-half years old had the vocabulary of a five-year-old, delighted in teaching him, 'doctoring' him and singing to him. Jeffrey was the center of attention at the Blair party that Christmas. Dot sang 'Rockabye Baby' to her little brother and everyone was sure to give her the applause she craved. Joseph and Claire brought Joseph's children and introduced them to their young cousins. Darby came alone giving some excuse for her husband's not being there and surprised everyone by announcing she was making a career of fortune telling. She angered Claire by telling her she would eventually marry three more times and kill her first husband.

"Claire, you know that's nonsense!" said Blanche. "You know how eccentric your sister is."

Blanche had decorated everything -- the front porch, the door, the kitchen, the hall -- and treated her guests to an enormous spread of turkey with all the trimmings. She made Addison's two favorite desserts, boiled egg custard and ambrosia. The crowd was growing and the fellowship was sweeter with each new face.

The children added a dimension to Addison's life he hadn't imagined. They were the focus of his existence and he delighted in presenting them to the community, spoiling them with attention and taking great delight in teasing them. He left most of the teaching to Blanche who instilled conscience, industry and respect in them, but, like most siblings they occasionally competed for recognition and quarreled over toys, food and especially their parents' affections.

On February 19, 1920, Addison and Blanche welcomed another daughter. This time Tutney had prevailed in convincing them to name the child for Dr. Sullivan, although they wondered how she had come to have such an obsessive admiration for him. Addison, having persuaded himself this child would be a boy, completed the birth certificate before the delivery. When to his surprise another girl was born he simply added an 'a' and she became 'Ivana Sullivan Blair'. She had wavy baby-fine hair, a straight nose like Tutney's and beautiful large gray eyes. Addison marveled at the uniqueness God had put into the design of each of his children who were so different in looks and temperament. By the time she was 18 months old it was obvious Ivana was a calm and gentle soul. She failed to talk as early as her siblings and it worried Blanche, but when she did begin to speak she had an impressive reserve of words, and Blanche realized she was by nature a listener.

One night the house was full of visitors. Claire and Joseph were there and had brought his children. There was a lot of jostling and confusion getting the children to bed, and Blanche had inadvertently forgotten to give Ivana her prize satin pillow when putting her down in the crib. The small pillow was Ivana's greatest source of comfort and the usually good-natured tot was for the first time in her life in terrible despair and refused to go to sleep.

"Col plo," she cried, big tears rolling down her face.

"What is it?" asked Blanche puzzled.

"Col plo," she repeated.

"I don't understand you, Ivana. Now go to bed! Mother's very tired."

Ivana began to cry even more loudly.

"Col plo, col plo!" Every now and then one of the older children would come to peek around the corner in an effort to see what was going on.

"Get back to bed!" Blanche said firmly. Blanche gave her youngest daughter an emphatic pat on the bottom.

"That's enough!" Ivana continued to cry, though more softly. She seemed to sense her mother was displeased but the sobs continued and every now and then she would repeat very softly 'col plo.' Addison, walking by, heard her sobs and could stand it no longer. He tiptoed into the room.

"What's wrong with Daddy's baby?" he asked sympathetically as he lifted her up into his arms.

"Col plo," said Ivana pointing her little finger toward the blanket chest.

Addison opened the chest and at the very top was a small pink satin pillow.

"Col plo, col plo," she began to repeat more excitedly wrenching her tiny hands with anticipation. Addison lay Ivana back into the crib, placing her 'cold pillow' into her arms and tucking her blanket around her little chin.

"Good night, Baby."

"Night Da-Da," she said and quickly drifted into sleep.

Ivana was extremely timid, unlike her precocious sister Dot or her mischievous brother Jeffrey. She was a good child, full of industry and quite intelligent, and Dot discovered she didn't much like sharing her physician father.

Blanche encouraged all the children to respect Addison and when they were disobedient she would exhort them.

"Do you know how disappointed your Daddy will be? He loves you so." She made sure each one washed his face and hands, brushed his hair and changed his clothes before appearing at the dinner table.

"You don't want your daddy to see you like that," she would say. She didn't have to worry about their loving him. He was so wrapped up in them they couldn't help adoring him in return. Often at bath time, especially during the dog days of summer when they were out of school, Blanche would fill a galvanized tub in the middle of the kitchen with hot water, and Addison and the three children would take their baths together in the kitchen. Addison would scrub each little back and shampoo each dirty little head; then, the three children would bicker about which one should get to scrub Daddy's back.

The Christmas Jeffrey was six years old, Blanche again invited all the family. Her cousin, Ian Reisdale from New Hampshire, was among those invited and Blanche prepared a "Yankee" meal of wonderful roast lamb with mint jelly, baked parsnips and rhubarb pie. The food was unfamiliar to most of the guests who were used to Southern fried chicken, but this didn't keep them from eating their fill. After the meal was over and everyone settled into the parlor for fellowship, Jeffrey and Dot got into a terrible quarrel while sitting together on the hearth.

"You're a lie!" shouted Jeffrey.

"I am not! You take it back!" protested Dot.

"You're a liar!" shouted Jeffrey louder.

"You take it back! If you say it one more time I'm gonna brand you with this fire poker," said Dot, slowly taking the hot poker from the hearth.

"You're a liar!" shouted Jeffrey boldly.

At that, although he tried to dodge it, a hot firebrand stuck solidly to his left cheek and he croaked with the agony of a scorched toad.

"Dot!" shouted Blanche, "What in the world have you done?"

"He called me a liar," said Dot breaking into sobs. "He always calls me a liar!"

"Addison!" cried Blanche. "Hurry!"

Addison grabbed Jeffrey up in his arms and hurried him over to the hospital. There was a buzz among the family about what had brought about this crisis, and after about thirty minutes Addison returned holding Jeffrey with a gauze bandage taped securely to the side of his face. Jeffrey was grinning from ear-to-ear from all the attention, but Dot was still sobbing.

It seemed that most of the time Jeffrey got the best of Dot, but she was the one who got to ride with her daddy all over the county when he made house calls. Addison talked with her about some of the cases he treated and she absorbed everything like a sponge and became quite good at medical terminology. As a fourth grader she absolutely worshiped her father who indulged her curiosity and made her his little medical assistant, allowing her to carry his bag. She'd wait on the porch or just inside the front door while Addison examined and treated his patients.

Although the children sometimes felt stifled by the strict Victorian expectations of their mother, Addison was careful to be sure Blanche had "the last word" and that all the children were obedient. Ivana was too young to have much of a chance when Dot and Jeffrey were together and generally took a back seat to their adventures. In self defense she developed a fast friendship with a little red-headed boy who lived next door named Harry Jackson. One afternoon during the summer the children were at play. Dot and Jeffrey had tied a string to the leg of a June bug and were spinning it around, listening to it buzz constantly in its circle of flight. Ivana and Harry crawled under the front porch to play 'house' and Ivana began to groom her doll.

"What are you doin'?" Harry asked Ivana.

"I'm combin' my doll's hair," said Ivana.

"I can cut it for you," said Harry confidently. "I'm really good at cuttin' hair!"

"You are?" asked Ivana seriously.

"Sure!" said Harry. "I cut my dog's hair all the time!"

"My mother has some scissors," said Ivana.

"Well, if you get 'em I'll cut your doll's hair for ya and you won't even have to pay me."

The offer was just too good to resist and trusting her little friend Ivana ran inside to Addison and Blanche's bedroom. She plundered eagerly through Blanche's sewing bag and pulled out a thimble, spools of thread and a box of needles before she finally found the scissors.

"Here they are!" she said triumphantly as she jumped from the porch into the yard.

"Great!" said Harry who promptly began his task. After only a few minutes, he presented his handiwork with a confident smile.

"See!"

Ivana looked tremulously at the doll, her hair cropped in chunks with bare patches in between; then, she looked accusingly at Harry. Her lips poking, her chin quivering, she suddenly began to scream inconsolably.

"My Babe-e-e-e!"

Mattie who was attending to the children for Blanche came running from the house to discover what was going on.

"What da matter wid you, chile?"

"My baby!" Ivana sobbed pointing to her doll.

"Lawd," shouted Mattie, "Mr. Harry, what you gone and done to dis here baby doll!"

"I just give her a hair cut," said Harry sincerely.

"You go on alongst ta home, Mr. Harry, 'fo you gets in some real trouble."

Harry gladly took his exit and Ivana stared at him teary-eyed as he left. It was a powerful test of their friendship, but somehow the two pals survived it.

Soon there was a substantial change in Blanche's and Addison's lives. They had telephones installed, one in their home and one in the hospital. Every call was initiated by the operator, whom everyone soon got to know well. It was a glorious invention and made life much more convenient. Hospital communications were easier and more efficient and appointments could be scheduled or canceled by phone. Blanche used her new telephone to invite family and friends to the frequent parties she hosted.

At the next social event Ivana and Jeffrey quarreled over dessert. Whenever there was conflict, Jeffrey seemed to be right in the middle.

"He got that teasin' from you, Addison. You ought to be ashamed!" Blanche would scold.

The two children were quarreling over 'Apple float,' which consisted of applesauce whipped with fresh cream and sugar. It was Ivana's favorite dessert and Jeffrey having finished his own, was threatening to get a mouthful from her bowl.

"I'm gon' get some of your Apple float!" Jeffrey taunted.

At first Ivana tried to ignore him, but he did his best to make sure she couldn't.

"I'm gon' get some," he taunted again, pushing his spoon toward her bowl.

"Don't you dare!" Ivana demanded guarding it closely.

"I'm gon' get some," Jeffrey insisted. Finally, he took his spoon and dipped out a big mouthful, savoring it gleefully.

Ivana picked up her fork. 'Z-i-i-i-n-n-g!' it hummed as it flew across the table and entrenched itself uprightly into Jeffrey's forehead.

"O-w-w-w-w!" shouted Jeffrey.

Ivana looked up at Addison with her big gray eyes and didn't say a word. Addison again gathered Jeffrey up and trekked to the hospital. In a few minutes the two of them returned, this time Jeffrey's forehead decorated with orange Merthiolate.

CHAPTER TWENTY-SEVEN

On a hot summer afternoon in 1925, the Blair children were out in the yard playing tag. Some peach trees Otis had planted for Addison years before were now loaded with peaches, and beetles buzzed from the trees to Blanche's flowers to the kitchen window where she had placed several peach pies to cool.

"Get away! Shoo!" Blanche demanded as she fanned the beetles away from the pies.

Suddenly, she heard a loud noise.

"What in the world is that?" she said aloud to herself.

The children had heard the noise and recognized it as the horn of an automobile and, as these were rare in Falkirk, the three of them ran toward the road to watch it go by. However, this time it turned into the yard, and the driver was none other than Dr. Addison Blair. He had gone to visit Claire and Joseph and while in Atlanta, decided to look into purchasing a car. He decided on a brand new Model T Ford complete with running boards, spare tire on the driver's side, roll-up top and upholstered seats. He was ecstatic!

The children were fascinated.

"Daddy, daddy," shouted Jeffrey. "Is this our automobile? Is it?"

"It sure is, Jeffrey."

"Can I drive it?"

"Maybe one day," said Addison.

"You're not old enough to drive," said Dot with the presumed authority of an older sister. While they argued, Ivana climbed up onto the seat beside her father and slid as close to him as possible.

"Go get your mother, Jeffrey," said Addison. Jeffrey ran inside and began to shout excitedly.

"Mother, Mother, come see, come see!"

"Come see what?" asked Blanche.

"Our new automobile," said Jeffrey.

"What has your Daddy gone and done now?" she asked as she retrieved the pies from the window sill and closed the window. She removed her apron and headed toward the front door.

"Come get in," Addison shouted to Blanche as she appeared on the porch. "We're going for a ride."

"What in the world do you want with an automobile, Addison? What's wrong with the buggy?"

"Blanche! Surely, you jest! It's the 20th century." Addison turned the hand crank and the automobile started. With everyone safely inside he drove out into the road and up to Tutney's. The children insisted on taking 'Aunt Tutney' for a short ride. They then headed to the Banks' house and took Otis and Mattie for a dusty tour of the countryside. When they finally returned home the children were exhausted and Blanche took them in to scrub their dirty necks, shampoo their heads and get them into bed.

"I do wish you'd let me know before you do these impulsive things," said Blanche to Addison as they dressed for bed.

"Why?" asked Addison. "What would you do?"

Blanche hesitated. "Well ... nothing I guess, but it would be nice to know just the same!"

After a few weeks Addison was a veteran driver of his new acquisition and decided to give his rig along with Mag and Mae to Otis for cleaning out the barn and converting it into a garage. From then on he made his house calls in the Model T.

Addison had a lot more help with the hospital now. He had hired Otis full-time to maintain the buildings and grounds. Shelton was trying his best to get him interested in politics but Addison declined and left this to the more civic-minded in the community. Nevertheless, he wanted to be a good citizen and to support industry, growth and good causes so he attended the town council meetings whenever he could. A meeting was coming up on the purchase of some private property for a new school in Falkirk. Belgrove School was bursting at the seams and the idea was that it would become the elementary school for first through seventh grades, and a new high school would be built. Tutney was very involved with the school board's budget committee, and had insisted Blanche and Addison attend the meeting. Addison was eager for Falkirk's educational system to improve for the sake of Dot, who he felt was a child prodigy. She was becoming accomplished on the piano and had a college vocabulary. Blanche made arrangements for Mattie to come stay with the children and as soon as supper was finished she and Addison left for the meeting.

Mattie cleaned up the kitchen and took the children into the parlor. It was a cold night and Addison had built a fire. It burned brightly and the logs popped and sizzled. The children were drawn to its warmth and gathered close to the hearth. They begged Mattie to tell them a ghost story.

"Once 'pon a time," began Mattie, "an ol' crooked woman was walkin' all by hussef down de road wid a cane, when out de woods jump a big bear!" The children huddled together in fright. Suddenly, they realized Mattie was staring at the window with a look of real fear on her face. The children saw what they thought was the glow of flames on the window panes.

"Mattie!" they pleaded. "Finish the story!"

"Hush, chilluns!" whispered Mattie. "Get down!"

Mattie turned off the lights, got down on her knees and crawled to the window. The children followed like little chicks following a mother hen.

"Sh-h-h-h," Mattie whispered softly, pressing her finger to her lips.

The children peeked through the window and saw what they thought were real ghosts carrying torches with white hoods over their heads and black holes for eyes.

"Are they haints?" asked Ivana.

"Don't be silly," said Jeffrey. "There's no such thing as haints."

"Dey is men," said Mattie softly. "Dey is de Ku Klux Klan."

"What are they doing?" asked Dorothy.

"Dey's comin' afta de likes of ol' Mattie," she said fearfully.

For several minutes the four of them watched in silence as hundreds of these ghoulish apparitions filed down St. Andrews Chapel Road and crossed the railroad tracks toward Main Street.

"We won't let 'em get you, Mattie," said Jeffrey heroically.

"No, we won't!" echoed Ivana.

Dorothy, old enough to sense Mattie was truly afraid, said nothing more. She wondered what could make these strange men in white so terrifying for Mattie. Soon they vanished as quickly as they had appeared.

"What is the Ku Klux Klan?" asked Jeffrey.

"Dey sons o' the confedrits," Mattie explained. "Dey say dey protectin' white folks from de colored."

"Are they?" asked Ivana.

"Chile," Mattie said wearily, "Has ol' Mattie evuh hut you?"

"No," said Ivana.

"Dey is bad in all mens," said Mattie. "We jes' gots to be thankful for de good ... and pray 'bout de bad."

Mattie got back up and sat in front of the fire. She was worried about Otis and Dudley ... about all the coloreds in Falkirk. Southern newspapers were full of stories of the hangings of negroes. The children sat at Mattie's feet until Addison and Blanche were home.

When they came in, the children rushed to tell them excitedly about what they'd seen.

"You mustn't be frightened by them, children," said Blanche. "Most of them are just misguided folks who are still bitter about the war."

"Dey bitter 'bout mo' dan de waw!" said Mattie. "I sorry, Miss Blanche, but dey sca'a's me!"

"We know, Mattie," said Addison, "and we want the children to realize they are to stand up against people who are so wrong in their thinking and so full of fear and prejudice."

It troubled Addison greatly that men he knew, upstanding citizens in the community, were members of the Ku Klux Klan. Many had forgotten their initial mission to protect women and children from thugs and carpet baggers who used the war as an excuse to take advantage of people in the South, and most of them were unaware of atrocities being committed right under their noses in the wee hours of the morning while decent people were home in their beds. Addison was disillusioned with Senator Tom Watson because he felt he sometimes changed his convictions for political reasons. Addison was devastated by the hanging of Leo Frank, a Jewish supervisor in an Atlanta pencil factory who had been likely falsely accused of raping and killing Mary Phagan, a thirteen-year-old factory worker who was one of his employees. He felt prejudice was what led to Frank's lynching in Marietta. It saddened him that Tutney flaunted photo postcards of Frank's hanging corpse, which she had received from fellow Klan supporters, to everyone in the community.

"Come on, Mattie. I'll take you home," said Addison. While he was gone, Blanche got the children ready for bed and together they had their nightly Bible reading.

> *Then Peter opened his mouth and said, "Of a truth I perceive that God is no respecter of persons; but in every nation he that feareth Him and worketh righteousness is accepted by Him." (Acts 10:34-35)*

That summer Jeffrey turned eight years old and began to get into trouble at school. Blanche supposed part of it was just his being a boy. She remembered Sammy's spirit and how his schemes got him into many an uncomfortable situation. Jeffrey' grades weren't good and he was often chastised for talking in class. Once he came home sick from sampling a wad of chewing tobacco he got from Roddy Campbell. Blanche was beside herself and asked Addison to have a talk with him.

"I don't understand you, son," said Addison. "Don't you know how disappointed we are when you get into trouble?"

"Yes, Daddy," replied Jeffrey.

"Then what is the problem? Tell me, so I can help you."

Jeffrey started to cry hysterically and could hardly talk.

"What is it son, tell Daddy."

Finally he shouted, "I'm dumb! Dumb, dumb, dumb!"

"Son, what in the world makes you think you're dumb? You're very bright!"

"I cain't spell good. I'll never be a doctor."

"And who said you had to be a doctor?"

"I gotta be a doctor like you, Daddy!" he said sobbing.

"Son, God pretty much makes each of us what we are and with His help we discover what that is. He gives us different talents. Why, I've seen you shoe your pony, Patsy, and I've never been able to shoe a horse."

"Joe Malone always helps me," said Jeffrey.

"Marie helps me when I'm practicing medicine ... your mother helps me when I'm being a daddy. We all need help from time to time."

"I wanna be a doctor like you, and I'm gonna be! I'll try harder and harder and I'll get smarter ... you'll see!" he shouted.

"Come on, son, Mother's got supper ready. Let's go eat. That'll make you feel better, and we'll talk about this again. Just remember, Daddy loves you just the way you are!"

Addison decided to buy Jeffrey a pony cart, thinking since he was the only boy it would help him identify with his father to have a rig like the one he had used for so many years to make house calls. Jeffrey had always seemed to love riding with Otis in the old rig, often taking the reins and sporting through town. For a short while, it worked magic. Jeffrey enjoyed taking the girls for rides around the hospital and seemed to be doing better in school, but after several weeks he seemed to grow tired of it. One afternoon Dot came home from school with the news that Jeffrey had not reported for class that day.

"On the way home I saw him and Roddy Campbell ridin' Patsy over the ice on the pond at Mayor Cole's place," Dot told Blanche.

"Oh, my goodness," said Blanche. "He'll be falling through that pond. Go get your Daddy."

Dot ran to the hospital to get Addison. When he came into the kitchen Blanche told him about Jeffrey and he left right away to find him. A few hours later the two of them appeared in the kitchen. Jeffrey looked like a scalded dog.

"Jeffrey!" said Blanche. "What in the world do you mean not going to school this morning?"

"I'm sorry, mother," said Jeffrey. "I just wanted to ride Patsy on the pond before the ice melted."

"Don't you know that's dangerous?" asked Blanche.

"Tell your mother about Patsy," Addison said to Jeffrey.

Jeffrey hesitated. He looked down at the floor and shuffled his feet.

"Tell her, Jeffrey," said Addison.

"I gave Patsy away."

Blanche looked quizzically at Addison.

"I explained to Jeffrey how much we love him and don't want anything to happen to him, and because of the dangerous thing he did he'll have to wait until he's older and more responsible before he can have another pony."

Blanche felt bad for Jeffrey and wondered if Addison's punishment was too harsh, but as always she backed him one hundred percent. She was determined she and Addison would present a solid front to avoid confusion in their children.

"Your father is right, Jeffrey." She said. "Sometimes we have to do things that make you sad to keep you from being seriously hurt or getting into trouble."

Jeffrey didn't say anything. He just kept looking at the floor.

"Now, go wash up and get ready for supper," said Blanche.

Part of Jeffrey's' problem was that his sisters were very academic. Both Dorothy and Ivana excelled in school. Dorothy was becoming quite a public speaker and Ivana had been spelling bee champion every year since the first grade. Addison and Blanche were very proud of them but Jeffrey felt studying for him was futile, and there was no way he could measure up. Addison had a long talk with Jeffrey about how Thomas Edison dropped out of school and how people thought Albert Einstein was a fool, but he knew instinctively it would be a long time before Jeffrey realized people truly are smart, as well as dumb, in different ways.

Tutney came over when she heard about Jeffrey's disobedience.

"He should be sent to a boarding school to learn some discipline!" she opined.

"We'll not send Jeffrey away, Tutney. We have a right to rear him as we see fit. You're far too bold when it comes to your opining about our affairs. I don't mind for myself but when the children are involved I won't have it."

"I'm not surprised that you don't know how to rear children when you're so manipulative yourself." Tutney retaliated. "Addison, you must instruct your overly indulgent wife to be more firm."

"No," said Addison. "If you're going to speak to Blanche that way you must leave."

"If she can't hear the truth, I won't speak to her, at all!" she said indignantly and stormed from the house.

Blanche went by Tutney's apartment to try and make amends but Tutney refused to acknowledge she was at the door. Tutney was furious and blamed Blanche for putting a wedge between her and Addison. She determined never to visit Addison's home again.

'If I want to see him,' she told herself, 'I'll go by the hospital, or I'll have him bring the children over to visit occasionally, but I never want to see Blanche again.'

She busied herself with household chores as she always did when disappointed. A violent storm blew up that evening and as thunder and lightning shook Malone House, she took her pen and poured out her feelings of abandonment and despair on the written page.

> *I seat me to write you when trial assails.*
> *My letter comprised now of woe stricken wails.*
>
> *Most especially I find this statement proves true*
> *When I pry into years that have bade me adieu,*
>
> *And dig up the relics of joy and of youth*
> *Not dimmed by the shadows of reason and truth.*
>
> *I look with regret on a life that's been shown*
> *But sorrow and strife ere the blossom was blown!*
>
> *A life nurtured long on Adversity's lap,*
> *Fed on defiance and quenched with the sap*
>
> *Of the Devil's own blood, fresh from the heart*
> *Of the Demon of Darkness with a Hell-heated dart*
>
> *That was dipped in a cauldron of withering blight*
> *And hurled by the Archer with fiendish delight.*
>
> *Oh, why should I look on a life so bereft*
> *Of its loveliest attributes – not a one left.*
>
> *Or show to the world that the spirit's still there*
> *Of the girl who triumphed o'er wrong and despair.*
>
> *Adversity taught me that life was not meant*

To be trifled away and in idleness spent.

The food was for strength, the drink to instill
A firm resolution my mission to fill.

As I sit here with thoughts running riot tonight,
I feel now a glimmer of radiant light.

A vision stands o'er me, an angel draws near
With waters of Lethe and words of good cheer.

Says he, "Bravely look to the future, nor fear,
For spirits watch o'er thee and are ever near.

Away with all thoughts thy peace would destroy,
And change moans of anguish for paeans of joy.

Drink, drink of these waters and let the drear past
Skulk ghoul-like away in the shadows at last.

Now comes the dawn of a glorious day
With new duties laden to brighten thy way."

I'll drink of the waters. On the past I'll not look.
I'll close it all up like the lids of a book.

In March of 1927, Tutney surprised everyone by packing up all her things in trunks and moving back to Marbleton. After a few months Addison received a letter.

Brother,

I will be moving next week to St. Anne, Georgia. Dr. Sullivan is opening a practice there and I am going to be his nurse. I love you.

Tutney

From that day Tutney ceased to be a part of Addison and Blanche's lives except for keeping in touch with their children. She still denied any romantic implications to her relationship with Dr. Sullivan but Addison knew she did this for Dr. Sullivan's sake and not her own, as she cared not a whit what people thought of her. Apparently, Tutney had actually fallen in love. How many years she had loved Dr. Sullivan or whether or not she had broken up his marriage, Addison didn't want to know, but he had suspected something years before when she was mailing all those letters to Dr. Sullivan's office in Marbleton. He was not surprised she was as adept at secrecy and deception as she was at cruel indifference.

Tutney found an old place in St. Anne built on pilings near the mouth of the St. John's River where it emptied into St. John's Bay. Later on she had all her furniture shipped down by freight train. She built a barn in the backyard and fenced in a small grazing area with her own two hands. She had lost almost every impulse for housekeeping and did very little to update the rooms. She put an oil cloth on the kitchen table and purchased some simple shades for the windows. In the kitchen, where she would spend most of her time, she hung the picture of Addison's anatomy class. She liked privacy and decided to build a wire fence enclosing a 6-foot strip of grass all the way around the house with a wooden gate at the foot of 18 stairs that descended from the front porch. The porch ran across the entire front of the house. At the extreme left was the door to the first bedroom. In the very middle at the top of the stairs was the entrance to the parlor, an over-sized double-door of dark oak with stained glass windows. At the extreme right of the porch was a door to the other bedroom. There was also a flight of stairs to the kitchen door at the back of the house.

Tutney immediately took a part-time job at the St. Anne library and as soon as she was settled, she notified Dr. Sullivan things were ready for him to come and live there. After he arrived, they renovated the dining room and parlor on the front of the house and made it his office. He hung a sign at the bottom of the stairs by the wooden gate. Tutney used the kitchen as a kind of laboratory where she kept the doctor's supplies and sterilized his instruments. Once he had taught her to give injections she became his nurse. Dr. Sullivan had become a rather eccentric character, preferring Khaki pants with matching belted waistcoats and a hat that made him look like a wealthy English gentleman on an African safari.

He always carried an ebony cane.

As soon as they were settled into a routine Tutney wrote Addison.

Brother,

I hope this letter finds you well. Dr. Sullivan and I have about gotten settled in this south Georgia town. We have bought a house. It was built in 1850, built of the best of lumber. There is room on our lot for 3 more houses, two on Conyers Street and one on Norris Street. There are four outside doors, and you are welcome. We do not have an ice box yet, so do not keep a supply of perishable "eats" on hand, but hope to have one by the time you come to see us.

People fish quite a lot out at Burell Creek where you cross the bridge, about two miles from St. Anne. They also go out with the shrimpers. If you come bring the children, I will tell you about another place that, if you can arrange it, would be a grand outing.

The season is getting so late that since the fair weather set in I have been using every minute of daylight toward getting some seed in the ground for vegetables and for our new cow. Today it is raining, the first rain we have had in four weeks tomorrow. I have half of the garden vegetables planted including carrots and beets for the cow and still have more space for the vegetables, but had to sow oats on two-thirds of the lot -- planted the oats Tuesday. This morning it began raining hard, I worked on the vegetable ground until I got wet. Anyway, some things are planted and some are already up, so there will soon be plenty of fresh vegetables.

Dr. Sullivan's practice is steadily growing. I think he will make a good living here.

I will be glad to have you and the children come whenever you want to, just feel free to come when it suits you. Write me.

With love,

Tutney

Addison noticed Tutney had not mentioned Blanche. He couldn't help but feel a little sorry for her, cutting herself off from her only family.

It meant she would seldom see the children, whom he knew she loved.

That fall, Dot and Jeffrey suffered from several bouts of ear infections and missed quite a lot of school. Addison made a decision to remove their tonsils. He canceled some of his clinic patients and moved another bed into one of the patient rooms so the two children could be together for recovery. They were extremely excited about their upcoming ordeal, as they had been promised ice cream every day for a week. Ice cream was Ivana's absolute favorite thing and Jeffrey, who knew this, couldn't resist throwing it up to her.

"We're getting ice cream, we're getting ice cream, and you can't have any!" he taunted.

"Yes, I can!" Ivana retaliated. "Daddy'll give me some!"

Addison came to collect the children at four o'clock, and when he headed back for the hospital Ivana started to cry.

"What's wrong, Ivana?"

"She'll be all right, Addison," said Blanche. "Jeffrey's been teasing her about getting ice cream and she thinks she wants to have her tonsils out, too. When she sees how weak they are she'll be glad she got left out."

"No, I won't, Mama. I'm a big girl and I can be brave and have my tonsils out. I can have ice cream."

Addison picked her up. "Come on, Ivana, let's show 'em how it's done!" Ivana flashed Addison an irresistible smile.

"Addison!" said Blanche. "You don't always have to give in to that child. You're spoiling her."

"I spoil them all," said Addison.

"Well, at least let me get her pajamas."

"Bring them over, Blanche. I need to get started, especially now that I have three patients."

Addison used ether to get Dot to sleep and while he did her surgery, he had Marie getting Jeffrey ready. Ivana was the last and in just two hours he had completed all three operations. They slept for a couple of hours, and when they awoke Addison was there holding their heads while they vomited up blood and clots. They were pretty uncomfortable for a while but soon they settled and began asking for their ice cream. Addison sent Marie across to the pharmacy and she came back with two

254

quarts of vanilla. Addison fixed them all a bowl, including himself.

"You didn't get your tonsils out!" said Ivana matter-of-factly.

"No, but I'm the doctor, and the doctor always has ice cream after surgery," said Addison.

"Oh," said Ivana, satisfied.

Addison stayed at the hospital with the children that night and Blanche enjoyed a very brief respite from her maternal responsibilities.

A few months later Blanche and Addison got notice Uncle Cambridge had died. They went down to Harrison for the funeral and stayed with Abigail for a week. Blanche helped her go through Uncle Cambridge's things. Jeffrey Clark came over with his wife Jeannette several mornings while they were there. Addison found this loss extremely difficult, as for him Cambridge had been the closest thing to a father and had always come through for him in a crisis. He knew he would miss him terribly.

CHAPTER TWENTY-EIGHT

Later that same year Blanche suspected she was pregnant again, and this time she didn't want to be. She panicked almost to the point of hysteria. Addison had her come by the clinic and after examination decided she was probably four to five weeks along. He knew he might regret it but out of concern for her nerves, and his fear she would go into another depression, he decided to delay telling her for awhile.

"I'm not sure its pregnancy, Blanche. It could just be a minor thing that's delayed your menstruation. Let's just see how things go."

"Are you sure it's not anything serious, Addison?" she asked him in earnest.

"I'm sure," he replied, hoping pregnancy would become less repugnant to her when she was further along, and then she would be more receptive to the news.

When Blanche's period didn't return she became obsessed with her health.

"I'm worried, Addison. Something is terribly wrong. I'm gaining weight and my stomach feels bloated."

"Give it a little more time, Blanche. If things don't get back to normal, I'll examine you again."

Of course, things didn't get back to normal and Blanche pleaded with Addison to send her to Athens Regional for some tests. At that point he decided he had to be honest and suggested she come back to the clinic. After a pretense at re-examination, he gave her the news.

"Well, Blanche, you don't have a problem, you're pregnant." Blanche was relieved in a way but puzzled.

"How far along am I, Addison."

"I'm not sure, eight to ten weeks."

"I guess that's better than being ill," she said, "but I'm not elated about it."

She dressed and returned home. Addison felt guilty about not being transparent but decided confessing would magnify things and make them worse. It wasn't long before Blanche began to suspect his deception.

'If I'm pregnant, I'm around four months,' she said to herself. She had experienced it enough to know her own body. One evening after the children went to bed she confronted Addison about it.

"Addison," she said angrily, "Did you lie to me when you said I wasn't pregnant?" Addison didn't answer. How he wished he could deny it.

"Say something!" she demanded.

"I didn't tell you the whole truth."

"You knew I was pregnant and told me you thought it might be some 'minor problem'. That was a lie!"

"You were so upset! I just wanted to give you more time. I was afraid you'd react like you did when Bitty died and go into depression for weeks. I believed it was better to tell you later when you were more accepting of the idea."

"Well, you were wrong, Addison! I'm your wife. I can't believe you'd deceive me about something like this. It was like denying your own flesh and blood!" After all the anguish from Ara Olivia's death he couldn't bear the thought of actually denying one of his own children and Blanche's words hurt more than she could have imagined.

"Blanche, I ... "

"I don't want to talk about this anymore," said Blanche quietly, and she didn't. Addison hoped Blanche's fury would blow over but for the first time in their marriage there was a wall between them. First they spoke politely only when necessary, and then not at all. Addison tried several times to ask for her forgiveness but she wouldn't discuss it. She became cold and distant and wouldn't let him touch her. It finally was bad enough that he went to talk to Pastor Reisdale who listened and advised him only that he needed to get Blanche to talk, but after several more attempts Addison quit trying. He felt all he could do was pray she would forgive and her trust in him would return.

"Lord, you know how I love Blanche and the children. I'd never deliberately hurt her!" But his own conscience convicted him that 'the road to Hell is paved with good intentions.'

The children sensed trouble between their parents for the first time in their young lives. Addison was a little short with them at times, which was unlike him, and there were no longer the delightful conversations they always had at the supper table about the town, school and the events of the day. Addison poured himself into his practice coming home from the hospital late most nights. Blanche would put his plate into the icebox. When she checked the next morning sometimes it would still be there. She longed to restore the relationship but was waiting for some sign from God that she should initiate a reconciliation. Addison ached for his wife, but soon weeks turned into months and he began to fear the damage he'd done was irreparable.

One Monday as he reviewed his schedule, Addison noticed Mrs. Eliza Sprayberry had an appointment with him that morning. She had provided money from her husband Edward's estate to build a carriage house with a second story apartment behind her sister-in-law's home where she stayed when she visited Falkirk. Eliza was from Boston. Her father was a physician who sent her to England as a young girl to be educated. After she married Edward Sprayberry, the two of them moved to North Carolina, but when her father died leaving her a generous estate they moved back to Boston to be near her family. Now she had no husband and only a few elderly family left, so her visits to Falkirk were more and more frequent.

Eliza was tall and blonde, pale in complexion.

"Good morning, Mrs. Sprayberry." Addison said shaking her hand when she came in. "How can I help you this morning?"

"Dr. Blair," she began, "I have ... had a lung condition, and my physician in Boston was seeing me routinely, but even if I return to Boston I'll be coming to Falkirk often and I'll need a physician to rely on when I'm here."

"Tuberculosis?" asked Addison as he reviewed her records.

"Yes. It's inactive now, but I'm afraid not to be seen routinely. It's a frightening illness."

"I understand."

With Marie beside him in the room, Addison examined Mrs. Sprayberry thoroughly, finding her to be in good health.

"You seem fine, Mrs. Sprayberry," said Addison, "I don't see any evidence of recurrence."

"Well, that's good news, Dr. Blair, but would it inconvenience you to see me every month while I'm here. I know that may seem foolish but I want to be sure this never catches me unaware again."

"Certainly," said Addison. "I'll have Marie set up an appointment for you next month."

Marie wasn't sure why but she took an instant dislike to Eliza. She felt she had a condescending air about her and the more she came to the office, the more enmity Marie felt.

Eliza kept extending her stay in Falkirk. When she came in for her September appointment she was looking very fashionable. Her sky-blue silk dress draped across her neck from shoulder to shoulder and bloused over a rather short pleated skirt. She wore stockings and matching high-heeled shoes. Blonde ringlets fell at her temples from underneath a soft blue hat and pearl earrings dangled from her ears.

Marie gave her a pert welcome.

"Good-day, Mrs. Sprayberry. You may have a seat."

"You don't like me, do you?" Eliza asked.

"I neither like nor dislike you, Mrs. Sprayberry," answered Marie. "I try to treat the patients with respect and not get involved personally."

"You don't apply that to Dr. Blair, do you Marie?"

"I don't know what you mean," said Marie astonished at her comment. "I'm very fond of Dr. Blair."

"So am I," said Eliza.

Marie escorted Eliza to the exam room and went down the hall to tell Addison his regularly scheduled patient had arrived. Addison detected displeasure on her face and intended to ask her about it later.

"Good afternoon, Mrs. Sprayberry," said Addison.

"Good afternoon, Dr. Blair. It's so good to see you again!"

"Good to see you," Addison replied. "Are you feeling well?"

"Better than ever thanks to my wonderful doctor!" Addison didn't quite know how to take her remark.

"My father was a physician, you know," she continued. "I guess that's why I'm drawn to them." Addison ordinarily found her conversation friendly and interesting but was feeling a little uncomfortable.

"I remember from your history your father was a doctor, Mrs.

Sprayberry," said Addison, trying to dismiss her comments.

"Please call me Eliza," she said.

After a limited examination he reassured her she was perfectly healthy. He left the room to update her chart and gave it to Marie, and after a few minutes returned.

"Well ... Eliza" he said finally, instinctively feeling he should stop her familiarity in its tracks. "I should hope to be as healthy as you are. I think it would be fine for you to wait awhile before returning. I know it gets pretty expensive coming in every month."

"Oh, I couldn't," said Eliza. "That is, I can't."

"I assure you your illness is practically non-existent. I can't keep taking advantage of you." He took her arm and led her toward the door. She pulled away and faced him.

"I mean, Dr. Blair, I can't wait any longer to tell you of my feelings. I want you to take advantage of me." Addison, now aware she was being intentionally provocative began to protest but she suddenly reached up and kissed him.

"Please, Mrs. Sprayberry," he said as he stood there frozen, unable to succumb but unable to move away. Feelings of Blanche's rejection, inevitably, spread over him. He had been so hungry for his wife's affection and closeness. Eliza's warmth and the scent of her hair enticed him and he felt himself losing control. His heart began to race. She stretched up to his mouth again and this time he responded. The newness, even the strangeness of her was incredibly exciting. Eventually, he pulled her dress from her shoulders and began to touch her breasts. They became enthralled in passion and Eliza's seduction was complete. She delighted in the glory of her conquest. Addison was stunned, overwhelmed. Sensation lingered in every nerve and he was breathless.

Eliza dressed and showed herself out of the clinic. As Addison washed his face and tried to regain his composure he kept asking himself, 'What happened?' When Marie presented the next patient he hoped she hadn't noticed how distracted he was. He didn't quite know how but somehow he had managed to get through the rest of the day. That night after they went to bed he heard Blanche's soft breathing. Occasionally, in her sleep she would roll over against him and he would feel the baby move. He couldn't lie there next to her. He got up, pulled on his robe and went to the parlor to read.

261

'What have I done?' he asked himself. He felt the need to pray but he couldn't. For the first time in his life he was unsure God would be there. Over the next few weeks the estrangement between him and Blanche worsened. He wanted to make things right, but the infidelity he had added to his dishonesty about her pregnancy made it impossible for him to approach her. He even found himself thinking about the next encounter with Eliza and was unsure if he dreaded or looked forward to seeing her again. He actually wrote to Tutney just so he could go by the post office on the pretense of mailing a letter. Eliza saw him come in.

"Hello, Dr. Blair!" she greeted.

"Good morning, Eliza," he said self-consciously. He suddenly noticed she was a very beautiful woman and wondered why he hadn't seen it before. Mrs. Sprayberry greeted him and never seemed to pick up on the tension between him and her sister-in-law.

"Meet me behind Belgrove school tonight," she whispered. Addison mailed his letter.

"Goodbye, ladies," he said simply.

Addison didn't have to make excuses for his departure that evening, as he and Blanche mostly ignored each other after they had eaten supper. While Blanche got the children in bed Addison left for Belgrove School. There was a chill in the air and everything seemed more intense--the dark silhouette of the trees against the dusky sky, the chattering of crickets, the occasional coo of doves. He parked his car discreetly near the back wall of the school and soon Eliza arrived and climbed out of her coupe and up onto the front seat of his automobile. Their kiss was warm and enduring. Her skin was soft against his cheek and he felt her curls brush his neck.

"Eliza," he whispered, as if the sound of her name was unlocking something in him he had never known. Again his heart was beating out of his chest and he was swept to the peak of ecstasy. Eliza, breathing heavily, relaxed and lay her head on his shoulder.

"When can I see you again?" she whispered. Addison smiled but didn't answer.

The next week she called his office and scheduled an impromptu appointment. Marie brought her back and after she left, Addison took a few minutes to make a pretense at an examination, then escorted her to his office and shut the door. Addison and Eliza irresistably embraced, drawn together by the bond of their common guilt. They found themselves once more in the throes of passion. It wasn't the same as with Blanche. Addison was out of control and obsessed with gratifying his desire. Eliza dressed and kissed his cheek.

"Darling," she said. Addison had begun to button his shirt when he heard the door softly open. He looked up astonished.

"Blanche!" he exclaimed guiltily. The door softly closed again.

"Who was that?" asked Eliza.

"My wife," he confessed soberly.

"Your wife?" she repeated.

"This has to end, Eliza. You must find another physician."

Eliza wasn't rattled, at all. She was used to getting what she wanted without regard for the feelings of others. She finished dressing and couldn't resist playing on Addison's feelings one more time.

"Don't be heroic, Dr. Blair," she said. "You may be sorry!"

Dorothy had come home from school and when her mother wasn't there had run to the hospital to find her. As she took off her sweater and put it on a chair in the lobby, Blanche rushed by her, obviously shaken, and crying.

"Mother!" she exclaimed.

"Run home, Dorothy. I'll be there in a little while." Dorothy was mystified. Shortly after, Eliza Sprayberry appeared.

"Hello, Dot," she said pertly as she left. Dorothy first felt afraid, then very angry.

"Daddy!" she shouted when she saw Addison come down the hall and up to Marie's desk.

"Dorothy!" said Addison with as much enthusiasm as he could muster in that moment. "Come have a seat in my office, young lady!"

Dot was in no mood to be patronized.

"What's wrong with Mother?" she demanded. "Why was she crying!"

"She's upset with me about ... something. Don't worry about it, baby."

"Does it have to do with Mrs. Sprayberry?" asked Dot intuitively. Addison took as much time as he dared to sort out how to answer his daughter.

"Dot," he said finally, "there are some things your mother and I can't discuss with you."

"You and Eliza Sprayberry!" said Dot. "Why? I thought you were a gentleman!"

She began to sob and pound fiercely on Addison's chest. He grabbed her hands and she fought frantically to free herself, then suddenly stopped and closed her arms about his waist, hugging him as tightly as her strength would allow.

"Oh, Daddy," she cried. "How could you?" After several minutes she looked up at him with tear-filled eyes. It was a look he would never forget. He had to say something. He walked with her into his office and sat her down as he took a seat in his desk chair.

"Dorothy," he said quietly, "you know I love your mother, don't you?"

"Yes."

"Then you have to know I'd never intentionally hurt her." For a few minutes they didn't speak. Dorothy sat there refusing to look at him.

"I'm going to tell you something you must never forget."

"What?" asked Dorothy.

"Your daddy has clay feet."

"What does that mean?"

"It means, Dorothy, I try to be a good man, but I can never be your hero. I'm your father and I love you, but you have only one champion in your life ... Jesus Christ ... not me, or any other man. Men are made of clay and sooner or later no matter how hard they try, they will in some way let you down."

He waited for Dot to respond but she stood there quietly.

"I have let you down, Dorothy!" She stood there contemplating what he had said.

"Do you understand?" asked Addison with tears in his eyes.

"I suppose," she replied.

"Then, please forgive me for not being all you wanted me to be, and promise me you'll remember what I've told you."

"I promise."

"Now, go on home ... and try not to worry about this. Your mother and I will work it out in time."

Dot retrieved her sweater and started across the yard for home.

Marie had seen Blanche storm from the hospital without speaking.

She knew something was amiss.

'This is not my business,' she told herself, and because of her loyalty she determined not to mention the incident to anyone.

Blanche had run wildly past the house and down St. Andrews Chapel Road without a thought as to where she was going. She didn't think of her condition or danger of causing problems in her pregnancy. She just wanted to escape from what she was feeling.

'How could Addison do this to me? The one person I trusted most.' She was angry and hurt and crying out to God. Tears streamed down her face and she could no longer see in front of her. She kept running until she reached St. Andrews Chapel Church. She ran across the cemetery and suddenly found herself at Ara Olivia's grave. She didn't know why she had come there unless it was because the loss of her first child was the closest thing to what she was now feeling. Deeply as that loss had wounded her, there had not been the sting of betrayal. She regretted she'd been unforgiving toward Addison for deceiving her about her pregnancy, but she knew she couldn't blame this on herself. He was a grown man. He knew the implications of what he had done. She didn't feel sorry he would have to suffer the consequences, just terribly angry for the pain she hadn't bargained for and didn't deserve.

"God," she whispered. "God, please ... I can't do this. I can't go through this. Please, help me ... h-e-l-l-p me." She threw herself down onto Ara Olivia's grave and began to heave and sob as she hadn't done since she was a small girl.

'How cruel! Why now? Why, when I had gotten up the courage to make amends ... to tell Addison I've missed our closeness. Oh-h-h, God!' Her stomach began to churn and cramp and she began to vomit violently. She wiped her mouth and face on her dress and lay down on Ara Olivia's grave. She stayed there for a long time trying not to think about what had happened. When she finally opened her eyes and sat up it was dusk. Twilight bathed the cemetery and the shadowy shapes of desolate tombstones appeared, but she didn't feel afraid. She didn't feel anything. She stood and took the agonizing walk back home.

Addison was on time that evening. Blanche was sitting out on the back steps by the kitchen when he arrived, her face and skirt smeared with red mud. She didn't look at him. He sat down beside her but neither of them spoke. He reached up and turned her face toward him.

Blanche thought she had cried all she could but at his touch her tears welled up again.

"How can you look me in the eyes?"

"I did a terrible thing," Addison confessed. An eternity passed as they sat there, Addison going over the things he wanted to say, trying to form the words in his mind.

"I love you, Blanche. I've missed your warmth so much. The tragedy is, all I am able to do is say I'm so very, very sorry! Please forgive me. It won't happen again. It meant nothing. I let my guard down and, ... it meant nothing!" He waited for Blanche to respond but she was silent.

"Please don't let this ruin our life together."

"Do I have a choice?" she finally asked. "I didn't do this." They sat through another long silence.

"Are you going to see her again?"

"No."

"I know you don't want me here tonight," Addison resigned. "I'll stay with the Malones." For a few minutes he looked at her sitting there, her abdomen bulging with his child, her ankles swollen, her eyes red from crying. He despised himself.

"Good night, Blanche," he said softly as he walked toward the door. "I do love you ... only you."

How could she let him leave? She was afraid if he did her life would be over forever. She didn't want the children, her friends, her family, anyone, to know he had failed her in this way. She didn't want Tutney to have the satisfaction of gloating over their problems. She felt the window of opportunity closing.

"Don't go, Addison," she said finally.

"But ... "

"Don't go!" she repeated. Addison walked back toward Blanche and again sat down on the steps beside her.

"I don't know if I can forgive you," she said without looking at him, "but I don't want to ruin the lives of our babies. They love you so much!" She began to cry.

"I wanted to hurt you for lying to me," she continued. "I knew when you began to work late every night and lost interest in coming home, even to see our children, that something had to be done. That's why I came to the hospital today and barged in on you without consulting

Marie. I wanted to tell you I was sorry for my anger and I wanted us to forgive each other and start again."

"Blanche," Addison said. "You had nothing to do with this. You could never hurt anyone. I knew I had wronged you by lying about your pregnancy. It's all my fault. I shouldn't have deceived you."

"No, Addison, you shouldn't have. This has broken my heart. You can't change what you did, but no one must know of our shame for the sake of the children."

"My shame, Blanche, not yours."

"It's my shame, too, Addison ..., and it's the children's shame if people hear of it. You know how they are. They'll make sure you pay, and that will mean we all must pay. We will act as if nothing happened. We'll take one day at a time, even if it changes our lives forever." Addison pulled her to her feet and full of sadness and regret tried to embrace her.

"Don't!" said Blanche. "I can't ... I don't ... I don't want you to touch me." She was numb and in the face of infidelity Addison's touch seemed totally foreign to her, but in that moment she determined no one must breathe a word of this terrible event. She would protect their marriage and their children, and besides, she thought, 'it is between us and God and no one else's business.'

Eliza came in once more to see Addison and it was obvious to him that, in her eyes, no harm had been done. Addison again told her she would have to find another physician.

"You can't face life, can you Dr. Blair?"

"Funny," said Addison, "I've heard that before, and maybe you're right, but I don't think so. Facing life is realizing when you've made a mistake and trying to rectify it and put it behind you. I'm sorry if you were hurt, but for both our sakes this has to stop and the easiest way to achieve that is by your finding another physician." Eliza didn't look the same to Addison. It was as if he now saw her in a completely different light, the light of truth, and she now seemed somehow very unappealing. The desire, lust, enchantment was gone.

"You need some time. You'll probably change your mind," said Eliza, but she sensed her fantasy concerning Dr. Blair was over. She was agonizingly sure their relationship had become totally insignificant in his eyes,--just a terrible "mistake" he would soon put behind him.

CHAPTER TWENTY-NINE

Even after their baby was born things continued to be difficult between Blanche and Addison. She still refused his affections, but they both tried not to let their problems affect the children. They conversed politely, even laughed occasionally, but never touched.

Blanche named her new daughter Blanche Reisdale Blair and called her "Little Blanche." There was something about her child that worried her from the very first. Addison feared Little Blanche had problems but didn't share this. One night when Little Blanche was almost a year old, Blanche climbed into bed and approached Addison about her misgivings.

"Is our baby all right, Addison? She's so different from the others. I can't put my finger on what it is, but I'm so afraid for her." She began to cry.

"Blanche," said Addison with compassion, cradling her in his arms.

"Oh, Addison ... Addison."

"Forgive me, darling Blanche," he whispered. "Please forgive me." Blanche's eyes spoke volumes, saying far more than she could say with words, expressing regret, forgiveness ... hope.

As Little Blanche grew older, she didn't seem to fit in with the other children. She couldn't focus on anything for very long. She was late walking and talking and incessantly sucked her thumb so that when her upper teeth came in they protruded. Blanche couldn't help feeling she was responsible for all these problems because she had not really wanted the pregnancy. Despite her apprehension, Little Blanche adored her and would seldom let her out of her sight. It was beginning to drain Blanche's emotions. She found herself being harsh and short and criticizing Little Blanche in a way she never had the other children.

Addison tried to set aside an hour each night to pray for his youngest child to be delivered from her apparent confusion and fear of him, but she continued to be a puzzle. Her problems tugged at his heart. He so wanted her to trust him but he was unable to get close to her, and wondered if God were punishing him. He was determined to find a way to make amends for the terrible mistakes he had made after she was conceived, but the more he tried the more she clung to her mother.

One evening at the dinner table Jeffrey shared some news.

"Guess who's leaving Falkirk!" he conveyed.

"Who?" They all asked.

"Eliza Sprayberry. She's moving back to Boston."

"I'm sure Ida will miss her," said Blanche. Addison said nothing.

At the age of five, Little Blanche was closest to Ivana but her rambunctious ways embarrassed the shy girl and Blanche knew Ivana needed a break from her younger sister. That summer she suggested Ivana visit Tutney, assuring Addison it would be safe for her to travel to St. Anne on her own by train. Arrangements were made and Tutney arrived to pick Ivana up at St. Anne Station in a brand new sedan.

When Ivana first saw the house, she was fascinated by how high it was off the ground and how steep were the many steps up to the porch.

"Why is the house so tall?" she asked.

"Well, that's because we live close to the river. Sometimes during storms the river will overflow and flood the low-lying houses near its banks, so most people try to build on pilings so the water can't reach the house and damage the furnishings inside."

"Oh," said Ivana. "Then, why did you move down here, Aunt Tutney?"

"When you spend some time with us, you'll understand. This is a lovely old town with a lot of history and it's very balmy and pleasant near the ocean."

"Are you rich?"

"I've always been rich, Ivana, in the things that mattered—culture, intellect, education, courage—didn't you know that?"

"I suppose," said Ivana agreeably. "Aunt Tutney?"

"Yes, Ivana."

"Do I have to drink the cow's milk while I'm here?"

"You certainly do!" said Tutney firmly. "It's good for you, and heaven knows your mother doesn't cook healthy food!"

Ivana resented this mean remark and Tutney sensed from Ivana's silence she must be careful not to be critical of Blanche.

The next day Tutney took Ivana down to the river giving her a bucket for collecting mussels, which Tutney steamed that night. Dr. Sullivan was very good to Ivana and seemed pleased she was his namesake.

"Are you going to be a doctor, Ivana?" He asked her at the dinner table.

"I'm a girl!" She said, as if it were settled. "I'm going to be a mother."

"Girls can be doctors, Ivana," said Tutney. "They have the same intelligence as men."

"That's true," added Dr. Sullivan. "And you have your father's blood in you, so you would probably have an inborn talent for medicine."

"Do you have to have special blood to be a doctor?" asked Ivana naively.

"You know," laughed Dr. Sullivan, "I believe you do! I worked with your father when he was a young man and he is the best diagnostician I've ever known. If he tells a patient after examining him he has a particular condition, you can bet he has it!"

"Are ya'll married?" Ivana asked innocently. It took them quite by surprise.

"No," said Tutney. "We have a professional relationship. I am Dr. Sullivan's nurse." Ivana took her at her word but Dr. Sullivan said nothing.

Every Friday evening after supper, and after Ivana had managed to choke down the extremely creamy glass of milk from Tutney's cow, Dr. Sullivan would give Tutney an envelope with money in it. Then, she and Ivana would walk down the block to the Kingsley house. The Kingsleys were a poor family who had an afflicted daughter, and Tutney would always take butter and milk and whatever leftovers she had to Mrs. Kingsley, along with the envelope of money from Dr. Sullivan. The lady was very kind and seemed grateful for the help. Their daughter, Mariah, was almost five years old but couldn't walk or talk so she stayed in the crib. She acted very much like a new baby, babbling and looking around but not responding much to the people around her.

On the way home Ivana asked about her.

"What's wrong with Mariah, Aunt Tutney? Did she fall or get hurt?"

"No, Ivana. Her mother had problems during her birth and Mariah was left with brain damage. She will never be normal like you are."

"Never? That's so sad. Isn't there something someone can do?"

"Ivana, one of these days when you are a lot older I'll tell you more about Mariah."

"I want to color pictures for her and mail them to her when I get home. Would that be all right, Aunt Tutney?"

"Yes, Ivana. That's very kind."

Tutney sent Ivana home with all sorts of presents for the other children, mostly to impress Blanche and Addison with her newfound prosperity and hoping to make Blanche sorry for imagined slights. Little Blanche was so happy to see Ivana and lavished her with hugs and kisses. Jeffrey was jealous he hadn't been allowed to visit Tutney's and made Addison promise he'd be the next to go to St. Anne.

In October, Velma Sims sent word to Addison that Henry Sims was sick. Addison found he had pneumonia and the case was so severe he had to send him to a hospital in Atlanta. It was at that moment Addison conceived the idea of building a colored wing onto Ara Olivia Hospital. He contacted Aubrey Reardon, the original architect, and discussed with Harley Anglin the details and costs of construction.

"You sure you wanna do this, Dr. Blair?" Harley asked. "Some folks around here will be wantin' to hang you."

"I think we're beyond that stage," said Addison.

"We're beyond that stage, but not everybody. Just last week they found a black man tied to a tree down by Wassabee. It looked as if he had starved to death. Apparently, someone tied him there and left him, and no one came to find him."

"That's all the more reason to fight that kind of thing," said Addison.

"You're a brave man," said Harley, "And I know better than to argue with you. When do we start?"

The dream was on its way to becoming a reality. The new wing would be added behind the nursing station and lab. There would be a long hall with four rooms on both sides and two common bathrooms at the end. Harley was again building contractor and Addison, though nearing middle age, was still strong and vigorous and wanted to help with some of the construction on the weekends. In the evenings after seeing patients Addison worked side by side with Harley and his crew plastering walls and ceilings, painting and even installing plumbing. Jeffrey went with him and helped with small jobs like bringing supplies and tools when needed and cleaning up construction debris.

"Is this gonna be a hospital for the niggers?" asked Jeffrey.

"Son, where have you heard that word?" he asked. Jeffrey sensed he had said something totally unacceptable. He hung his head.

"Roddy Campbell says that all the time," he defended.

"Roddy Campbell doesn't know any better, Jeffrey, but you ... you love Mattie and Otis and Dudley. Dudley's son is one of your best friends. He'd do anything for you. Don't you realize how much it would hurt him if he heard you say such things?"

"Yes," said Jeffrey. "I'm sorry."

"I know you are, Son, and I know I can depend on you not to make that word a part of your vocabulary."

"Yes, Daddy."

Things went smoothly with the construction for the first three months, then it became apparent someone didn't want the building to reach completion. One morning Addison discovered all the window panes broken and he and Harley spent a week replacing them. Later, the new plumbing fixtures were stolen before being installed and had to be repurchased.

"I warned you," said Harley. "There are always going to be people who ain't happy unless they're looking down on somebody."

"We can't let them win," said Addison. "We have to fight for what we believe."

"Yeah, I guess so," replied Harley, "But you better get ready for anything 'cause it ain't over yet."

Addison wasn't about to be discouraged. He worked all the harder, saving as much money from his practice and the hospital as was possible to finance the new addition. Finally, the construction was in its final stages and the colored of Falkirk were about to have access to hospital care.

On Friday, the twentieth of March 1927, Addison came home about eight-thirty in the evening exhausted. He and Harley were done. By helping, Addison had saved hundreds of dollars, but trying to do it in addition to keeping up with his patients had drained him of all his resources—physical, emotional and financial. His consolation was that it was finally ready. All that remained was a good cleaning up of the construction site for which he hired Otis, and a thorough cleaning of the new wing by Velma and Annie Sims.

"It's going to happen, Blanche," he said wearily. "The colored folks are going to have a hospital right here in their own town."

"I'm happy for you Addison. I know how much you wanted this ... and how hard you've worked!"

"It's been worth it!" declared Addison. "It'll be great to see the Negro children and old people getting the care they need without having to be shipped off to Atlanta or suffer through illness at home with no nursing. God's been so good."

"Let's go to bed," said Blanche. "You look exhausted. We'll talk more in the morning."

Addison drifted off to sleep but Blanche lay awake thinking about the new addition to the hospital, their drained finances and Little Blanche. God had brought them through some tough times and they had made it. Addison had realized his dream, but they had depleted their savings and she worried about the future. Finally, she closed her eyes.

At three a.m. the telephone rang but neither Blanche nor Addison heard it. Blanche was having strange, chaotic dreams about the children. They appeared in her dreams dressed in yellow knickers and all had mallets in their hands. They were chasing a white dog through the brush and suddenly spied a door amongst the weeds and briars. They pulled at the door and it wouldn't open, so they began to pound on it with their mallets but nothing happened. Blanche tossed and rolled, then opened her eyes, realizing there really was a pounding. It was at their front door. Addison was sleeping soundly and she didn't want to disturb him so she put on her robe and slippers and hurried down the hall. She could see people peering through the stained-glass windows. Someone began knocking again, this time more loudly and frantically, shouting, 'Dr. Blair! Dr. Blair!'

274

Finally, Blanche reached the door and opened it.

"Mrs. Blair!" shouted Shelton Cole, "Is Addison awake?"

"What's wrong?" said Blanche.

"I tried to call you. It's the hospital. It's on fire!"

"Oh, no!" cried Blanche. "I'll get Addison." She could smell the smoke drifting in from outside.

"Addison, Addison, wake up!" she shouted. He was so exhausted she had to nudge him several times.

When he opened his eyes she blurted out, "The hospital's on fire, Addison. Hurry!"

"Oh, God!" said Addison. He dressed and met Shelton Cole at the door.

"It looks bad, Addison. The fire seems to have a strong grip on the new wing. Someone called the Fire Department and they called me. They're already fighting the flames. Edna is evacuating all the patients and Marie is trying to arrange for their transfer to Atlanta. I came to get you!" Addison and the Mayor rushed across the yard to the burning building. Blanche awoke the children and told them to get on their clothes. The fire had apparently started in the new colored wing and was slowly burning its way to the lab and registration area. The firefighters were working diligently but it seemed to be spreading to the point they were unsure if it could be stopped. Blanche held Little Blanche in her arms and despite her reluctance, sent the other children to help Addison. He recruited them into an assembly line to pass buckets of water to he and Mayor Cole as they tried to help the firemen put out the flames, which were edging closer and closer to the other two wings and into the woods towards the house. The children were like soldiers coming to the rescue of their adored general, but it was far too late. Soon the flames consumed the lobby and began to engulf the other patient wings. Everyone realized it was a lost cause. The fire was becoming more and more dangerous and Addison sent the children, coughing, back to Blanche's side. He was coughing himself, violently.

"Get back, Addison!" shouted Shelton. "Get back! There's nothing you can do!" He grabbed Addison's sleeve and pulled him away from the flames to the edge of the parking area. From that distance he and Shelton watched the hospital burn, mesmerized by the fire's destructive power as it consumed the roof, the walls, the furniture inside. Finally, everything was falling into the flames like cardboard. Addison and Shelton, Blanche, the children and even the fire crew stood spellbound, unable to speak as they watched for the next hour as the last vestige of the hospital crumbled. They stood there for two more hours until nothing was left but burning timber and glowing ashes.

"I'm sorry, Addison," said Shelton finally. "We tried."

"Everything I've worked for is gone, Shelton. Everything."

Shelton just stood there knowing words at this point were futile. Finally, he turned to Addison.

"Let me take you home with me. The firemen have things under control. I'll fix you a good pot of coffee and we'll discuss the steps to rebuild."

"Thanks, Shelton," said Addison wearily, "but I just want to stay here for awhile. I hope you understand."

"You don't have to say another word, Addison," said Shelton. "I'm going home." He started to walk away, then suddenly stopped and turned around.

"I love you, Addison." Addison nodded.

Blanche took the children home, cleaned them up, sent them back to bed and waited for Addison's return. She was afraid this was a blow from which he would never recover.

Addison watched until the last flame died, until everything was gone-- the hospital, the lifelong work, the dream-- and there were only embers. The firemen left and still stunned, Addison made his way across the yard to the back door. It was almost daylight. Blanche had fallen asleep in a kitchen chair with a dishcloth in her hand. When Addison walked in she opened her eyes. She got up and with the cloth began to wipe the black soot from Addison's face. Each looked at the other as tears welled up in their eyes. They had lost Ara Olivia Hospital and they stood in an embrace, just as they had stood years before when they lost Ara Olivia.

Ivana wrote Tutney about the fire and Tutney promptly sent Addison a letter expressing her empathy, then added, 'It was that scoundrel, Slye Campbell. You need to have him arrested.' It was ironic coming from her. She was a die-hard confederate who never used anything but the word 'nigger' when referring to the colored. Addison wasn't about to prosecute anyone or even have the incident investigated. It didn't matter who had done it. Every violence, every slight came from the same twisted source. Punishing Campbell would only incite the hatred of others like him and, anyway, if Slye Campbell were the culprit it wouldn't do any good to sue. He didn't have anything. Addison felt the fact he was underinsured was his own fault. Things would never be the same. Addison didn't feel he could ever put his heart into it again even if rebuilding were possible.

In the following weeks Addison went over and over patient accounts to find those in arrears, and to try to collect the unresolved debt. He feared losing the hospital was going to destroy him financially.

"Russell Cobb has a balance of seven-hundred dollars," said Blanche. "You should call him and explain our circumstances. He has the means to make his debt good now."

Addison couldn't bring himself to embarrass Russell, as he and his wife Evelyn had been loyal friends. He determined to pull himself together and start making house calls and get Harley to convert Blanche's living and dining rooms into an office and examining room. Harley enclosed the front porch and converted it to a waiting area. In a little over a month Addison was able to reopen his practice in his home. He had to let Marie and Edna go. Marie, ready for retirement, decided to continue living in Joe Malone's apartment and helped Blanche out with the children whenever she could. When she was not in school, Dot rode with Addison on his house calls. She had dreams of pursuing the medical career that Jeffrey, after years of less than stellar grades, had finally given up.

Blanche solicited Mattie's help in planting a large plot with turnip greens that fall. She sold them door-to-door, along with jars of vegetables she'd canned during the summer. She was out in the neighborhoods so often people began to call her the "turnip green lady." It was a far cry from 'Mrs. Doctor Blair,' but she didn't mind. She wanted to be a help to Addison who had always provided without complaining and she prayed he would soon be himself again.

When Addison continued to be depressed, she deliberately got pregnant hoping another child would lift his spirits. Another baby girl was born January 10, 1929. Blanche named her Marilyn and allowed Addison to give her the middle name of Tutney as a tribute to the sister he loved, but had never been fully able to understand.

Marilyn was a happy child with big round eyes blue as the sky and with Blanche's full mouth. Naturally, she adored her father just as the other children, all but Little Blanche who was still a Mama's girl. Addison carried Marilyn around in his arms as he had the others and when he wasn't holding her, Ivana was. Quite captured by her new little sister Ivana became a second mother while Blanche was out selling greens. Marie had taught Ivana how to sew and cook, and she made clothes for little Marilyn and helped her mother every night with dinner.

Little Blanche, who was now six years old, didn't seem to be able to adjust to the baby. She teased her inappropriately and Blanche constantly had to reprimand her. One day Little Blanche came into the house screaming with excitement.

"Mother, come see what I did to my little duck!"

Blanche pulled off her apron and followed her outside. She was horrified at what she found. There on a stump beside the wood pile lay the little duck, his feet all bloody and broken.

"What have you done, Little Blanche?"

"I beat his feet with a rock so he couldn't walk. Now, he'll have to fly!" she said almost proudly. Blanche told Addison what had happened and he killed the young duck to put it out of its misery. They both knew Little Blanche needed special attention but mental and emotional illness was something medicine didn't yet understand.   Not knowing where to turn, Addison and Blanche just hoped she would outgrow her problems.

CHAPTER THIRTY

Despite everything Blanche tried, Addison couldn't recapture his enthusiasm. Years before he had told Blanche about a place called South River Shoals. She had heard of it from neighborhood children but had never been there. She felt a change might help Addison and that it would be good for the children to be out in the country. When some physicians in Decatur approached him about joining their practice Blanche talked Addison into it. Addison closed his own practice and he and Blanche sold their home and bought a place by the river near the shoals. It was as beautiful as Addison had said. You could hear the river from the house and there was a continuous summer breeze, so they called their new home 'River Breeze.' Where the old Stoneville Road crossed, a large covered suspension bridge spanned the shoals from one side of the river to the other. The South River Lighting and Power plant was close to the river upstream. Their new home was not large but a back porch ran the entire length of the house on the back and reminded Blanche of her childhood home. She and Addison enclosed the porch, bought several single beds and turned it into sleeping quarters for the children, and in the summer their Hammond cousins would come and visit to swim and play in the river.

Addison acquired privileges at Leslie Memorial Hospital on the outskirts of Atlanta, which allegedly led to his effectively treating the first case of lockjaw ever cured there. He was honored by his colleagues with a banquet but he didn't like a fuss to be made over him and was actually relieved when one of his patients went into labor and he could notify them he was 'unable to attend'.

Addison missed Falkirk but Blanche never looked back. She still believed in living each moment to its fullest. She resolved her children would not be robbed of feeling secure and savoring whatever life held in store for them.

Addison moved Mattie and Otis onto the property in a small tenant house at the back, furnishing it with things he and Blanche no longer needed. Mattie helped Blanche start a new garden and can vegetables for the winter. Blanche continued to have her elaborate Christmas gatherings. Claire and Joseph would always come and bring Joseph's children and after the meal, everyone would sing carols and the children would perform skits of The Marx Brothers, The Three Stooges, Charlie Chaplain, or just do a satire on a family member who had managed some sort of achievement or debacle, whichever the case might be.

Addison took the children to school in Falkirk each morning -- Dot, Jeffrey and Ivana to the high school and Little Blanche and Marilyn to the grammar school -- then headed to Decatur. Otis picked the children up in the afternoon in the old Model T Addison had given him years before. Addison would get back to River Breeze in the evenings about six o'clock.

The children were changing every day. It wasn't long before Addison and Blanche realized they were becoming young adults. Dot reclaimed the name "Dorothy" and at the age of seventeen her piano playing was often requested at church or at school for special events. She was extremely outgoing and bold, which enabled her to maintain first place on the Falkirk High School debate team. Although she had ridden with Addison at every opportunity on his house calls to the colored since the age of five, her life now took a turn toward independence. She was awarded an academic scholarship to Agnes Scott College and was to start classes in the fall.

Jeffrey decided he wanted to live with Joseph and Claire and attend Boys' High School in Atlanta with Joseph's two sons. Addison and Blanche allowed it, believing being with the boys would be good for Jeffrey. The three boys worked in the afternoons after school at Joseph's store. Jeffrey soon met a young Atlanta coed named Sara Brown and they began dating regularly.

Ivana was just a freshman in high school and a member of the Beta Club and National Honor Society. She idolized her father and spent hours reading his medical journals. She was as matter-of-fact about the physical anatomy as her father, but guarded her virtue according to her mother's staunch Methodist teachings. She had met an Atlanta boy named Kevin Lauren, a friend of Jeffrey's, while visiting with James at the Hammond house on Clifton Road. Kevin's family had a lucrative business, which manufactured commercial refrigerators and distributed them throughout the southeastern states. Kevin was outgoing and personable and when he began to court Ivana he began immediately asking her to marry him. At first she found this amusing, but soon she realized he was serious and he began to make headway into her heart. One weekend as Addison was getting ready to leave for evening rounds at the hospital Ivana walked into his bedroom.

"Daddy," she said matter-of-factly. "Am I pretty?"

Addison looked up to find his young daughter completely naked. He was stunned at her beauty but hurriedly removed his coat and wrapped it around her shoulders.

"Yes, Baby," he said softly. "You're beautiful. Now go get some clothes on before you show your butt!" Ivana had wanted affirmation of the beauty she one day hoped to present to her future husband and she asked the man she most admired, her father. Addison always encouraged his children to be transparent and he understood his daughter, but Ivana realized she had made her father uncomfortable and was somewhat remiss.

CHAPTER THIRTY-ONE

The children received letters from Tutney occasionally, always inquiring as to their father's health, but she no longer corresponded with Addison. She had written the children how hurt she had been that he didn't respond to her letter when the hospital burned. She didn't understand how shaken he was and how it affected all his relationships.

When the moments with the children began to be fewer for Addison and Blanche they found it difficult. Dorothy was soon in the midst of her college years and dating. She loved drama and found it thrilling when two young men fought each other for her affections, and a tall young man from Decatur named B. H. Douglas won out, and they were married. Soon after, Jeffrey came home for a visit and introduced his new bride, Sara Brown, to the family. They had eloped without telling anyone. Kevin Lauren was still spending quite a bit of time at River Breeze on the weekends to court Ivana.

One weekend when B.H. and Dorothy were visiting they decided B.H.'s brother, Kenneth, would be a good match for Ivana and brought him along. Early that Saturday morning at Dot's urging, B.H. and Kenneth awoke Ivana and the four of them crept out of the house and went down to the shoals. It wasn't long before Kevin arrived and not finding Ivana at the house walked down to the covered bridge. As he started across he peered down through the planks and caught sight of Ivana and Kenneth in the water. Kenneth was carrying her across the deepest part of the river over the slimy river reeds.

"Kiss me," said Kenneth, "or I'll drop you."

"I'm not going to kiss you and you're definitely not going to drop me," she said confidently.

"Kiss me," he warned. "I'll count to three, one ... two ... "

"That's enough of that!" bellowed Kevin, startling Kenneth so, he dropped Ivana and she disappeared under the water. In a few moments she came up breathless and decorated with algae and seaweed. When Addison heard about this he roared with laughter.

Kevin had lost his mother when he was thirteen, and his father had a problem with alcohol, so he wasn't used to the kind of family Ivana had and Blanche took him under her wing. Addison loved to tease him. Once Kevin cut his hand while helping Ivana peel potatoes and she quickly solicited her father's help. Addison could see Kevin was quite distraught. He studied the bloody thumb and shook his head.

"Maybe you'll live," he said. Kevin dropped promptly to the floor, out cold, and Addison learned he must be a little more careful about teasing his prospective son-in-law.

Jeffrey and Sara visited River Breeze one weekend bringing news of Blanche's sister Claire. She was pregnant and according to everyone glowing with anticipation over the prospect of being a mother for the first time. They soon heard, however, that her joy was short-lived, as a physician had discovered her pregnancy was actually a malignant tumor, which he expediently removed. Claire almost lost her mind over this so Blanche invited her to come and stay for a few weeks. While there, Claire told Addison she'd never stopped bleeding and was feeling tired and weak, so he agreed to examine her.

"Who confirmed you had a tumor, Claire?" he asked.

"Dr. Leon Carter, Joseph's company physician," said Claire. "I told Joseph I was pregnant, and he made an appointment for me to see Dr. Carter. I was terribly upset when Dr. Carter told me about the tumor but he was kind and removed it that very day."

"I see," said Addison. "Well, I'm going to do a D and C. I think the bleeding will stop in a couple of days." He anesthetized her locally and performed the procedure. He dreaded telling Blanche what he suspected but felt he must, so that night after the girls were in bed he spoke to her.

"Blanche," he said soberly, "I believe Claire has had an abortion."

"Are you sure?" asked Blanche shocked.

"I discovered it when I examined her. When Joseph learned Claire was pregnant, he asked Dr. Carter to see her. I'm sure Dr. Carter knew

Joseph didn't want another child. I believe, on the pretense of doing an examination to confirm her pregnancy, he diagnosed her with a tumor and did an abortion."

"Poor thing! She wants a baby so bad."

"She'll never experience motherhood now, Blanche. Her ovaries and uterus are too damaged."

"Do you think Joseph knows?"

"I have no idea," said Addison, "but I do know, Joseph has always wanted Claire all to himself. He probably feels relieved."

"Claire must never know. It would kill her!"

Little Blanche finally became so unruly in school that Blanche convinced Addison the best thing would be to send her to a Catholic school, believing the religious training and strict routine would help their young daughter. Blanche could no longer take her obsessive affection, her outbursts and the way she embarrassed Marilyn with her foul language and harangued Addison whenever he tried to discipline her. By the end of the school year, however, the Catholic School wrote Addison little Blanche had formed an 'unhealthy attachment' to one of the nuns and would be unable to return to school the following year. Addison felt Little Blanche had projected her affections for her mother whom she missed, onto the kind nun.

'Why is it when people find love in unexpected places they are sure it must be 'evil'?' Addison asked himself. Mental problems were gravely misunderstood and psychiatric help was difficult to come by. That fall Addison put Little Blanche back into the public school system and he and Blanche continued to cope with her episodes as best they could. She was constantly talking, singing out loud, failing to do homework, disrupting class and sassing her teacher. She would have been expelled but because she was Dr. Blair's child, her teachers managed to keep her in school.

One afternoon in the spring of 1935, Dudley Banks came into Addison's office with word that Otis was very sick. Addison immediately closed his office and left for River Breeze to check on his friend.

"How are you doing, Mattie?" asked Addison.

"I's the same ol' Mattie, Dr. Blair, goin' strong. It my man I's worried 'bout. He ain't doin' too good."

Addison placed his bag on the bed and put on his stethoscope to listen to Otis' lungs and heart. Otis didn't open his eyes. There was a terrible rattle in his breathing and he seemed to be in a deep sleep.

"What's going on?" he asked Mattie.

"Well, he got sickly las' Sunday night aftah suppah and fell, and hit his head on de fireplace when he fell. We gots 'im in bed, but he ain't et fo' three days."

"I tell you what, Mattie," said Addison as he removed the stethoscope,

"Get me a good rocking chair and give me a pillow and blanket. I'm just going to sit with Otis tonight and keep him company." Mattie complied and didn't even ask what Addison thought about Otis' illness. She had known Dr. Blair for a long time and knew Otis was going to die that night and Dr. Blair was determined to stay by his side and see it through. At five a.m. that morning Otis took his last breath. Addison closed his eyes and covered him with the sheet.

"I knows you done yo' best, Dr. Blair. You always been heah fo' us and I thanks de Lawd fo' ya." Addison hugged Mattie heartily, took out his handkerchief and wiped the tears from her eyes, then wiped them from his own.

"Otis was a good man, Mattie ... a good man!"

"Yessuh, Dr. Blair, he wuz!"

"I'll take him to the funeral home for you, Mattie, and you ride along." Addison now owned a 1935 Plymouth sedan. He wrapped Otis' body in a blanket and put it in the back seat, and he and Mattie climbed in the front. When he reached the funeral home he helped the director carry Otis' body inside and promised to pay all the expenses. He told Mattie to call Dudley about his father, then went by the coroner's office to fill out the death certificate. It was going to be hard to tell Blanche about Otis' death.

Blanche was sewing when Addison came in late that afternoon.

"How is Otis?" she asked as she pushed a garment along to the hum of her machine, waiting for his answer.

"Otis died this morning, Blanche."

"Oh, no!" exclaimed Blanche.

"He went into a coma and never woke up."

"Is Mattie all right?"

"Mattie's always all right," said Addison. "She lives her life day by day and does what she has to do. I've learned a lot from Mattie."

"What will we do without Otis?" said Blanche, not really expecting an answer.

Addison and Blanche and all the children attended Otis' funeral two days later. Addison was a pallbearer. Carrying his friend to the grave was one of the hardest things he had ever had to do. Death was becoming more real to him than he cared to admit.

That summer Blanche went into menopause with heavy bleeding and terrible emotional ups and downs. Addison decided to prescribe pain medication and Blanche took to the bed. Addison had to prepare the meals when he could get her to eat. When she began pleading with him for another pill long before due, he realized she had become addicted to the pain relievers and he'd have to wean her off the drugs. She wasn't very cooperative and protested strongly when he refused to oblige with more medicine. Addison asked Mattie to come to the house during the week to help with cooking and solicited Ivana's help with the housekeeping. Even little Marilyn tried to distract her mother by reading to her in the afternoons after school or taking her on walks down by the river. It took a lot of support from both Addison and the children, but after several months Blanche's moods stabilized and she eventually became herself again.

The tragedies Addison and Blanche had suffered began to be magnified in Addison's mind -- losing Ara Olivia, the burning of the hospital, Little Blanche whose love he'd never been able to win. He began to be unable to sleep, getting up several times during the night, always tired. His legs began to ache so much at night he'd drink a glass of wine. This became more and more frequent and Blanche feared it would get out of control.

"Addison, you must get hold of yourself," she told him. "I know you're in pain but you can't throw away your reputation. I won't let you. Leave the Decatur Clinic. We can get by if you just make house calls. I'll drive you until your health is better." For once in his life, Addison needed Blanche to take care of him. At her request he retired from the clinic and decided only to make occasional house calls, and from then on Blanche was constantly with him. She faithfully drove him to see

287

every patient. On one occasion as they parked the car on Ponce de Leon Avenue, Addison spotted a former patient from Falkirk strolling up the sidewalk.

"Why it's Russell Cobb," he said throwing up his hand.

"Russell!" he shouted loudly, obviously within the man's hearing distance. Mr. Cobb didn't look in his direction but turned into a building close by without speaking.

"What's the matter with him?" Addison asked Blanche.

"Remember," said Blanche. "He owes you money ... people don't want to be recognized when they owe you money, no matter how good you may have been to them."

"If he only knew," said Addison, "how I'd love to talk with him for just a few minutes about Falkirk and the good times."

Blanche turned her face away to hide her tears.

Addison seemed grateful to have Blanche with him but despite all she did, with every passing day she watched his health deteriorate. He was losing too much weight. One morning as they were preparing to leave on a house call, he gave her some devastating news.

"I have diabetes," he said calmly.

"Diabetes! How do you know?"

"I'm a physician, Blanche, remember?" he said laughing.

"Don't laugh!" she said in horror. "It isn't funny!"

"I know, Blanche," he said, "But if I don't laugh, I'll cry."

"You're teasing me again."

"No, Blanche, I'm not. Tests confirm it."

"What can we do?"

"Deal with it, I guess."

"Is there a cure?"

"No, unfortunately, there isn't. There are some physicians at a clinic in New York experimenting with a drug called insulin."

"Then we'll go there!" said Blanche emphatically.

"We can't afford that, Blanche!" Addison protested.

"We can't afford not to! I'm not going to lose you!"

Blanche had saved some money. She sold her engagement and wedding rings and a brooch that had belonged to her mother, raising almost enough for she and Addison to make the trip to New York, and borrowed the rest from Joseph Hammond. Mattie agreed to stay with

Little Blanche and Marilyn for the week and Blanche made arrangements for she and Addison to travel by train to New York City.

It was Blanche's first train ride. She loved looking out at the countryside as it rushed by. The sky was clear blue as they traveled through eastern cities and towns along the way. Blanche had purchased a Pullman car so Addison could rest at night. It was early Autumn and when they left Georgia the leaves had just begun to turn. It took them a day-and-a-half to reach their destination and in New York City many of the leaves had already fallen. The big city was rather intimidating for them both. Blanche had never been out of Georgia except for their honeymoon trip to St. Augustine. On top of this, they had trouble getting to Mayo Clinic, having to switch trolleys several times. Blanche was amused everyone in the city seemed always to be in a terrible hurry.

Finally, they reached the clinic and were thankful to only wait a few minutes before being seen. Addison was impressed with the modern facilities. They had equipment he'd heard about but never seen, and some he didn't know existed. They called him back to an examining room and a young physician introduced himself.

"Dr. Blair, I'm Dr. Justin Hunter. How are you feeling today?"

"Mean," said Addison jokingly.

"Uh-oh, I better watch my P's and Q's."

"Don't worry," said Addison, "I'm harmless." After the examination, Dr. Hunter took Addison back to his office.

"Have you heard about insulin?" he asked.

"Oh, yes," said Addison. "Is it as good as they say?"

"Yes, I'm excited about this medicine and believe it will help you, but your diabetes has, apparently, been out of control for some time." Dr. Hunter took a great deal of time discussing the new drug with Addison and the nurse instructed him in how to give himself injections.

"You'll be the first patient in Georgia to be on insulin, Dr. Blair," he said.

"That's wonderful, Doctor-- one of my few achievements!"

When Addison related the details to Blanche who waited in the lobby, she was filled with hope this was the miracle she'd been praying for, and Addison would be fully restored to health by this amazing new medicine. It put her into such a good mood she decided while they were in New York the two of them should do some sightseeing. They visited

Times Square, the Empire State Building, the Statue of Liberty and ate at an automat. They took a few photographs to show the children. The next day they boarded the train and it seemed in no time at all were back home.

CHAPTER THIRTY-TWO

Blanche was relieved Addison was receiving treatment now and not left to his own defenses. The two of them continued to drive to his house calls. They managed for a time to get by but the insulin was expensive and eventually they were forced to sell River Breeze, and she and Addison and the three girls rented a house in Decatur where most of Dr. Blair's current patients lived. They found a two-bedroom house with a front porch and a garage. They had to leave Mattie behind, who moved in with Dudley's family in Falkirk. When Blanche was able she drove to Falkirk to pick Mattie up and bring her to Decatur for the weekend, putting her up for the night in a room over the garage. Ivana, Little Blanche and Marilyn shared a bedroom. Ivana and Blanche transferred to Decatur High School and Marilyn attended Glenwood Elementary School on Ponce de Leon Avenue.

Despite the insulin and all the care Blanche provided, Addison still had a lot of pain in his legs. Apparently, his heart and kidneys were paying their dues to his diabetes. Eventually, he became so fatigued he had to give up practicing altogether, and his own medical care was becoming more and more expensive. In order to give them some financial relief Dot asked Blanche and Addison to let Ivana move in with her and B.H., and they reluctantly agreed. Though she missed her mother and father terribly, Ivana was ecstatic about being able to see Kevin more often.

One day at Decatur High School, Miss Ledford, an old maid English teacher, noticed Ivana as she rushed into class that morning. Ivana was not wearing a brassiere under her dress. When class was over, she pulled the girl aside.

"What do you mean coming to this school without the proper underwear, Miss Blair!" she said indignantly. "I should have you expelled!"

"Miss Ledford," Ivana replied. "My father's very sick and I'm living with my sister and her husband because it takes all Daddy and Mother can scrape up to pay for his medicine. He's a wonderful proud man who loves me very much, and I'm just thankful for the fabric he and my Mother send me to make dresses to wear to school. I won't ask them for what I know they can't provide. You don't have to expel me. I quit!"

Miss Ledford watched, astonished, as Ivana laid down her books and walked out. A few weeks later Ivana told Addison and Blanche she was leaving school to get married. Blanche was devastated. Addison knew his daughter well and realized she'd made up her mind. He was fond of Kevin but couldn't resist teasing Ivana a little.

"Ivana," he said, "Before I consent to let Kevin marry you I have to know a little about his credentials."

"Well," Ivana replied, "I've seen him in a bathing suit!"

"Ivana!" exclaimed Blanche. "Why, you should be ashamed ..., and so should you, Addison, encouraging our children to be so frank!"

Blanche and Addison went with Kevin and Ivana the following week to the Justice of the Peace and acted as their witnesses. Blanche cried a few tears at Decatur High's graduation ceremony that spring. The National Honor Society had honored the valedictorian, Ivana Blair, with an elaborately decorated, but quite empty chair.

A few months later Little Blanche shocked everyone by eloping with a young American Indian from Ohio who was in the army and based in Atlanta. His name was Jimmy Simmons. He was clean-cut and polite and they were relieved she had someone who seemed to love her and to want to take care of her. Blanche and Addison accepted the decisions made by their children, but they were very sorry they had not been able to do for them all the things they had dreamed. Blanche especially regretted she couldn't give her daughters weddings like the one she had.

After their marriage, Kevin and Ivana moved into his grandfather's grand home on Ponce de Leon Avenue near Leslie Memorial Hospital, where Addison had practiced. They shared the home with Kevin's grandfather and his widowed great aunt. Ivana became pregnant right away and Kevin's father helped him build a small Cape Cod on

Wright Street, which was finished just before the baby was born. The child was a boy whom Kevin named Everett Parrish Lauren, II, after his grandfather.

Marilyn, now nine years old, adored Everett and spent quite a lot of time with Kevin and Ivana. She carried the baby around the way Ivana had carried her when she was small. That same year Dorothy and Sarah also gave birth to boys, Benjamin Hall Douglas and Jeffrey Addison Blair, III. Addison hadn't delivered them but he was there when they were born and he was so happy to have children in his life again. He had a special affinity for the comic strip 'Li'l Abner' and made an announcement.

"We are now 'Mammy' and 'Pappy'.

"If that makes you happy!" said Blanche.

Ivana and Kevin lived nearby and brought their baby by to see Addison as often as they could. Everett was a quiet, intelligent child and Addison called him his "little old man." He took him on walks on the sidewalks of town and introduced him to 'Pappy's moon'. The children very quickly learned they couldn't be around Pappy long without finding laughter.

That winter, Addison got word from Tutney that Dr. Sullivan had died. Kevin and Ivana drove her mother and father to St. Anne for his funeral. Dr. Blair grieved for Tutney and for the loss of his friend from Marbleton, with whom he shared so much in his younger years. After they left Tutney decided to sit down and write her brother one last time.

Dear Brother,

It was so good to see you again, but you did not look well. You must begin to take better care of yourself. You've always worked too hard for your own good. I guess you noticed I still try to keep a cow, and still plant a small garden in the spring. It helps me to remember the years in Marbleton and Falkirk.

Occasionally, Dr. Sullivan and I would go down to the beach to dig for clams but I will have to find someone else to go with me now, maybe Merry Wilson, my neighbor's daughter.

It has been too lonesome to be by myself and I have got myself a cat. He is getting fat from the milk I give him everyday. I named him Brother, but he's a poor substitute for you.

Wish I could see you more, but we're both getting too old to do much traveling. Tell my children to come and see me.

Love,

Tutney

In early 1939, Addison took a turn for the worse. Blanche took him to see Dr. Sedrick Ingram, who admitted him to Leslie Memorial Hospital. Dr. Ingram got his blood sugars under control but wasn't making much progress in getting the fluid off his heart. He finally told Blanche there was nothing more he could do, so she took him home.

They spent hours reminiscing about the years they'd had together. This was going to be so hard for Blanche to accept. She knew Addison had been a dedicated physician, a good man and the best father in the world. He deserved a long life and plenty of time to spend with his grandchildren, those living and those who'd come later. She stayed on her knees in prayer for her husband's health but she recognized the inevitable. Addison eventually became so weak she decided it would be best to send Marilyn to stay with Tutney until things changed for better or worse.

"I don't want to leave Daddy," Marilyn told Blanche.

"It'll be all right, Marilyn ... it's just for a little while."

Blanche got Ivana to call Tutney and make the arrangements and that weekend Kevin drove Marilyn to the train station. Blanche felt so alone after she'd gone but knew Addison was going to require constant attention, and was glad Marilyn was not there to see him languish. Blanche was very angry.

"It isn't fair for you to suffer so, Addison. You've been so faithful and so giving. If it hadn't been for Slye Campbell, our lives would have been very different. Don't you feel bitter?" she asked.

"I don't want to be bitter, Blanche. I'd rather remember the good times ... remember you as you were the first time I saw you, your big green eyes and that feather hat. You were the prettiest thing."

"That was a long time ago," said Blanche.

"To me it was yesterday, and you're still beautiful."

"Addison," she said, "I'm old, and you're a hopeless romantic!"

"Hopelessly in love!" said Addison then added weakly, "Help me sit up, Darling ... I can't breathe."

She helped Addison sit up in the bed. She offered him a glass of water. She suspected his blood sugar was probably very high, and felt some light exercise would help him.

"Do you feel like walking, Addison? It would be good for you."

"I'm sorry, Blanche. I just don't feel like getting up. Let me rest a while and maybe I'll feel stronger." Blanche had never seen Addison so pale and weak. He was trying to protect her but she knew how serious this was. She decided she had better call the children and went into the kitchen. She first called Ivana and asked her to get in touch with Tutney, then called the other children.

When Tutney answered the phone Ivana had trouble holding back her tears.

"Aunt Tutney," Ivana said softly, "Daddy is dying and Mother wants you to get Marilyn on the train for home right away!"

Tutney wasn't one to mince words.

"I'm coming, too, Ivana. I want to see Brother. We'll take the afternoon train and be there sometime in the morning."

The next day the children arrived one by one with their spouses, all but Little Blanche who had moved to Ohio with her new husband and would come later. Blanche and Addison's three grandsons were visiting with Kevin's aunt. The family gathered in the living room. Addison was sleeping, but they could hear the sound of his coughing coming from the back of the house. Blanche stayed by Addison's bedside and every now and then one of the children would tiptoe into the room. As evening fell Addison's breathing became heavier and Blanche sensed the eminence of death. She went to the door and motioned for the children to come. As they gathered in the hall, she whispered.

"You had better say your goodbyes."

She nudged Addison.

"Addison," she said, "The children are here to see you."

Dorothy, Ivana and Jeffrey crowded into their father's bedroom while Sarah, Kevin and B. H. waited in the hallway.

"I love you, Daddy," said Dorothy kissing Addison's forehead.

"I know you do, Baby," he answered weakly.

Ivana bent over and held her father's big hand. "Daddy ... " she started, then choked up, unable to speak. Addison squeezed her hand in understanding.

"You're going to be all right, Daddy," said Jeffrey, always the optimist ... perhaps the one who felt most desperately he could not go on without his father.

"You're going to be all right," he repeated.

"Where's your Mother?" he asked.

"I'm here," said Blanche.

"Got to ..." Addison began. "Got to tell my little old man I love him. Don't let him forget his 'Pappy.' "

Blanche swallowed hard not wanting to break down for the children's sake, but couldn't stop her tears. Addison was always aware when she was upset and his last thought was for her.

"Don't cry, love," he said, "I'm going to be with Bitty."

For a few moments longer they heard the sound of Addison's labored breathing, then the room became completely quiet. Ivana bent over and closed her father's eyes. For an hour they sat in his room but none of them could speak.

A little while later Tutney arrived with Marilyn. Marilyn hurried into the house and hugged her mother. Blanche was unable to hold onto her. She pulled away and ran straight to the bedroom, falling on Addison's chest.

"Daddy! Daddy!" She immediately knew something was wrong with her father and began to sob hysterically. Blanche pulled her away from him.

"It's all right, darling." Blanche began wiping Marilyn's tears with her apron. "Your daddy is in heaven now with Jesus."

Ivana went out to greet Tutney at the car.

"Daddy died about an hour ago," she said. "Do you want to come in?"

"No," said Tutney. "I learned long ago about the cruelty of Death. He leaves no vestige of our loved ones in their shells."

Dorothy and B. H. took Tutney with them. They went by to get the boys so Tutney could spend some time with Addison's grandchildren. Ivana and Jeffrey stayed with Blanche to help plan the funeral.

Blanche had never seen so many people in one place as gathered at Henderson's Funeral Home that Sunday. The families of the children's spouses, many of the townspeople of Falkirk, Marie, Edna, Michael Balfour from Athens, all of the Reisdales, Darby and her husband from Jacksonville, Claire and Joseph and their children and many of Addison's patients who were still living. Blanche was grateful for this tremendous show of love and respect for Addison. Mattie was there, walking with a cane but still bright and alert.

Tutney came into the chapel and walked to Addison's coffin. It was not surprising this staunch, strong-willed woman who still refused to accept her sister-in-law had outlived her younger brother. She kissed her hand and touched Addison's cheek.

"Good-bye, Brother," she said.

Dorothy delivered the eulogy. She spoke of her father's undying love for her mother and his exceptional devotion to his children. She held nothing back. She praised his intellect, his medical and surgical skills and his exceptional compassion. There were some there who didn't understand this incredible break in tradition, 'a daughter speaking at her own father's funeral', but those who loved him understood no one could have done better than the precocious little prodigy who had sat beside him in his old Ford looking up with a child's devotion at her physician father as he went from house to house healing the suffering-- sometimes for watermelons, sometimes for chickens, and sometimes for just a smile.

When Dorothy's remarks were done and people began to mingle throughout the chapel, Tutney found Ivana and placed in her hand a small package. For the first time Ivana saw tears in her Aunt's eyes.

"The only thing about us that is sure, is death," said Tutney. After Tutney left, Ivana carefully untied the string and unwrapped the brown paper. Inside was a small ruby crystal shot glass and a diamond ring that Dr. Sullivan had given Tutney years before, along with a note from Tutney.

Dear Ivana,

I would like for you to have this ring, given to me by Dr. Sullivan years ago. Besides my beloved Brother, you have always been my dearest.

I'm afraid I won't be far behind your father. My religion has been all right for me in life, but it may not fair me well in death. The most extraordinary thing about your father was his forgiving spirit. He made everyone, even this stubborn old woman, feel as if she'd never done anything he needed to forgive.

I told you one day I would tell you about Mariah Kingsley. The truth is, Mariah is my daughter. Dr. Sullivan was her father. We never married and because Mariah was disabled, and for the sake of Dr. Sullivan's reputation, we arranged for Mrs. Kingsley to take Mariah in. She and Mr. Kingsley had four children and were very poor. They were glad to do it. They agreed to accept a reasonable sum for her keep, and they have always treated her as their own. When I'm gone, I am going to make you executor of my will. I want you to liquidate all I have and be sure half of it is put in a trust for Mariah. The rest is yours. I have complete faith in you to honor my wishes. You are a Blair.

With love always,

Aunt Tutney

Kevin, who had recently been ordained as a minister, led a prayer at the graveside for Addison's homegoing. Afterwards, Blanche went up to Mattie and embraced her and they both cried.

"How you doin', Miss Blanche?" she asked.

"I'm all right, Mattie," she said, "but it's hard." Mattie then approached Dorothy as she started to leave.

"Oh, Mattie," Dorothy said sobbing. "How will we get along without him? What are we going to do?"

"Lawd knows, Miss Do'thy, I loved Doctah Blair. It sho' is ha'ad for me to say goodbye to our 'white angel'.

"I know, Mattie," Dorothy replied. "Sometimes I have to remind myself Daddy had feet of clay."